Theories of the New Class

Contradictions

Edited by Craig Calhoun, Social Science Research Council

Theories of the New Class

Intellectuals and Power

Lawrence Peter King and Iván Szelényi

Contradictions, Volume 20

 University of Minnesota Press
Minneapolis
London

Published by the University of Minnesota Press
111 Third Avenue South, Suite 290
Minneapolis, MN 55401-2520
http://www.upress.umn.edu

Library of Congress Cataloging-in-Publication Data

King, Lawrence P.
   Theories of the New Class : intellectuals and power / Lawrence Peter King and Iván Szelényi.
      p.   cm. — (Contradictions ; 20)
   Includes bibliographical references and index.
   ISBN 0-8166-4343-1 (HC : alk. paper) — ISBN 0-8166-4344-X (PB : alk. paper)
      1. Communism and intellectuals.   2. Power (Social sciences)
   3. Socialism.   I. Szelényi, Iván.   II. Title.   III. Contradictions (Minneapolis, Minn.) ; 20.
      HX528.K56 2004
      335.4'11—dc22

                                                      2003022320

Printed in the United States of America on acid-free paper

The University of Minnesota is an equal-opportunity educator and employer.

12 11 10 09 08 07 06 05 04   10 9 8 7 6 5 4 3 2 1

Contents

Preface

The purpose of this book is to tell the history of the idea of the "New Class" as a history of—so far always unsuccessful, but while pursued not necessarily unviable—"power plays" or even "class projects" by various fractions of intellectuals.

The term "New Class" was coined by the anarchist Bakunin around 1870. Bakunin accused Marx of advancing a theory that was actually a project by the intelligentsia to exploit the working-class movement. By pretending to represent working-class interests, intellectuals sought to establish themselves as a new dominant class after the fall of capitalism and the propertied bourgeoisie. History did not follow Bakunin's forecast: while intellectuals in the first Marxist-inspired revolution, the Russian Revolution of 1917, did play a formidable role, soon after their victory not only were they squeezed out of power positions by the Stalinist bureaucracies, but many of them perished in the Gulag.

Future generations of New Class theorists, however, were not discouraged by this historically falsified prediction. Repeatedly during the twentieth century, social theorists came forward with new scenarios in which the propertied bourgeoisie eventually would lose power. These theorists argued that while the working class was an unlikely candidate to replace the bourgeoisie, different fractions of intellectuals,

bureaucrats, technocrats, managers, and left-wing humanistic intellectuals would be likely to grab that power.

Frederick Taylor was the first New Class theorist in the West.
When he formulated the idea of scientific management at the end of
the nineteenth century, the concept arguably represented a rather
radical project by university-trained engineers to remove owners and
financiers from the command positions of corporations and replace
them with scientifically trained personnel. During the early twentieth
century these radical engineers inspired Thorstein Veblen to consider
the possibility of "Soviets of engineers" as the force for postcapitalism
in the United States. Similarly, during the 1960s there were enough
radical humanistic intellectuals taking an anticapitalist and anti-
individualist stance to be considered a political force to reckon with.
None of these projects resulted, however, in any fundamental change
of power structure of capitalist societies, and none of these actors
succeeded in constituting themselves as a class, certainly not as a new
dominant class.

During the late nineteenth century and during the whole of the
twentieth century, no new dominant class emerged; the bourgeoisie
retained its position of hegemony. Where capitalism became fully established, intellectuals were effectively co-opted by the bourgeoisie,
and transformed themselves into professionals. Thus engineers and
managers learned how to manage capitalism efficiently, and by the
end of the century they learned from Irving Kristol to salute capitalism with, in that author's terms, "two cheers." The radical humanistic
intellectuals of the 1960s were quickly marginalized and some even
turned into yuppies, discovering a good side of capitalism. The most
recent blow to New Class theory occurred in 1989: after the fall of
bureaucratic communism, which was at least in part caused by the activity of dissident intellegentsia and technocrats, intellectuals did not
establish a postcapitalist social order in which they were dominant;
rather, they accepted the vanguard role of making capitalism on the
ruins of socialism.

What is the point in studying an idea that has so far produced only
systematically false predictions? We believe there are at least three good
reasons to do so.

First, the fact that the projects pursued by different segments of
intellectuals to collectively occupy major positions of authority failed,
does not mean that such projects did not exist. What if intellectuals are

guilty as charged by New Class theories—only they failed to achieve their aims?

Second, intellectuals like to think of themselves as ironic, and they are. They are also prone to lose the wit of their irony, when it comes to self-reflection. Intellectuals who demonstrate a superb sense of irony in writing about other social actors often turn pathetic when analyzing themselves or fellow intellectuals. Too often theories about intellectuals present knowledge producers as altruistic, as a social category standing outside the major cleavages of society, as a set of people who articulate the interests of others, but not their own. If there are or have been self-serving power projects by intellectuals, one has to be rather innovative to spot these plans, since normally they will be hidden within ideological self-portraits. It may be worth overstating our case; enlarging a picture may be a good strategy to find what is meant to be well-hidden.

Third, while the main assertion of this book is that no fraction of the intelligentsia—much less the intelligentsia as a whole—succeeded in establishing itself as a new dominant class anywhere, over the past century, the balance of power among social actors has nonetheless shifted and some types of intellectuals are the clear beneficiaries of this change. In Eastern Europe, intellectuals have played a prominent role in bringing communism down. After the fall of state socialism they undoubtedly filled the power vacuum created by the disintegration of the old communist bureaucratic ruling estate, a vacuum that, in the absence of a propertied bourgeoisie, could only be occupied by intellectuals. Now, East European technocrats in alliance with former dissident intellectuals are busy making capitalism from above, enlisting the help of foreign capitalists. It remains to be seen what kind of capitalism will be the end result of their labor and what sort of positions they will be able to secure for themselves.

In the advanced West, no fraction of the intelligentsia plays such a prominent role in society. However, with the globalization of economies and politics, some intellectuals, in particular members of the technocracy, and especially supranational governmental technocrats, have been gaining more clout and relative autonomy from the owners of capital. If the New Deal of the 1930s, and similar social democratic policies, were built on a compromise between domestic capital and labor, any similar new social contract may have to stand on three legs rather than just two. If there is to be a New New Deal, it probably has to be made among capital, labor, and the new technostructure.

In the East as well as in the West, intellectuals eventually may be ready to confront themselves and acknowledge their own interests, to dare speak with their own voices rather than feel obliged to present themselves as speaking on someone else's behalf. We believe the history of the New Class will come to an end when we arrive at this brave new world. To put it bluntly: a tour around the history of the idea of the New Class may serve the purpose of some sort of collective psychotherapy for modern intellectuals. It may confront them with their most secret and suppressed desires of the past, and make them more comfortable operating in the real world.

Introduction

Intellectuals and the End of History

The collapse of Communism in Russia and Eastern Europe was a moment of such obvious historical importance that Francis Fukuyama (1989) was able to advance his now-famous thesis that this change was inevitable, given the existence of a world-historical, evolutionary trend toward liberal capitalism. In this view, liberal capitalism is the "end of history," the most rational and enlightened way of organizing society. With the death of communism, Fukuyama makes clear, the hopes that the working class will unseat the bourgeoisie fade into the past. The "end of history" thesis, however, also directly challenges another body of theories that predict that the rule of the bourgeoisie will indeed pass. These theorists agree with Marxists that a new class will replace the bourgeoisie, only they identify intellectuals and not workers as this new dominant class.

We believe that a comprehensive and holistic appraisal of these New Class and related theories, an appraisal that combines a history of ideas and a sociology of knowledge, is necessary to fully evaluate the "end of history" hypothesis. First we put New Class theories into a broader historical framework and show that the idea of the New Class over the last century has been stubbornly re-entering the agenda of critical social theorizing. Our key hypothesis is that the last century can be interpreted as a history of projects by different groups of the highly educated to gain ultimate power. Up to now, all these projects failed, but the projects were real and there is no reason to believe that we have seen the last such attempt.

Second, while indeed there is good reason to be skeptical whether the New Class is a *class* at all, the application of the method of class analysis to intellectuals—or, to put it more generally, to those who have claims for power and privilege based on the grounds of knowledge monopoly—is at least insightful. New Class theorists since Bakunin repeatedly reminded social scientists to subject the power-knowledge link to critical scrutiny. New Class theorists were the first to emphasize that knowledge could and should not be understood simply as an epiphenomenon of power; knowledge can be the source of power too. In this sense New Class theorizing addresses one of the questions at the core of social theory since the 1980s: the relationship between knowledge and power.

By analyzing these theories and placing them in historical context, we by necessity provide a historical account of the transformations of the social structures of capitalist and socialist societies. This allows us to evaluate Fukuyama's claims that the fall of socialism was inevitable and that liberal capitalism is the "last social formation" or the "end of history." We will argue that socialism's fall was not inevitable, but must be understood above all as the product of struggles among groups of New Class actors such as technocrats, managers, bureaucrats, and humanistic intellectuals. Moreover, our analysis will suggest that, by the time Fukuyama and others have declared liberal capitalism the ultimate victor in history, the neoliberal state so admired by Fukuyama is already in a profound crisis. This crisis is partly a result of not coming to terms with the changes in the structure of advanced capitalism that have indeed created New Class actors who must be involved with any renegotiation of power between labor and capital. We believe that finding a solution to the crisis of advanced capitalism necessitates a clear understanding of the place of intellectuals in the structure of Western society.

New Class Theories: Definitions and Social-Theoretical Relevance

The term "New Class" was coined by Mikhail Bakunin around 1870 in his book *The Knoto-Germanic Empire and the Social Revolution*. In analyzing the possible social consequences of the Marxist scenario of socialism, he wrote: "There will be . . . an extremely complex government, which will not content itself with governing and administering the masses politically, as all governments do today, but which will also administer them economically. . . . All that will demand an immense knowledge. . . . It will be the reign of scientific intelligence, the most aristocratic, despotic, arrogant and contemptuous of all regimes. There will be a new class, a new hierarchy of real and pretended scientists and scholars, and the world will be divided into a minority ruling in the name of knowledge and the immense ignorant majority" (Bakunin 1966, 80–97). The idea of this New Class, the possibility or the danger of a postcapitalist class society, in which domination is based not on ownership of wealth but on monopoly of knowledge, has haunted the social sciences ever since.

The term "New Class theory" describes a variety of approaches. In our search to provide an all-encompassing definition of New Class theory, we found only two points that New Class theorists tend to agree upon: (1) Marx was correct in predicting that the class rule of the bourgeoisie under capitalism will not last forever; but (2) Marx was incorrect in hoping that the formation that will follow capitalism will be either classless or the "dictatorship of the proletariat." All New Class theorists claim that postcapitalist society will be a new class society in which a new class, other than the proletarian, will rule. But beyond this claim there may be no common ground for New Class theorists; the history of New Class theories is a history of political and theoretical controversies.

After a century of prolific debate, New Class theorizing is still in shambles. New Class theorists are unable to agree as to who would be the likely candidate for the new dominant class position: bureaucrats, technocrats, engineers, managers, or what Alvin Gouldner calls the "critical, counter-cultural, adversary-culture intellectuals." On what grounds will the New Class rule? Will it be on the basis of its bureaucratic position within the state, or by knowledge monopoly? What type of knowledge will those agents most likely to form the New Class need: technocratic or teleocratic, technical or theoretical? In what kind of society will the New Class become dominant: state capitalist, socialist, or bureaucratic collectivist? Where is the New Class more likely to emerge: in Soviet-type societies, in the West, or in both systems simultaneously? Will this New Class be progressive, "our best card in history" (Gouldner 1979), or will it be the most despotic of all dominant classes? Is the New Class a "class" at all, or rather it is an "estate," a dominant "group" (Feher et al. 1983), "officialdom" (Bauman 1974) or a "new priesthood" (Schelsky 1974)?

Different theorists have come forward with diametrically opposed answers to these questions. To make matters difficult, they have given little guidance as to what sort of empirical evidence we need to test these claims. How can we know whether the New Class is or is not in the making? What sort of evidence do we need to decide whether the formation of such a class progressed more in what used to be the socialist East, in the capitalist West, in social-democratic Sweden, in the technocratic United States, or in postcommunist Eastern Europe or Russia? When will we know that the New Class has succeeded to unseat the old dominant class? When can we decide that it has failed to do so and that we should therefore forget about the New Class project altogether?

In this book, we attempt to move towards a synthesis of previous New Class theories and to develop a research agenda to assess, in a comparative framework, how far advanced the formation of the New Class is in different national and historical settings. Again, to avoid pre-empting the crucial question of the "classness" of the New Class, we may pose our research question this way: what are the indications, if any, that a new type of domination, based on monopoly of knowledge, is challenging or replacing domination based on ownership of wealth or on bureaucratic position?

We hope that our attempt to achieve such a synthesis will be a worthwhile venture. Although we read quite extensively in the New Class literature, we could not find a satisfactory theory, and we were also often irritated by the lack of specificity and lucidity in this literature. Nevertheless, our intellectual journey around New Class theories turned out an exciting one. We gained refreshingly new insights invaluable toward rethinking critically, mainstream—Marxist or stratificationist— explanations of the position of the highly educated in the social structure. The more sophisticated among the New Class theorists often demonstrate a sense of irony and a kind of self-reflexivity typically absent in Marxist or stratificationist analyses of the power and privilege of intellectuals. Critical reflections on the New Class are critical reflections on ourselves: if there is a New Class, we the critical intellectuals are, in one way or another, more centrally or more peripherally, part of it. Gouldner formulated quite formidably the central question of New Class research when he asked "Where does the cameraman fit in?" (Gouldner 1979, 9). In other words, where do we intellectuals fit in? Where does the power—if any—of the knowledge producers as knowledge producers come from? Indeed, the main strength of New Class theorizing is *critical self-reflexivity*.

While exploring this question, New Class theorists in essence are practicing critical theory. The authors of the more sophisticated New Class theories have radicalized the sociology of knowledge. Since the famous passage in "The German Ideology," in which Marx and Engels hypothesized that the dominant ideas of each epoch represent the ideas of the ruling classes (Marx and Engels 1972, 44), and more specifically, since the contributions of Karl Mannheim, we are aware that all knowledge is existentially based (Mannheim 1971, 59–115). We know that there is an intimate linkage between knowledge and interest, knowledge and power. But the first wave of Marxist and non-Marxist sociology of knowledge assumes that the knowledge producer is a neutral instrument through which particularistic interests of other social agents, classes, generations, ethnic groups, etc. are formulated. Neither Marx nor Mannheim asked the question: does the interest of the knowledge producer as knowledge producer have any impact on knowledge? For the Marxists, knowledge producers are "organic intellectuals" (Gramsci 1980, 5–23) of one class or another; for Mannheim, knowledge producers are "socially unattached" (Mannheim 1972). New Class theories, however, push one step further along the frontiers of the critical-theory project; they now subject the theorist (that is, the knowledge producer) to critical scrutiny. Hence the irony and the novelty of their insights.

Paralleling such radicalization of the sociology of knowledge by some New Class theories is the radicalization of critical theory or theory of knowledge by Jürgen Habermas, Pierre Bourdieu, and Michel Foucault. None of these authors believe in the existence or even in the possibility of a new dominant class, with its power based on knowledge monopoly. Instead, they call for a domination-free discourse as the precondition of genuine human emancipation (Habermas 1979); emphasize cultural capital or symbolic domination as a relatively autonomous source or form of power and privilege (Bourdieu 1977, 487–511); and, more importantly, insist on the twin concepts of power/knowledge and the implied inseparability of the two phenomena (Foucault 1980), thus indicating that some New Class theorists (most typically Alvin Gouldner) do address the same questions as the most creative and influential social theorists of the last two or three decades. Thus New Class theories may make contributions toward the very central debates surrounding contemporary social theory.

On these pages, we try to achieve three tasks. First, we try to identify different types or waves of New Class theories, demonstrate where the strength of each theory lies, and suggest particular insights to be gained from them. In this way, we attempt to offer a history of the idea of the New Class and an immanent critique of each wave of theories. Second, we complement this task with a sociology of knowledge approach. That is, we try to link the waves of theories to failed attempts at the formation of the New Class. Our central hypothesis is that, over the past century, groups of the highly educated did indeed have power aspirations of their own and, at different historical conjunctures, did pursue "collective mobility projects" (Sarfatti-Larson 1977) or "New Class projects" (Gouldner 1979). Until now, all of these collective mobility or New Class projects have proved failures, and so the New Class theories could be interpreted as critical or apologetical, overgeneralized or premature reflections of these projects. The primary reason, therefore, why the theories are incomplete or fragmented is not because the theorists made analytical errors, but because the empirically identifiable projects they generalized from were premature, incoherent, and contradictory. Finally, we try to develop a synthetic theory of the New Class. Tongue in cheek, we turn from being critics of the New Class to being its ideologues. We ask the question, can the highly educated learn from the lessons of history and formulate a project that will bring intellectuals to class power? How would a complete theory and a successful class project of the highly educated look? We also try to assess the prospects for a successful New Class project in light of such a synthetic theory, first in the West, then in the East.

Waves of New Class Theories

We distinguish three waves of New Class theories: the anarchist theories of the intellectual class of the late nineteenth and early twentieth centuries; the bureaucratic-technocratic class theories of the 1930s, 1940s, and 1950s; and the knowledge-class theories of the 1970s. Each wave offers different insights; each wave captures in a fragmented manner different aspects, or dimensions, of a New Class formation.

From a textual analysis of New Class theories, we identified three such dimensions of class formation: agency, structural position, and consciousness. While theorists in each wave capture features in each dimension, they put particular emphasis on selected dimensions. Thus the first wave of theories emphasizes agency, the second structural position, and the third consciousness.

Our key assumption is that a successful formation of a new class requires that all three preconditions are present: there are agents who are ready to assume class power; a new structural position is created from which class power can be exercised; and, finally, the new agents with class aspiration have the appropriate consciousness, necessary to exercise class power. We believe that an analysis of these three dimensions of class formation could be applied to the study of any class. The making of the bourgeoisie or the modern proletariat may also be assessed this way, but such a distinction may be particularly pertinent for the understanding of the phenomenon we call New Class. As the New Class, at least up to this historical moment, is a particularly unevenly formed class, its history is more a history of failures than of successes.

The Anarchist Theories (1870–1917)

The anarchists spotted early the latent scientism and elitism of the Marxian project of socialism. Bakunin's attack against Marx during their collaboration in the First International focused on the statist features of the Marxist conception of socialism. He argued that the complexity of the knowledge that a government-run economy and society requires will inevitably lead to rule by scholars and intellectuals.

Jan W. Machajski, the Polish-Ukrainian anarchist, following the anarchist line of argument, suggested that there are two different visions of socialism: workers expect socialism to be egalitarian, while intellectuals see the essence of socialism in state power (Machajski 1937; Nomad 1959). Machajski believed that this intellectuals' vision of socialism is self-serving, intellectuals wanting to use the working-class movement to promote their own rise to power through the state bureaucracies. The society that would emerge would be as inegalitarian as capitalism, except that privilege based on private capital ownership would be replaced by privilege based on the monopoly of knowledge.

Thus both Bakunin and Machajski were skeptical with regard to the role intellectuals would play in the socialist movement. To give primacy to the political over the economic in mass struggles, to under-emphasize equality as a goal, and to concentrate on the nature of state power are ideologies that serve the power aspirations of the intellectuals but do not contribute to the emancipation of the manual workers.

The first wave of theorizing concentrates on the question of agency: who are the agents who may attempt to form a New Class? Why do intellectuals play such a prominent role in the working-class movement? Can one accept on faith that such intellectuals are indeed altruistic, acting as the mouthpiece of the proletariat (as Marx and Engels suggested in *The Holy Family*), or is there good reason to suspect that they may in the end serve their own particularistic interests, pursue their own power aspirations?

Technocratic-Bureaucratic Class Theories

From the late 1930s onward, several theories have emerged claiming that a bureaucratic, a technocratic, or a managerial new dominant class is in the making or already in power in the (former) Soviet Union, in Western capitalism, or in both. These theories are rather heterogeneous: the agents each suggests will become the core of the New Class are quite different (from Stalinist bureaucrats to American managers). Some theories insisted that the New Class formation was limited to the Soviet Union, while others would describe the evolution of a new dominant class under both capitalism and socialism. Still, the common feature of all these theories is the claim that class power based on individual ownership of capital has been superseded and a *new structural position* created from which economic power can be exercised.

Although in the works of Thorstein Veblen as well as of Adolf Berle and Gardiner Means (Veblen 1963; Berle and Means 1932) such an analysis began to develop independently for Western societies alone, most of the bureaucratic class theories could be traced back to the work of Leon Trotsky (Trotsky 1974) and to the empirical analysis of the early Stalinist Soviet Union.

Trotsky himself was of course not a New Class theorist. He emphatically denied the class character of the bureaucracy and emphasized that the Soviet Union, even after the rise of the Stalinist bureaucracy, remained a workers' state (though a deformed one). Still, Trotsky powerfully documented the conflicts of interest between the ruling Stalinist bureaucracy and the working class during the 1930s in the Soviet Union, and so opened up the theoretical space for bureaucratic class theories.

Indeed, the first comprehensive theories that described the Soviet Union as a society dominated by a bureaucratic class were developed by former Trotskyites who, particularly under the influence of the Stalin-Hitler pact, found it unacceptable to believe that the Soviet Union was a workers' state. Thus Trotsky's former disciples moved beyond their teacher by pointing out the class nature of the ruling Soviet bureaucracy and thus offering a more radical analysis of the character of the Soviet Union. Two versions of such post-Trotskyist bureaucratic class theories could be distinguished: according to some (for instance, Tony Cliff), the Soviet Union was state-capitalist, and capitalism was restored by the Stalinist bureaucracy (Cliff 1979); according to others, under the influence of Bruno Rizzi (Rizzi 1985), the Soviet Union represented a fundamentally new social system that was different from either capitalism or socialism, and that rightfully should be called bureaucratic collectivism (Shachtman 1962). Bureaucratic-collectivist societies are ruled by the state bureaucracy, constituted as the new dominant class. However, both the early state-capitalism theories and the bureaucratic-collectivism theories assumed that the class power of the bureaucracy was based in a new form of ownership: the bureaucrats collectively owned the means of production.

These early theories of the Soviet Union as a New Class society dominated by a collective ownership class, the bureaucracy, remained influential for some time. Elements of their impacts can be traced to theories emerging as late as the early 1970s. There are, however, three reformulations of these early bureaucratic class theories in the post-Stalinist epoch. Milovan Djilas and, in the late 1960s, Jacek Kuron and Karol Modzelewski accepted the idea of a new dominant bureaucratic class whose power is based on collective ownership, but they still regarded Soviet-type societies as "communist" or "state monopoly socialist."[1]

Maoists, such as Charles Bettelheim (1976), developed a new version of the state-capitalism theory. The Maoists argued that the Soviet Union restored capitalism and became a New Class society, but, unlike the post-Trotskyist theorists, they also believed that the agents who carried out this restoration were not Stalinist bureaucrats but enterprise managers. However, in a crucial respect both Bettelheim and the post-Trotskyist bureaucratic-class theorists were in agreement: both identified the base of the class power of the managerial technocracy in its collective ownership of the means of production.

During the early 1970s, a new version of bureaucratic collectivism emerged in the works of Antonio Carlo (in his case traces of the Maoist influence can be found) and, to an extent, in some writings of Cornelius Castoriadis (Carlo 1974; Castoriadis 1978–79, 212–48). Both Carlo and Castoriadis believed that the Soviet Union was obsessed with economic growth and consequently produced an economic system with "production for production sake." Since this production would serve the interest of *production* rather than the satisfaction of genuine social needs, Soviet bureaucratic collectivism (Carlo) or total bureaucratic capitalism (Castoriadis) would, in the last analysis, serve bureaucratic class interests.

The idea that in Soviet-type societies individual private property withers away, and that the class power of the old bourgeoisie is replaced by the power of whoever de facto controls the means of production, influenced the thinking of those who analyzed the transformation of social structure in Western societies.

Some of these Western New Class theories are spin-offs from Trotskyist analysis of the Soviet Union. James Burnham, a former Trotskyist, developed in the early 1940s the theory of "managerial society" (Burnham 1964), where he claimed that the Russian revolution replaced the bourgeoisie with managers as a dominant class. He also stated that the managerial revolution was a worldwide phenomenon, with fascist Japan and Germany also appearing to be moving towards managerialism, as the United States did with the New Deal. Thus Burnham developed an East-West theory of the New Class, which forecast the evolution of a new dominant class for the Western world, too.

During the 1930s, the idea of a technocratic-managerial transformation of modern capitalism had been emphasized by some with apologetical, others with critical, overtones. Berle and Means (Berle and Means 1932) reported approvingly the advance of managerial power in the United States. They claimed that capitalism was undergoing a major transformation, with private property being dissolved and private owners replaced by managers in the position of economic power.[2]

Several theorists of the Frankfurt School, and even Habermas in his early writings, have had an analogous, though critical, analysis of modern capitalism, fascism, and Stalinism (Habermas 1970). Some Frankfurt School authors regard these societies as being technocratically deformed.[3] They portray early capitalism as liberal-democratic, and so focus their criticism against advanced, technocratic capitalism. Technology, they say, intrudes increasingly on all spheres of life, even culture and politics; Fascism and Stalinism are extreme expressions of such a scientistic, technocratic development. The theorists of the Frankfurt School in such writings come close to a theory of postcapitalist, or state-capitalist, society in which the technocracy or the positivist scientists rule (though, in the last instance, none of the critical theorists accept New Class theory).

The second generation of New Class theorists concentrated their attention on the question of structural position: what kind of positions do New Class agents have to occupy in the system of social reproduction to qualify as the new dominant class, and is there a new structural position in modern societies that replaces the position guaranteed under classical capitalism by private, individual ownership of capital? A few of the theorists argued that in postcapitalist societies, incumbents of state bureaucratic positions perform functions similar to or equivalent to those performed by private owners under capitalism. The same argument has been made about the replacement of the position of "owners" by "managers" or "technocrats."

The Knowledge-Class Theories of the 1970s

During the 1970s, for the first time, the political right (the neoconservatives) began to develop their own New Class theories; earlier theories were typically, though with a few exceptions, left-wing critiques of Marxist theory or of Marxist-Leninist political practices. The neoconservative argument was that the left intelligentsia has developed an "adversary culture" that seeks to undermine the value system of modern democratic society and establish the power of a modern "priesthood" comprised of moralizing left intelligentsia (Schelsky 1974).[4] The left intelligentsia, this argument contends, exercises undemocratic pressures through the media, or uses the welfare state, academia, or the combination of these institutions to create its own class domination (Moynihan 1982).

Daniel Bell, in *The Coming of Post-Industrial Society* (Bell 1976), develops a politically less charged but in certain respects similar argument.[5] According to Bell, scientists are believed to play a fundamentally new role in postindustrial society. Scientific-theoretical knowledge accordingly becomes a major force of economic growth and social progress in the postindustrial epoch. Under such circumstances, there is room for a new, socially progressive knowledge class.[6]

Both Bell and the neoconservatives are knowledge-class theorists. Like Bell, the neoconservatives point to the existence of a new quality of knowledge upon which rests the class aspiration of the intelligentsia. But while for Bell this new quality is theoreticity, for the neoconservatives it is simply the destructive and subversive aspects of the new culture that the left intellectuals advocate.

Alvin Gouldner offers the most comprehensive knowledge-class theory. Gouldner's research project on the New Class begins as a sociology-of-knowledge critique of Marxism and the role of the left revolutionary intellectuals (Gouldner 1975–76, 3–36). Gouldner spots certain features of Marxism—in particular its "metaphoricality" (Gouldner 1974, 387–414), which makes it suitable for the Marxist intellectuals to pursue self-interested goals while pretending to represent universal interests. Armed with this knowledge, the revolutionary intelligentsia can substitute itself for the proletariat and emerge from the revolution as a new dominant class. In his two major works on the subject, *The Dialectics of Ideology and Technology* (Gouldner 1976, 9–13, 23–63, 195–294) and of course *The Future of Intellectuals and the Rise of the New Class* (Gouldner 1979), Gouldner develops a New Class theory that not only encompasses the power aspirations of the Marxist revolutionary vanguards but also reflects on the increasing power of the technocrats/scientists. The key concept Gouldner develops is the notion of a "culture of critical discourse," which captures the common feature, the common quality of knowledge shared by Marxist radicals, professionals, the technical-intelligentsia, and adversary or countercultural intellectuals. As the knowledge of the highly educated takes the form of this culture of critical discourse, the cultural capital thus acquired enables them to "usurp" from the position of power both "old line bureaucrats" of state socialism and private capitalists.

Typically, knowledge-class theories were reflections of the changing social relations in the West. But one author of the present work
developed, in his book *The Intellectuals on the Road to Class Power*
(Konrád and Szelényi 1979), an analysis quite similar to that of Gouldner. Konrád and Szelényi argued that the intelligentsia in Eastern Europe,
by virtue of its monopoly over "teleological knowledge," formulates
claims for class power, and in the post-Stalinist epoch there has indeed
been a trend for the bureaucracy to open up and join forces with the
intelligentsia, thereby becoming a new dominant class.

The last New Class theories explore the changing nature of knowledge. They typically argue that a new type of knowledge (call it adversary culture, teleological knowledge, cultural capital, etc.) is gaining
ground and the possessors of this knowledge are in a radically new relationship to domination. It is assumed that the possessors of this new
type of knowledge can now make an autonomous bid for power.

Our main criticism of existing New Class theories is that they are
incomplete: they overemphasize one dimension of the New Class phenomenon, of the process of the formation of the New Class. In Table 1
we assess schematically the waves of New Class theories (more "+"
[plus signs] in the chart means more emphasis put on such a dimension by the wave's theories). The central task of theory-building is to
combine these fragmented insights into a coherent theory that combines all three dimensions.

Incomplete Theories as Reflections of Incomplete Projects

It is possible to interpret the history of the past two centuries as the
history of several failed attempts at the formation of the New Class.
The incompleteness of the theories is nothing else but the theoretical
reflection of these unsuccessful collective mobility projects.

Table 1. Insights, by wave of New Class theories, on dimensions of the formation of
the New Class (plus signs denote a wave's emphasis on a given area)

Wave of New Class theories	Agency position	Structural	Type of knowledge
Intellectual class	+++	++	+
Bureaucratic-technocratic class	++	+++	+
Knowledge class	++	+	+++

The first such project was attempted by what Karl Mannheim termed the "socially unattached intellectuals" of the nineteenth century. They were the uprooted intellectuals who had lost their traditional social position, but were unable or unwilling to accept the new position market capitalism offered them.[7] It was quite clear who the agents were who aspired to a new social position; it was, however, less obvious what that position might be and what sort of knowledge it called for, or how the agents would go about acquiring such a position.

Bakunin and Machajski were critical theorists of such "agents." The empirical reality they were confronted with was the overrepresentation of intellectuals in the social democratic movement of the nineteenth century and their unshakable belief that they are the "true" representatives of working-class interests. The anarchists' suspicions were not without basis; these intellectuals were not as altruistic as they claimed. But on the other hand, the anarchists' predictions did not come true. The intellectuals certainly did not come to power with the Russian Revolution. On the contrary, most perished in the concentration camps during the 1920s and 1930s at the hands of the newly emerging Stalinist bureaucracy. Still, our main point is that there was a project of the radical, socially unattached intelligentsia for power of their own during the late nineteenth century. This project certainly failed, particularly since the agents of the project were utopian; they did not have a clear enough vision of the structural position they would need in order to fulfill their power aspirations. But the project existed; hence the realistic core of Bakunin's theory.

The second wave of New Class theories reflect several projects. These projects—namely, the Soviet bureaucratic project, the technocratic project, and the managerial project—are not identical, but they show certain similarities despite the significant differences in the social and historical circumstances under which they originated. It was probably the Soviet bureaucratic project that came closest to acquiring class power. It may be that Djilas, after all, in the whole New Class literature had the most convincing case. The Soviet-type bureaucracy undoubtedly succeeded in creating a new structural position in the system of bureaucratic planning upon which a New Class formation would appear quite plausible. Curiously enough, on the other hand, this new structural position has been occupied by quite "archaic agents"—a bureaucracy possessing "Asiatic," "pre-modern" characteristics.[8]

This Soviet-type bureaucracy does not deserve to be called a class, however, since the type of power it exercises is of pre-class character. Particularly in the Stalinist epoch, the bureaucracy's domination required the systematic use of coercion. To transform Soviet-type societies into "modern class societies," this bureaucratic power had to be rationalized, gain rationalistic legitimacy. The main weakness of the Soviet bureaucratic project is the weakness of its rationalistic appeal.

In *The Intellectuals on the Road to Class Power*, Konrád and Szelényi tried to capture the spirit of the rationalistic, scientistic reform movements of the late 1960s and the early 1970s. These reform movements had the potential to found Soviet-type societies on rationalistic principles of legitimacy while widening the circle of those who possess decision-making powers. That book's critics, on the other hand, are probably correct in pointing out that it underestimated the resilience and the stubbornness of the Stalinist bureaucracies. For example, the manner in which the Polish bureaucracy during the 1970s sabotaged the cause of rationalistic economic, social, and political reforms indicated what a long way these societies still had to go before they could be transformed into modern class societies.

Our primary contention here is that even this bureaucratic project failed to achieve a new type of class power. The strength of the project was that it succeeded in creating a new structural position, but it was occupied by the wrong agents—namely, agents who were unable or unwilling to develop a rationalistic system of domination, a prerequisite for class power.

In the West, too, from the turn of the twentieth century onward, a group of highly educated, more specifically the technically skilled, came forward with a new claim for power. The Progressive Era in the United States, the ideology (and organizations) of the "scientific management movements" among engineers in particular, signaled the beginning of this technocratic project. Apologetic and critical, the works of Veblen and those of the Frankfurt School described this project as the increase of power of the technically highly trained personnel in a technologically complex economy. This technocratic project had a significant impact on the Soviet bureaucracy, too. During the 1930s, even the Soviet bureaucracy attempted to use technology—for instance, Soviet success in aviation—to legitimate itself. There were also movements among Soviet engineers to import the idea of scientific management, to try to promote engineers into bureaucratic positions, in short, to "technocratize" the Soviet bureaucracy (Bailes 1979).

But this technocratic project also failed. In the Soviet Union, it was defeated by the bureaucracy; in the West it proved less of a challenge to the existing system of domination than advocates and critiques of "technocracy" thought during the 1930s and 1940s. Technocratic power was co-opted. Like the bureaucratic project, the technocratic one was weak in terms of the "consciousness" dimension; technocratic consciousness in the end proved less subversive than anticipated by many.

Contemporary Western theories of the New Class emphasize the "knowledge" dimension. This indeed may capture the uniqueness and relative strength of the contemporary project of the highly educated in Western societies. We may label this wave the "teleocratic" project. In the "knowledge class" literature of the 1970s, the New Left intelligentsia—the so-called adversary-culture intellectuals—is regarded as the core of this new teleocracy, who construct a new meaning-system to foist upon society, thereby attempting to undermine the existing system of authority. They are seen as self-righteous, terrorizing society with their moralistic view of the world and politics. In other words, this teleocracy has power, not by virtue of a particularly important structural position, but because they have succeeded in developing a genuinely subversive consciousness. The essence of the teleocratic project is to gain power by constructing or reconstructing the system of meanings, thus preempting the democratic discourse by monopolizing meanings.

The teleocratic project is just the opposite of the Soviet bureaucratic project. The strength of the Soviet bureaucrats is derived from the position they occupy; their weakness is their "consciousness." Conversely, the strength of the teleocrats is the type of knowledge they possess; their weakness is that they barely have anything else, just this consciousness.

The knowledge-class theories lack credibility, since we doubt very much if a bunch of New Left ideologues, armed with subversive ideas, will be able to subvert the existing system of domination. Furthermore, it is also questionable how committed these agents are to this "teleocratic project." Those who are behind the teleocratic project are not uprooted as the agents of the project of the socially unattached intellectuals were; the culture industry, the academia, and the mass media are able to (quite effectively, for that matter) integrate them into the status quo. As the New Right started to gain ground, from the mid-1970s onward, the weaknesses of the New Left teleocratic project became obvious. Adversary culture lost its impact; many agents of the teleocratic project "deserted the camp" and, hence, betrayed the project.

We should not dismiss, though, too easily the chances of recovery for the teleocratic project. After all, it may be possible to look at the new fundamentalist right as another right-wing version of the teleocratic project. Earlier theories too easily, and perhaps erroneously, assumed that the knowledge class must come from the left, that its knowledge must be universalistic and secular. If, on the other hand, the essence of the teleocratic project is to monopolize the system of meanings, then the fundamentalist New Right, particularly the Christian Right in the United States, also pursues a teleocratic project. If Schelsky is right—that is, if one could regard the critical New Left intellectuals as a kind of new "priesthood"—then what about the intellectuals of the fundamentalist Christian Right? It is ironic that in the late 1960s and early 1970s, the emerging neoconservatives (or neoliberals?) were criticizing the left intelligentsia for moralizing politics and exercising a moralistic terror, but by the mid-1980s the intellectuals of the fundamentalist New Right had emerged as the new moralizers. The teleocratic project of the left intelligentsia suffered a serious defeat as politics moved to the right since the 1990s, but the left's cause may not be irreversibly lost.

We try to comprehend the incompleteness, muddiness, and self-contradictoriness of the different types of New Class theories as reflections of the inconsistencies in different types of New Class projects, inconsistencies that are at the root of their subsequent failures. But since the "empirical materials" we are working with are theories and not the historical contingencies surrounding the emergence and evolution of different New Class projects, we cannot give a satisfactory sociological description of these projects.

All that we expect to achieve in this book is to work out a research agenda, to identify those movements of the highly educated during the last century that could be meaningfully interpreted as failed New Class projects, and to leave it to future empirical research to reconstruct the histories of these movements.

Prospects for the New Class

At this point, we can attempt to construct a synthetic theory that measures the formation of the New Class in all three dimensions and that tries to avoid the error previous theories made—to avoid, that is, declaring the emergence of the New Class prematurely just because it made progress in one or two dimensions. In our view, it is rather difficult to answer the question of what the prospects are that a New Class will eventually form, satisfying the criteria of classness in all three dimensions. In this concluding section, we address this issue, too.

However, just because previous New Class projects have failed, we should not simply conclude that the New Class has no chance in the future. While we do not see the formation of the New Class along all three dimensions as very likely in the near future, we believe that structural changes in the social system in the East and West make New Class actors increasingly powerful. Even if they do not make a successful bid for class power, these actors will be crucial players in all substantial political and economic changes.

The New Class in the West

As we noted earlier, the main weakness of the New Class in the West during the last few decades has been its inability to find an institutional position. At the same time, of course, with increasing state intervention a new structural position around the institutions of government planning has been gradually created. This change in the social system in the West toward a statist capitalism creates the structural position from which New Class actors may make a claim for class power. If the social structure further evolves in the statist direction, creating a postcapitalist future, it is most likely that the New Class, rather than any subordinated class, will become dominant.

For those who want such a postcapitalist society, Gouldner may be right again in saying that the New Class may be the "best card" history has. It is indeed probable that an effective anticapitalist strategy can only be based on an alliance between forces of labor and the New Class. On the other hand, such a development is far from a historical inevitability.

There are two major limits to the emergence of such a statist postcapitalist class society. First, why could not society learn the lesson that it must resist simultaneously the forces of commodification and bureaucratization? The New Class may be the best card history has for us, but we may be better off if we do not play this card. Instead, we can try to maintain a more complex system of social domination. We may be better off by having two masters, rather than swapping our old master for a new one. The idea of the "New Social Movement," which is not a class-based movement attacking one dimension of domination by allying with another dimension of power, but is a broadly based social movement attacking both systems of domination, may be the most viable strategy at this moment.

Second, most New Class theories too readily assume that the agents who can become the New Class will also want the "class power" emanating from that position. Gouldner did consider this possibility, and so did Konrád and Szelényi in *The Intellectuals on the Road to Class Power*. But now we are becoming more skeptical about this possibility. It is not clear that the intellectuals, the highly educated, want class power. Even if they can have it, even if a structural position is open to them and even if "society" lets them become the new masters, it is not certain that they would seize upon this opportunity. There may be good reasons why they would not. Our tour around New Class theories and the experiences of previous New Class projects suggest that the highly educated will have to pay a very high price for class power: this price is bureaucratization. Bourgeois society at least offers the freedom of the "professions libres" and of the academia with economic security and privileges for the highly educated. Statist bureaucratization, on the other hand, would endanger such privileges. Would the intellectuals and the highly educated knowingly and willingly forgo these privileges just to exercise power? Paradoxically, the highly educated may resist the temptation of its own class power, not out of any altruistic dedication to social causes, but out of self-interest. Further, intellectuals, by resisting the temptation of class power, may actually gain a different type of power—namely, symbolic domination. This has been always an attraction to ideologues, on both the political left and the political right: to exercise influence through the possession of knowledge or information, to remain "behind the curtains" in the theater of power.

In summary, postcapitalist society under a New Class domination is possible, but not very probable.

Still, contemporary capitalist society remains mired in a long-term crisis that started in the late 1960s and early 1970s. The New Deal, representing a compromise between labor and capital, has slowly been dismantled in favor of the neoliberal state. This new regime does not rest on any social compromise; the bourgeoisie rules without any partners. As a result, the neoliberal state is weak and unsustainable. Any solution to the current systemic crisis must be based on a coalition of social forces. We believe that any such coalition must include New Class actors in addition to labor and capital to succeed. Whereas the New Deal was a compromise between labor and capital managed by the state, a "New New Deal" must contend with the social actors created by the last New Deal. New Class actors must be brought into the deal, creating a tripartite class coalition, if such a movement is to have a chance of success. In particular, international technocrats who staff governmental and nongovernmental international financial institutions must consent to this deal.

The New Class in the East

The Intellectuals on the Road to Class Power ended with these sentences:

> Paradoxically, no transcendent intellectual activity is thinkable in Eastern Europe so long as intellectuals do not formulate the immanence of the intelligentsia's evolution into a class. That however must wait for the abolition of the ruling elite's hegemony and the consolidation of the power of intellectual class as a whole. As to when that hypothetical third period of socialism will arrive, we can only say that when some East European publisher accepts this essay for publication it will be here, and not before.

In November 1989, in the midst of the tumbling walls of communist regimes, *Intellectuals on the Road to Class Power* was finally published in Budapest by Gondolat, a government-owned publishing company. Is this an indication that intellectuals have formed a new dominant class? Did the Gorbachev project, which ultimately led to system breakdown, represent the activity of this New Class of specialists and experts on its way to ascendancy? Does this support the claim that "with the rise of Gorbachev to power, one could detect a revitalization of the New Class project"?

If the answer is yes, it still has to be decided whether the newly won power of the intellectuals is a lasting phenomenon or is just a brief era of transition. If it is likely to constitute a whole epoch, what is the character of the social system that it creates? Is it a variety of capitalism, socialism, or a "mixed" system?

In this book we offer a qualified "yes" to the first question. The bureaucratic rank order collapsed all over in Eastern Europe and it was in shambles even in the imploding U.S.S.R. This is consistent with the

New Class theory advanced in *The Intellectuals on the Road to Class Power* in two ways.

First, what could be called the intellectualization of the bureaucracy undoubtedly played a significant role in the rather unexpected collapse of communism. It accounts for the bloodless "velvet revolutions" against the bureaucracy, which were only possible because of the astonishing readiness of the ruling elite to dissolve itself and its organizations, such as the Communist Party. Certainly one of the reasons the bureaucracy demonstrated so little resistance can be attributed to the changing pattern of recruitment into the party and state bureaucracy over the last two decades.

In Hungary, at least during the Kadarist consolidation, the party consciously tried to appeal to the highly educated and went out of its way to bring good young professionals into nomenklatura position, in particular into the party apparatus. Indeed the overwhelming majority of the party apparatus under forty in Hungary by the late 1980s were highly trained professionals. As these "communist yuppies" replaced the old-line bureaucrats, the ethos of the party apparatus changed. These young professional cadres, unlike those who were recruited from the working class and peasantry, did not depend exclusively on political bosses; their personal fate was not tied to the future of the party. They believed they had marketable skills, and if their party job went they could return to their professions and earn better salaries by working for multinational corporations. This turned out to be a highly bourgeoisified party elite, whose loyalties did not lie with communism. While some critics of *The Intellectuals on the Road to Class Power* ridiculed the book for suggesting that party cadre could be intellectuals, the prediction about the intellectualization of the bureaucracy (and its devastating impact on the bureaucratic rank order) proved surprisingly accurate.

Further, there is a power vacuum today in Eastern Europe. The old elite collapsed and, in the absence of a domestic propertied bourgeoisie, the only serious contender for the role of elite is the intelligentsia. A new political class is in formation, and this emergent new elite is exclusively recruited from the intelligentsia. Its members are historians, economists, sociologists, jurists, media professionals, and they all claim power; they all aspire for positions such as members of parliament, government ministers, presidents, and mayors, on the grounds of their expertise as professionals.

If one wanted to describe the power structure of Eastern Europe in 1990–91, one could fairly confidently have said it could be characterized by the power struggles between different fractions of the intelligentsia. In Hungary the society silently, and quite apathetically, watched this struggle. The Polish working class looked at the new elite with increasing nervousness, if not hostility or disgust. The new elite froze wages and boosted prices, tried to control strikes, and offered the Lenin shipyard for sale to Mrs. Johnson, while promising her industrial peace. Undoubtedly intellectuals at the time in Eastern Europe had more power than ever in history. And what used to be conflict between society and power was rapidly becoming a conflict between intellectual elites and the rest of the society.

Our answer to the second question, whether the new class would hold power long, is: we do not know. Intellectuals usually play a prominent, vanguard role in revolutionary social change, when one social formation collapses and a new one is emerging. But these vanguard intellectuals usually are unable to keep the power they grab during revolutions. As the new social order consolidates itself, they lose power and surrender some of their political privileges to other classes or social categories, such as the propertied bourgeoisie or the bureaucracy (the former happened after the French, the later after the Russian, revolution). Will the intelligentsia be able to set a historic precedent this time—to keep its power and to constitute itself as a genuine New Class, which can reproduce itself in the position of power—or will it simply surrender power to a new bourgeoisie? In other words, is the current revolution (which, for those who subscribe to a Marxian theory of philosophy, thus who believe that historical progress leads from capitalism to socialism, may really be a *counterrevolution*) much else than a probably historically brief period of transition from socialism or communism to capitalism?

We will argue that intellectuals are not constituting themselves as a New Class. Although the agents of the New Class now command the power positions in political, cultural, and economic institutions, they paradoxically abandon the consciousness necessary to rule as a class, and have dismantled the structural positions around which they could exercise class power (the redistributive integration of the economy).

Liberalism holds ideological supremacy. Relying on neoclassical economics and with deep sympathies toward the economic policies of Margaret Thatcher and Ronald Reagan, intellectuals call for a shock therapy, an unrestrained reprivatization, the wholesale, unrestricted transformation of public property into private property. This reprivatization may mean just passing the public firms into private property of managers (according to Elemér Hankiss and Jadwiga Staniszkis, a lot of this has happened in Hungary and in Poland), or it may mean passing Hungarian and Polish firms into the hand of foreigners.

Intellectuals, rather than assume class power, have taken the task upon themselves of making capitalism in Eastern Europe. The struggles among groups of intellectuals, in varying alliances with other social groups, will determine the nature of the postcommunist system; in some regions, such as Central Europe, they have already succeeded in creating a type of capitalist economy. The nature of these capitalist systems are different for every country in the region, reflecting the local balance of social forces and the outcomes of prior struggles. Perhaps the most interesting feature of this system (still rapidly transforming itself) is that it is thus far a capitalist system in which there is no dominant capitalist class; there is no grand bourgeoisie. There is the requisite consciousness (liberalism), structural positions (market-dependent firms); only the agents have not yet arrived. Who will become these agents, or even whether these agents will ever come, will be the focus of social conflict in this region for a long time. The technocracy, foreign capital, and former socialist entrepreneurs (private domestic businesspersons who started during late state socialism) will all contend for this spot.

As in the West, a clear understanding of the position of intellectuals in the postcommunist societies (and indeed of their historical roles during communism) is necessary for societal reconstruction. As intellectuals never acknowledged their own interest in socialism, they again fail to acknowledge their interests in postcommunism. They now confidently proclaim that creating a market society requires dismantling the "redistributive state" that was created during the socialist period. Thus, redistribution in the form of social welfare is "drastically overgrown" and must be seriously trimmed back to accommodate the current "stage" of development of capitalism in these societies. But New Class theory reveals that socialist redistribution benefited intellectuals, and was not "welfare" as known in the West: it did not correct for social inequalities; rather it generated them. Paradoxically, it was market mechanisms that were utilized by workers to correct for inequalities caused by redistribution.

With postcommunism, intellectuals have mostly dismantled the system of socialist redistribution. They "make capitalism" for the good of society, but in the meantime the project means that they can get well-paying jobs in the marketized sector of the economy, can serve as highly paid and rewarded "comprador intelligentsia" that assist foreign capital in penetrating the domestic market, or can become owners of businesses. They no longer need redistribution, so they wish to eliminate it. The result, in some postcommunist economies like Hungary, is skyrocketing social inequality, the weakening of domestic demand, and, most important, misery and poverty for the losers in the transition.

One

Proto-Theories of the New Class: Hegel, Saint-Simon, and Marx

In the introduction we called Bakunin the first New Class theorist. This is only correct if we understand New Class theories as critical assessments of Marxist forecast concerning the class character of postcapitalism. From Bakunin to Gouldner the social analysts whom we call New Class theorists all agreed with Marx that a postcapitalist future was inevitable, though they did not think that this society would be either classless or a dictatorship of the proletariat. They all predicted the rise of a new dominant class, which—if one used a broad enough definition of intellectuals—was likely to be composed of some fraction of intellectuals or the intelligentsia as a whole. Given this definition of New Class theories, Bakunin is indeed the first in line.

There are, however, earlier theories that foreshadow this position. The idea that the monopoly of knowledge of one sort or another may be—or, if it is not, should be—one or even the main source of power and privilege has been around since the dawn of philosophy. Plato's "philosopher king" may have been the first fully fledged formulation of the idea of "rule by reason."

In this chapter, we present three proto-theories of the New Class. All the proto-theories reviewed here share the usually normative character of earlier philosophies about the desirability and superiority of the rule of reason over other forms of social domination.

These proto-theories are already motivated by disenchantment with the emerging civil, or capitalist, society; thus, they are historically contextualized theories that formulate the dominant themes of the subsequent major waves of New Class theories. We still call them *proto*-theories, however, since they precede the idea of a classless post-capitalist future. They pave the way to the mature Marxist vision of socialism, and at the same time they identify those crucial contradictions of the Marxist analysis of capitalism and project for socialism that New Class theories will critically reflect.

The three proto-theories are: Hegel's theory of the civil servants as the "universal class"; Saint-Simon's yearning for a society ruled by scientists; and, finally, the crucial role the young Marx in his "Hegelian epoch" attributed to the critical intelligentsia, to the theorists of the socialist revolution.

The aging Hegel, an earlier enthusiast of the French Revolution, became bitterly disappointed with what he saw as the hopeless particularism of class egoism in civil society. In search of a universal viewpoint, he found the ideal state, the embodiment of the Hegelian system. This universal viewpoint was supposed to be carried out by the enlightened civil servants who could be seen as the only universal class standing above the particularistic classes of civil society.

Saint-Simon saw with anguish the anarchy that was unleashed by the forces of the market, and he saw in science and in the scientists the promise of a new, rational order.

The young Marx is inspired by both of these traditions. In his writings between 1843 and late 1844 he is searching for an agent who can indeed represent the universal viewpoint. He is also committed to Enlightenment rationalism and sees markets as a source of anarchy. Marx, however, transcends both the Hegelian and the Saint-Simonian perspectives. He is attracted early by the critique of Hegel advanced by the young Hegelians; like other young Hegelians, he objects to what he believes is Hegel's inclination to reify the state. The task for Marx, too, is to turn the Hegelian critical method against the Hegelian system and the state itself. In this process, the "critical critics," the critical intelligentsia, play a crucial role. However Marx— under the influence of anarchists, especially Proudhon—becomes irritated with the futility of criticism for criticism's sake. Thus, as early as the spring of 1844, he identifies the proletariat and not the critical intelligentsia as the universal agent of history; however, while the proletariat forms the "heart" of the revolution, its "head" remains the critical intelligentsia.

In other words, the three proto-theories foreshadow three New Class actors that will occupy the center stage of various later New Class theories: the bureaucracy, the technocracy, and the critical intelligentsia.

The Hegelian Concept of the Universal Class of Civil Servants

Hegel developed his theory of the "universal class of civil servants" in his *Philosophy of Right* (Hegel 1942). First published in 1821, this book is the work of the aging Hegel. During the last years of his life, Hegel was turning politically more conservative and he was losing his earlier enthusiasm for the ideals of the French Revolution. In developing the philosophy of the state, this conservative turn of political beliefs played an important role. Hegel made a crucial distinction in this book between the political state and civil society. This distinction expressed his changing political views and at the same time opened up important new theoretical perspectives.

Eighteenth-century French social philosophers and the classical British political theorists regarded civil society as the arena of civil liberties, the approximation of the democratic ideal of the state. As Hegel became disillusioned with the bourgeois revolution he began to look at bourgeois or civil society as an arena of rather disgraceful particularistic struggles that would keep society in turmoil unless they could be regulated by the state, expressing the spirit of the universal order. While civil society expresses particularism, the state is the embodiment of universalism: "The state is the actuality of the ethical Idea. It is ethical mind qua the substantial will manifest and revealed to itself. . . . The state is absolutely rational inasmuch as it is the actuality of the substantial will which possesses in the particular self-consciousness of its universality. This substantial unity is an absolute unmoved end in itself. . . . This final end has supreme right against the individual. . . . If the state is confused with civil society, and if its specific end is laid down as the security and protection of property and personal freedom, then the interest of the individual as such becomes the ultimate end of their association" (Hegel 1942, 155–56).

This is a critique of bourgeois democracy, and in a sense an opening to radical political theory. As Marx noted in his "Contribution to the Critique of Hegel's Philosophy of Law": "It shows Hegel's profundity that he sees the separation of civil from political society as a contradiction. He is wrong, however, to be content with the appearance of this resolution and to pretend it is the substance, whereas the 'so-called theories' he despises demand the 'separation' of the civil from the political estates . . . and rightly so. . . . The representative constitution is a great advance, since it is the frank, undistorted, consistent expression of the modern condition of the state. It is an unconcealed contradiction" (Marx and Engels 1975, 3:75).

Hegel after all did not move in the direction of a radical political theory; he thought he could resolve the contradiction, noted by Marx in the quoted passage, between the particularism of civil society and the apparent universalism of the political state by state institutions that are above civil society. Here he clearly had the Prussian state as a model in mind. At this point, the Hegelian radical left-wing critique of "bourgeois democracy" turned into a romantic, conservative one.

Despite its romantic, conservative ideological and political implications, the Hegelian theory of the state and civil society was a major advancement, when compared with French social philosophy or English classical political theory, toward the foundation of a sociological conceptualization of the state. While earlier views of civil society were operating with the concept of individual will and with the idea of contract based on an arbitrary will, for Hegel the relationship between state and civil society appeared as a problem of classes. "The merit of Rousseau's contribution to the search for this concept is that, by adducing the will as the principle of the state, he is adducing a principle which has thought both for its form and its content. . . . Unfortunately, however . . . he takes the will only in a determinate form as the individual will, and he regards the universal will not as the absolutely rational element in the will, but only as a 'general' will which proceeds out of the individual will as out of a conscious will. The result is that he reduces the union of individuals in the state to a contract and therefore to something based on their arbitrary wills" (Hegel 1942, 156–57). According to Hegel, the universalism expressed by the state was sui generis; it was irreducible to the individual will; it could be grasped only at the level of classes.

Hegel does not reduce the essence of the state to the contract between individuals; he thinks that the universality of the state is carried by one class, the "class of civil servants," that he calls the "universal class" (Hegel 1942, 131–34 and 197–200, paragraphs 202–208 and 303–307). The other two classes in society cannot express the universal will. The "substantial" or "agricultural" class can express only an implicit universality, since it is locked into immediacy, especially, the immediacy of family life. In contrast, the "business" or "industrial" class already shows reflectivity, but this is only an advance from implicit universality to explicit particularity. The emergence of this second class also signifies the movement from life based on family to life based on civil society. The political state and the universal class of civil servants is the synthesis of all earlier developments. (See the note of T. M. Knox to paragraph 202 in Hegel 1942, 356.) The explicit particularism of the business class is now superseded by this explicit universalism of the "universal civil servant class"; social life based on family or on civil society is superseded by life based on the state. "The universal class (the class of civil servants) has for its task the universal interest of the community. It must, therefore, be relieved from direct labor to supply its needs, either by having private means or by receiving an allowance from the state which claims its industry in its work for the universal" (Hegel 1942, 132, paragraph 205).

Saint-Simon and Auguste Comte on Science

Saint-Simon and Auguste Comte share with Hegel a disenchantment with the French Revolution. They, like Hegel, were particularly concerned with the deleterious societal effects of individuals pursuing particularistic goals, which they saw as a recipe for anarchy. All three searched for ways to bring order to their societies.

In Saint-Simon's view, the French Revolution induced "an upheaval in which all the existing relations between the members of a nation become precarious, and anarchy, the greatest of all scourges, rages unchecked, until the misery in which it plunges the nation afflicted by it arouses a desire for the restoration of order even in the most ignorant of its members" (Saint-Simon [1803] 1952, 5).

Neither Hegel nor Saint-Simon nor Comte, however, advocated a romantic or reactionary response to the emergence of bourgeois society. Saint-Simon, in spite of his aristocratic origins, did not champion reinstating the old order. Like Hegel, he did not want to return to feudalism, but rather to move past France's anarchic society toward a new organic social order.

Hegel's solution relied on enlightened civil service bureaucrats staffing the state. In contrast, Saint-Simon and Comte inherited an anti-statist bias from the French intellectual tradition. They were also greatly influenced by the "scientistic" bias of French social thought. Rather than identify the state as the instrument of order and freedom, they viewed science as the instrument of human emancipation. Thus, Saint-Simon and Comte drew on themes deeply rooted in eighteenth- and nineteenth-century French philosophy, which replaced religion with science as the basis for social thought and the salvation of humanity.

Saint-Simon, writing during the first years of the nineteenth century, offered a critique of the previous century and a program for the future, in works like *Letters from an Inhabitant of Geneva* (1803) and *Essays on the Science of Man* (1813). The eighteenth century was dominated by critical thought and social disorganization, he argued, and the task of the nineteenth century was to move to positive thinking and create a new social order. In this process, the development of positive sciences, especially the positive science of "man," or society, was crucial: "Already astronomy, physics and chemistry have been reorganized on this positive basis: these sciences are nowadays an essential part, the very foundation of education. It follows necessarily that physiology, of which the science of man is a part, will be brought under the same method as the other physical sciences, and that it will be introduced into education when it has been made *positive*" (Saint-Simon [1813] 1952, 21; Ansart 1970, 10–11).

Saint-Simon hoped that the evolution of positive social science would fill the vacuum created by the decay of traditional religious beliefs and institutions. "Having rendered . . . important services, the Christian religion . . . had fulfilled its function and completed the useful part of its career: it had attained old age. This institution . . . had become a burden on society" (Saint-Simon [1813] 1952, 23). Elsewhere, in his *Introduction to Scientific Studies of Nineteenth Century*, he further elaborates this point: "Deism is a belief which lags behind the present stage of enlightenment. . . . [T]he human mind owes the great progress which it has made in the mathematical and physical sciences . . . to the weakening of belief in God" (Saint-Simon [1813] 1952, 19).

The "science of man," though, served a dual purpose for Saint-Simon: beyond the accumulation of knowledge, necessary for the rational administration of society, it would also help stabilize the new social system, necessary since order had been destroyed in the previous century. This new science therefore would have to function as a secular religion; scientists would have to act like modern priests: "I have shown that the idea of God should not be used in the physical sciences, but . . . it is the best means that has been discovered of managing the fundamental political relations. . . . The scientific opinions . . . should be clothed in forms which make them sacred, in order that they can be taught to the children of all classes and the illiterate, whatever their age" (Saint-Simon [1813] 1952, 20).

Saint-Simon saw this emergent social order as an industrial society in which inequalities—necessary or even desirable—would be based on knowledge, merit, competence, on the one hand, and property on the other (Ansart 1970, 174). While Saint-Simon was in no way opposed to private property, he saw problems if it was not under the tutelage of competence. Property ownership per se, he argued, did not guarantee that proprietors would be committed to the tasks of production; they indeed might even abandon this task and "live in the style of nobles" (Saint-Simon [1819] 1952, 73; Ansart 1970, 213). Thus, not proprietors but scientists and artists were more important for the rational and effective organization of the society and the economy.

According to Pierre Ansart, Saint-Simon in *Catechisme des industriels* (Saint-Simon 1824) "gives a privileged role to industrial leaders and he sees them as being responsible for the organization of future society. In Saint-Simon's view the superiority of industrialists is not based on their wealth, since he rejects idle proprietors as one of those forces hostile towards industry, but it is based on their competence" (Ansart 1970, 165). In Saint-Simon's own words, "[T]he scientists, artists and industrialists, and the heads of industrial concerns are the men who possess the most eminent, varied and most positively useful ability, for the guidance of men's minds at the present time. . . . [T]he work of the scientists, artists, and industrialists is that which, in discovery and application, contributes most to national prosperity" (Saint-Simon [1825] 1952, 78).

Auguste Comte, who was Saint-Simon's secretary from 1818 to 1822, left the sectarian excesses of some of Saint-Simon's followers for the academy. He stayed faithful to Saint-Simon's philosophy, however, extending Saint-Simon's early formulation of positivism. For Comte, as for Saint-Simon, positivism meant the objective study of a phenomenon to find a "positive" solution based on logic as opposed to superstition or some other nonrational approach. Comte also used the word "positivism" to attack French enlightenment figures, such as Voltaire and Rousseau, for "negative thinking" that helped destroy the old order through criticism. Because these figures did not advance positive solutions to the problems they highlighted, the disintegration of the old order brought chaos. Comte also extended Saint-Simon's solution to disorder. While Saint-Simon identified agents that would exercise essentially technocratic solutions to social problems, Comte merged this idea with his desire for a positive study of society. Whereas Saint-Simon had essentially a technocratic solution to the problems of disorder, Comte saw the need for social engineering, which would be based on "sociologie," his name for the scientific study of society.

While Marx acknowledged his inspiration from German Idealism, there are also obvious links between Marx and Saint-Simon and Comte. In fact, Marx's socialism is in many respects a combination of Hegel's statism with Saint-Simon and Comte's scientific solution. Marx shares with the French the criticism of capitalism as anarchy, as well as a belief that a solution to this problem can be found only if utopian socialism is replaced by a socialism rooted in scientific rational discourse (although this reliance on science was more pronounced in Engels' writings than in Marx's own work). For Marx, as for Saint-Simon and Comte, scientific information used by planners would overcome the anarchy of the market. Marx criticized utopian socialists because they critiqued capitalism on ethical grounds, and not on a scientific understanding of society leading to an analysis of how it could realistically be transformed. This was similar to Marx's critique of the anarchists for their overemphasis on the role of spontaneous activity of the workers in social transformation and their rejection of reliance on the state to organize the economy.

Marx, like Saint-Simon and Comte but unlike the anarchists, assigned a large role to the social theorist in social transformation. The anarchists believed revolutionary consciousness would be formed spontaneously by what Marx termed the lumpen proletariat without any help from intellectuals. However, unlike Comte's and Saint-Simon's, Marx's view of the role of intellectuals is informed by his bottom-up approach to history. Saint-Simon and Comte view society from above, and want to impose order through a scientific elite. In contrast, Marx sees the structural basis of the new society in the workers. To the extent that intellectuals, or "bourgeois ideologists, who have raised themselves to the level of comprehending theoretically the historical movement as a whole," as he refers to them in the *Communist Manifesto* (Tucker 1978, 481), understand the historic mission of the workers, based on a scientific understanding of capitalism, they can react back upon history by providing leadership and a revolutionary consciousness for the proletariat. However, not just any consciousness can be inscribed on the proletariat by revolutionary theorists. Rather, the theory must be ad hominem to the worker. It must describe a reality that the worker experiences but does not have the concepts or theories to make sense of.

The Proletariat as a Universal Class

In the development of the Marxist theory of classes, the critique of the Hegelian theory of the state and "universal class" played a decisive role. During 1843 and 1844, in those crucial years during which Marx and Engels prepared their epistemological break with Hegel, they subjected the views of Hegel and the Young Hegelians to systematic critique. The first major piece was the "Contribution to the Critique of Hegel's Philosophy of Law," a work that Marx left incomplete in the summer of 1843. This book attempted to demystify the idea of the "universalism of the state." The "Contribution to the Critique of Hegel's Philosophy of Law. Introduction" (in Marx and Engels 1975, vol. 3) written some six months after the "Critique" itself, is a major breakthrough.

While, in his critique of Hegel, Marx simply rejected the Hegelian notion of the civil servants as the universal class, in this introduction for the first time he identified the new universal agent as the proletariat. In 1844 Marx and Engels joined forces and, in "The Holy Family" (Marx and Engels 1975, vol. 4), concentrated their attack on the Young Hegelians. In objecting to the role that some Young Hegelian philosophers attributed to the "critical critics" (critical intellectuals), they substantially expanded their theory of the "universal class of the proletariat." Lukács found these works the key to the understanding of the Marxist concept of class (Georg Lukács 1971, particularly section 3, 149–209; see also material about Lukács's application of the concept of the "proletarian universal class" in I. Mészáros 1971, 91–94). Lenin also regarded the "Contribution to the critique of

Hegel's philosophy of law. Introduction," among other works written in this epoch, as a crucial link in the development of the theory of the proletarian revolution (Lenin 1960, 21–47).

The Critique of the Universalism of the State

In the "Contribution to the Critique of Hegel's Philosophy of Law"— if we may use Gouldner's terminology (Gouldner 1979, 7)—Marx documents how "badly flawed" is the universalism of the state in general and the state bureaucracy in particular. Marx's critique of Hegel is, in fact, as much anti-feudal as anticapitalist. The argument Marx develops in this essay has two components.

First, Marx shows the pseudo-universalism of the kind of political rule represented by the estates in the Prussian State, and in this sense he offers an anti-feudal critique of the early- and mid-nineteenth-century German political system. This analysis still belongs to the bourgeois-liberal epoch of Marx. His early journalism in the *Deutsche Jahrbucher* and in the *Rheinische Zeitung* was still very much a rejection of prebourgeois, feudalistic, and authoritarian German political machinery. The main concerns of the young journalist Marx were civil liberties, universal suffrage, and other sorts of what he would later come to call "bourgeois rights." In other words, in unmasking the particularism hidden behind the pretended universalism of the political system of the German State, and especially of Prussia, Marx offered a critique of the political system from the point of view of civil society. The political program to gain "bourgeois citizenship rights" was very much on Marx's agenda; he defended bourgeois democratic institutions and found the demand for the separation of civil society from the political state justified. Marx also thought that the replacement of the monarchy with a representative constitution would be an advance (Marx and Engels 1975, 3:75 and see also footnote 3:77).

Already, in this work, however, Marx began to move significantly beyond such a "bourgeois liberal critique." He desired the separation of civil society and the political state because it would reveal the unconcealed contradictions in the modern state (Marx and Engels 1975, 3:75). He believed that, in the final analysis, in spite of pretensions to universalism, the state is a universalized expression only of the particularistic interests of the dominant class of the civil society: "The bureaucracy must therefore protect the imaginary generality of the particular interest, the spirit of the corporations, in order to protect the imaginary particularity of the general interest—its own spirit" (Marx and Engels 1975, 3:46). Marx found the Hegelian scenario not only false, but also dangerous. A reformed Prussian state, with an enlightened civil service bureaucracy, conceals rather than alters the character of the modern state. The removal of the feudal facade and the establishment of bourgeois democratic institutions would only make it more obvious that bourgeois political emancipation in no way resolves the fundamental problems of human emancipation.

That Marx defended the bourgeois policy of the separation of the political state and civil society was not because he suspected or despised the resulting domination by the particularistic bourgeois interests less than Hegel did. Marx shared with Hegel a belief in the need for a universal viewpoint, for universal emancipation, but Marx thought that Hegel was searching for the agent of such emancipation in the wrong place.

The Problem of Human or Universal Emancipation

The question of universal emancipation, the identification of the agent who represents the universal interest of humankind, was permanently on Marx's mind during these months. In his essay "On the Jewish Question," written immediately after he ceased work on the unfinished manuscript of the "Critique," Marx continued the search for his solution (Marx and Engels 1975, vol. 3).

While, in the "Critique" Marx established the need for bourgeois political emancipation that would "unconceal," but not resolve, the contradictions of civil society, in "On the Jewish Question" he tried to be more specific and offer a solution to these contradictions. This essay is a critique of Bruno Bauer, a Young Hegelian, who argued that the Jewish question could be solved by a radical political emancipation of the Jews. Marx agreed that such a political emancipation would be necessary. However, as in the "Critique," he reconfirmed his belief that it would not be sufficient for real emancipation: "Political emancipation is . . . a big step forward. True it is not the final form of human emancipation in general, but it is the final form of human emancipation within the hitherto existing world order" (Marx and Engels 1975, 3:155). All that political emancipation can achieve is the "reduction of man . . . to a member of civil society" (3:168).

It was human emancipation in general that was really needed, a form of emancipation that would transcend civil society, the society of egoistic, independent individuals. In terms of the Jewish question, this meant that it was not sufficient to make the state genuinely universal, as Bauer wished. Bauer recommended a state that regarded religion as the private affair of individuals; Marx believed this insufficient. The final emancipation of the Jews would come only if society was also emancipated from Judaism and all other religion (Marx and Engels 1975, 3:174). While in the "Critique" Marx only demystified the imaginary universalism of the state, in "On the Jewish Question" he states the need for a universal emancipation, which cannot be carried out by the state or by state bureaucracies. In neither of these works, however, could he explain how such a universal emancipation was possible and which social force could carry it out.

After Marx finished "On the Jewish Question," he returned to his work on the critique of Hegel's philosophy of law. He wrote an "Introduction" incorporating the new discoveries of "On the Jewish Question" into this critique of the Hegelian theory of the state. Marx restated that a political emancipation—in a country like Germany, which had only the illusions of a constitutional state—was necessary, but it would not be sufficient to achieve general human emancipation. In the "Introduction," Marx moved one step beyond this position: he identified the force that could carry out the task of such a universal emancipation. This was "the class with radical chains, a class of civil society which is not of civil society" (Marx and Engels 1975, 3:186). This class—the proletariat—has a "universal character by its universal suffering"(3:186). Marx moved therefore beyond the unmasking of the "flawed universal character" of the class of civil servants; he identified his own universal class. In his view, it was a Hegelian illusion that a civil servant class could ever impose the universal will on the bourgeoisie and resolve the contradiction between the particularism of civil society and the universalism assumedly expressed by the state. No class of civil society, no class of state bureaucrats, could emancipate the whole of society. The only solution is the transcendence of civil society, of all class particularism, of the separation of state and civil society. The only class that has the interest, and may have the will as well, to transcend civil society, is the class that can only lose "its chains"; that is, of course, the working class. In the "Poverty of Philosophy," this view was formulated powerfully: "The condition of the emancipation of the working class is the abolition of every class, just as the condition for the liberation of the Third Estate, of the bourgeois order, was the abolition of all estates and all orders" (vol. 5).

The same theme is formulated in a more philosophical language in the "Economic and Philosophical Manuscripts of 1844": "[T]he emancipation of society from private property . . . is expressed in the political form of the emancipation of the workers; not that their emancipation alone is at stake, but because the emancipation of the workers contains universal human emancipation" (Marx and Engels 1975, 3:280). In the terminology of the "Manuscripts," the working class will carry out this universal emancipation, since the historical process of alienation has produced its most extreme form in the alienation of wage laborers. The total negation of wage labor will be universal emancipation.

Here we reach the most controversial point in the Marxist theory of the universal class. If in their particularistic existence the wage laborers are indeed found in the most extreme form of alienation, how can they transcend their alienated condition? How can we expect the workers in their universal suffering, alienation, and immiseration to develop the consciousness adequate to their universal historic task?

Proletariat and Philosophers: Which Is the Universal Class?

Marx confronted this question already in the "Contribution to Hegel's Philosophy of Right: Introduction." For the proletariat to fulfill its mission of universal emancipation, it has to rise from its present conditions "to the rank of a principle of society" (Marx and Engels 1975, 3:187). This cannot happen without philosophy. The universal emancipation will be achieved when philosophy and the proletariat meet: "[P]hilosophy finds its material weapon in the proletariat." And again: "The head of this emancipation is philosophy, its heart is the proletariat" (3:187).

This explanation of the transformation of the proletariat from its totally alienated condition into the complete negation of this alienation was borrowed from Hegel. "Already in Hegel the Absolute Spirit of history has its material in the Mass and finds its appropriate expression only in philosophy" (Marx and Engels 1975, 4:85). But Marx and Engels begin to see the difficulties of this explanation. For Hegel it was the Absolute Spirit that made history, and philosophy appeared on the scene only *post festum*. This view was unacceptable for Marx and Engels because of its idealism. They insisted that history cannot be made in "speculative imagination," but only by practical activity (4:86) that is guided by "actual philosophical individuals." In order to comprehend the formation of the "proletarian universal class," it was not sufficient to explore the relation between "idea" and "mass"; the relation between the philosopher and the worker was the one that required reflection. This question was discussed rather systematically in the critique of Bruno Bauer and of other Young Hegelians.

Bruno Bauer did not leave Marx's attack on him in "On the Jewish Question" without reply, but went on the counterattack (Marx and Engels 1975, 4:106–18). In Bauer's view, Marx was uncritical, since he expected the universal emancipation from an inert and passive mass; Bauer attempted to offer an alternative by revising Hegel. In Bauer's conception, the place of Absolute Spirit was taken by Criticism. Criticism furthermore was not incarnated in a mass, but in a handful of Critics. The Critics, although they reflected on history only in the imagination, still executed history, while the Mass remained the passive, material element of history (4:86).

Bauer in a sense here foreshadows the coming debate about the New Class. He doubted that the proletariat could develop the necessary consciousness to perform its function as the universal class. Bauer looked at the "critical critics" (in our contemporary terminology we may call them intelligentsia or humanistic intellectuals) as the real agents of universal emancipation, or the real universal class.

In response to Bauer, Marx and Engels elaborated their most candid and fullest account of the relations between the proletariat and the philosophers/ideologues, in *The Holy Family*. This book is the summary of their criticism of the Young Hegelian philosophy and particularly of the Bauer brothers. Despite the vitriolic language used in the book, Marx and Engels take Bauer's disrespect for the "mass" seriously. They did not want to assume that the working class will develop automatically an emancipatory consciousness, but neither did they want to degrade the workers to the role of the passive mass. They tried to strike a balance between the naive "ouvrierism" of Proudhon (whom they still admired for his dedication to the French proletariat) and the elitism of the Young Hegelians. They started their criticism of Bauer by ridiculing the idea that the act of transforming society can be "reduced to the cerebral activity of Critical Criticism" (Marx and

Engels 1975, 4:86). Against Bruno Bauer and other Young Hegelians, Marx and Engels sided with the French socialists, and particularly with Proudhon. They emphatically claimed, "Critical Criticism creates nothing, the worker creates everything" (4:20).

The method of historical materialism had not yet been fully developed, but Marx and Engels were materialist enough at that time to doubt that "critical critics," who "create nothing," could carry out the task of universal emancipation. The two began to write *The Holy Family* in September 1844, immediately after Marx ceased working on the *Economic and Philosophic Manuscripts of 1844*. During the summer of 1844, while working on the manuscripts, Marx made significant progress toward a materialist reinterpretation of the problem of alienation/emancipation. He radically reinterpreted Hegel, who understood alienation in terms of the development of the "Spirit" as a stage in the evolution of self-consciousness. In the *Manuscripts,* Marx rooted the problem of alienation in the process of commodity exchange. The proletariat for him is the best suited to carry out the task of universal emancipation since it suffers the most from the commodification of economic and social relationships. These materialistic arguments were not repeated in *The Holy Family*.

It is impossible, from the text of *The Holy Family* alone, to see how far Marxist theory had already moved away from Hegel. Lukács's analysis of class consciousness (in his *History and Class Consciousness*) is based mainly on *The Holy Family,* and therefore he overemphasized the Hegelian bias in the Marxian theory of the "proletarian universal class." We know from the 1967 introduction to *History and Class Consciousness* (Lukács 1971) how surprised Lukács was when, about a decade later, while in Moscow during his years in Soviet exile, he had a chance to read the still unpublished *Manuscripts* and to gain new insights about the materialist foundation of the concept of the "proletarian universal class." Lukács in his auto-critique subsequently acknowledged that his view of the development of proletarian revolutionary consciousness, the "ascribed consciousness of the proletariat," had been too "subjectivistic."

Indeed, if one reads *The Holy Family* after the *Economic and Philosophical Manuscripts of 1844,* one can better understand why "the proletariat . . . is compelled as a proletariat to abolish itself and thereby its opposite, private property" (Marx and Engels 1975, 4:36). Marx and Engels tried to establish what the objective reasons are for the proletariat's having a universal character. For them, the proletariat is a universal class irrespectively of its actual consciousness: "It is not a question of what this or that proletarian, or even the whole proletariat, at the moment regards as its aim. It is a question of what the proletariat is, and what in accordance with its being, it will historically be compelled to do" (4:37).

It may be possible to interpret the contribution of the Young Hegelians to Hegelian theory as an attempt to replace the civil servants by the "critical intelligentsia" as the "universal class." When confronted with the initial Hegelian position, Marx argued that the state, staffed by civil servants, could not express genuine universalism. When Marx and Engels confronted the Young Hegelian proposition, they did not really question the universalism of the point of view of critical intellectuals, but rather questioned this group's ability and interest to carry out the tasks of universal emancipation.

While Marx and Engels insisted that the revision of Hegel by the Young Hegelians was inadequate and that their own theory of the "proletarian universal class" was the only valid theory, they did not want to underestimate the role of "critical intellectuals." Marx and Engels did not commit the error Bauer thought they committed; they did not blindly believe in the revolutionary potentials of the "passive Mass." While, as a result of its objective position, the proletariat is the universal class, it can not, Marx and Engels believed, fulfill its historic task by itself. The "socialist writers ascribe this world-historic role to the proletariat" (Marx and Engels 1975, 4:36).

The wage laborers represent an objective potential for universal emancipation, but this potential will not become reality until this objective condition is theoretically reflected upon. The "universal class of proletariat" will carry out the historic task as this theoretical consciousness developed by the "socialist writers," by the "critical intellectuals," is absorbed by the working class.

This position is not an "idealist bias" in Marx and Engels, or a "concession" to the Young Hegelians. On the contrary, it is a rather mature reformulation of the idea that "philosophy finds its material weapon in the proletariat." In this new formulation, thought is replaced by real people, philosophy is replaced by the socialist writers. The Leninist view, according to which the revolutionary consciousness has to be brought into the working class from the outside, by the revolutionary vanguard, is an authentic interpretation of this Marxian theory of the proletarian universal class.

In their mature works, Marx and Engels concentrated their efforts on explaining the objective conditions of the working class. In most of their scholarly work after 1844–45, they attempted to explain why the proletariat is compelled to perform its historic task. With the exception of the *Grundrisse,* the question of universal emancipation did not receive much attention. But the idea of the proletarian universal class is never abandoned. The problematic reemerges in the work of Lenin on the revolutionary vanguard. The idea that the proletariat will have to carry out a world historic task that is beyond its immediate, particularistic interests, and will be able to do this only because an intellectual vanguard theoretically formulates such a universal task, was, and has remained, an absolutely central component of the Marxist theory of the dictatorship of the proletariat and the Marxist scenario for the emergence of socialism. Attempts to deviate from this, to "subordinate" the historical strategy to the immediate interests of the workers, to devalue the significance of the vanguard, were and will be branded as "revisionism," fatal deviations from the genuine spirit of Marxism.

Let us briefly summarize: in what way can the young Marx be seen as a proto-theorist of the New Class, and how did his early work along these lines remain consequential for the mature theory of postcapitalism as a classless society, or of the dictatorship of the proletariat?

Marx in his early work on the "universal class" offers a synthesis of Hegel and Saint-Simon. Marx adapted from Hegel the idea of universal class, the need for the universal standpoint, but he did not see the civil servants as the proper candidates for this historic role. Early on, under the influence of Proudhon, Marx found the proletariat as the only class with interest in universal emancipation. Marx's position was formulated in response to the Young Hegelian criticism of his then-recent position—that he blindly believed in the "passive Mass"—and in admiration for Saint-Simon's celebration of science. Marx qualifies as a proto-theorist of the New Class because he attributed a crucial role to philosophy and science, to critical intellectuals and social scientists, in formulating the historic task that the proletariat will have to eventually carry out.

In the mature work of Marx and Engels, the main task is to show why objectively the working class will have to carry out the task of revolution. Those who, like Lukács, overemphasize the importance of "ascribed consciousness" are usually criticized as being Hegelian Marxists. Still, the figures of scientists and critical intellectuals cast their shadow onto the proletariat, as well as upon the whole history of Marxism, including the history of concrete attempts to implement the Marxist scenario of socialism.

Two

The Vanguard Project

As the Marxist scenario of socialism was gradually turning from intellectual speculation into a political force, with the establishment of the International and, even more, with launching of the Second International and of social democratic parties, the relationship between intellectual theorists and the working class gained new importance.

In the Marxist-inspired working-class movement, intellectuals, usually from bourgeois and gentry families, played a disproportionate role, as if it might be easier for them to see the light, to understand the "historic mission of the proletariat," than for ordinary workers. Furthermore, particularly by the end of the nineteenth century, those movements in which working-class involvement was more active began to move away from the revolutionary spirit of Marxism.

As parties of the Second International gained the widespread support of the working class, they shifted in the direction of "economism"—in the language of the "authentic" Marxist critics. These working-class parties became bogged down in trade union struggles, and were charged by Marxist theorists with excessive concern with wages, working hours, and working conditions at the cost of losing sight of revolutionary goals. Intellectuals began to develop a critique of this trade-unionist "deformation," and by the early twentieth century began to formulate Bolshevik strategies in which the key argument was that the working class, left to its own devices, would only develop "trade union mentality" (as Lenin formulated in his path-breaking 1902 work, "What is to be done?"). For Lenin and other Marxist intellectuals, revolutionary consciousness would have to be brought into the working class from the outside, by "revolutionary theorists."

After the Great War, revolutionary movements spread everywhere in Europe. However, they were defeated, ironically, in those countries where the working class was the strongest. The Marxist revolutionaries' only lasting victory was in the most backward country in Europe, Russia. In this primarily agrarian society, the revolution was carried out by radicalized intellectuals in order to create the proletariat. The working-class movement during the late nineteenth and early twentieth century could only stay on a consistently radical or revolutionary path, and could have hopes for a successful revolutionary transformation, when led by a vanguard. This vanguard was by definition smaller than the working class, and the majority of its members were men of ideas, often the children of teachers, doctors, bankers, or clergy. The revolutionary vanguard, a small group of professional revolutionaries (as envisaged by Lenin during the first years of this century), by definition could not be composed of ordinary workers. Workers were busy feeding their families; they could not sacrifice their lives for the cause of the movement. Not surprisingly, the army of professional revolutionaries mainly came from the ranks of intellectuals, who either could live on family wealth or could make ends meet with incomes earned from intellectual activities.

Under these historical circumstances, the questions of why "bourgeois" intellectuals were frequently attracted to the working-class movement, how genuine was their commitment to the "proletarian cause," and to what extent they used this movement for self-serving purposes were inevitably raised. The relation between the "class" and the "theorists," the "class" and its "vanguard," had to be scrutinized.

The first to undertake this task were the anarchists. They saw the relationship between actual workers and the intellectuals who claimed to articulate the interests of these workers—if necessary even against the workers themselves—as a vulnerable point in Marxism. Bakunin offered interesting insights along these lines as early as his disputes with Marx in the International around 1870. Some three decades later, Jan Waclaw Machajski, who tried to combine the anarchist and Marxist perspectives, began to develop a quite systematic theoretical critique of the Marxist scenario of socialism along these lines, as well.

Marxists were slow to respond to this challenge. Marx, an enthusiastic debater, quite surprisingly never bothered to respond to Bakunin. Lenin and Lukács glossed over the relationship between the class and its theorists, and the issue was only first seriously discussed within Marxists circles during the 1920s, by Antonio Gramsci and Karl Korsch. In the works of Karl Mannheim, the critical analysis of this social relationship became—driven by his intellectual competition with Lukács—the foundation of a new discipline in sociology, the sociology of knowledge.

The Anarchist Critique of the Marxist Scenario

Bakunin's critique of Marx during the late 1860s and early 1870s formulated many of the themes to be taken up by different waves of New Class theories during the next century.

Bakunin on the "Flower of the Proletariat" and the New Class

In 1869 Bakunin joined the International with Marx and Engels in the belief that the slogan of this movement, "The emancipation of the toilers can be the work only of the toilers themselves," could serve as a joint program for him and Marx (Kolakowski 1981, 247). But he quickly became disillusioned. Bakunin was influenced by Proudon's anti-statism and ouvrierism, and he soon became suspicious of Marx's belief in the necessity of a strong state as a vehicle for the transition to socialism. He was particularly disturbed by Marx's notion that the proletariat was a "universal class" that had to "abolish itself" to fulfill its historic mission assigned by "socialist writers" who advocated scientific socialism. "Is it not astonishing," writes Bakunin, "that Marx has believed it possible to graft on this nevertheless so precise declaration [i.e., 'The emancipation of the toilers,' etc.], which he probably drafted himself, his *scientific Socialism*? That is to say, the organization and the government of the new society by Socialistic scientists and professors—the worst of all despotic government!" (Bakunin 1966, 97).

The disagreement between Marx and Bakunin goes back to what they regarded as the revolutionary core of the proletariat. Bakunin believed that for Marxists the revolutionary core of the workers were those fractions that were likely to become state bureaucrats or intellectual workers themselves—the highly skilled strata within the working class such as skilled workers, foremen, and the like. For Bakunin, in contrast, the revolutionary core, or the "flower" of the proletariat, was exactly that mass of unskilled workers labeled by Marx and Engels the "lumpen proletariat." Bakunin writes, "By the flower of the proletariat I mean above all, the great mass, those millions of non-civilized, disinherited, wretched and illiterates whom Messrs. Engels and Marx mean to subject to the paternal regime of a very strong government, to employ an expression used by Engels in a letter to our friend Cafiero. . . . By the flower of the proletariat I mean precisely that eternal 'meat' for governments . . . designated by Messrs Marx and Engels by the phrase . . . 'lumpen proletariat' . . . which, being . . . nearly unpolluted by all bourgeois civilization . . . carries . . . all germs of the socialism of the future, and which alone is powerful enough today to inaugurate the Social Revolution and bring it to triumph." And he adds: "To me . . . the flower of the proletariat does not mean, as it does to the Marxians, the upper layer, the most civilized and comfortably off in the working world, that layer of semi-bourgeois workers, which is precisely the class the Marxians want to use to constitute the fourth governing class, and which is really capable of forming one if things are not set to rights in the interest of the great mass of the proletariat" (Bakunin 1966, 89–90).

There is, we think, more theoretical insight behind this somewhat inflated, overheated rhetoric, than meets the eye at first glance.[1] In Bakunin's view, it is no coincidence that Marx misidentified the "flower" of the proletariat; rather, this error follows from his views about the role of the state in socialist transition: "According to the theory of M. Marx, the people not only should not destroy the State but should strengthen and reinforce it and transfer it in this form into the hands of its benefactors, guardians and teachers, the chiefs of the Communist Party" (Bakunin [1873] 1953, 288–289). Bakunin foresaw with unusual clarity the implicit totalitarianism of the Marxist statist road to socialism. He argued that while bourgeois governments administered the masses "politically," in the Marxian scenario the government would administer them "economically" as well (Bakunin 1966, 87).

According to Bakunin, as the government extends its power to control the economy, the class character of society also changes. This, of course, does not serve the purposes of the emancipation of the working class. On the contrary, as the state begins to administer the masses economically a new "reign" emerges, the reign of "scientific intelligence" (Bakunin 1966, 87). The rise of this new ruling group is the result of the need for "immense knowledge" to run the complex state machinery: "They [Marxist socialists] will concentrate all the powers of government in strong hands, because the very fact that the people are ignorant necessitates strong, solicitous care by the government. They will create a single state bank, concentrating in its hands all the commercial, industrial, agricultural and even scientific production; and they will divide the mass of people into two armies, industrial and agricultural armies under the direct command of State engineers who will constitute the new privileged scientific-political class."[2] These predictions, written in 1870, show extraordinary foresight. How much better these described the coming realities of the Soviet Union than did Marx's own ideas about socialism.

Bakunin has a few interesting ideas about class structure and he even begins to formulate the problem of cultural capital. As we will see, Machajski's more elaborate theory is to a significant extent built on these theoretical fragments. Bakunin calls the new scientific-political class the "fourth ruling class." He claims that three privileged classes have existed up to this point in history: the priestly class, the aristocratic class, and the bourgeois class.[3] As the bourgeois becomes "exhausted" with the emergence of state economic power, a new dominant class emerges, interchangeably labeled in different essays as bureaucrats, state engineers, or scientists. (He does not use the term "cultural bourgeoisie," but this may be the most appropriate.)

When Bakunin tries to define what distinguishes this "fourth ruling class" from the "third ruling class," the bourgeoisie proper, he identifies two sources of class power, property and education.[4] Marx's theory of class based on property was standing on only one leg, in Bakunin's view, and had to be balanced with an emphasis on education. Or, more politically: the weakness of the Marxian analysis was that it attacked only one dimension of social power or privilege—namely, property—but regarded educational inequalities as merely derivative or epiphenomena of differences in wealth. For

Bakunin the monopoly of knowledge was an independent dimension of social privilege, and, if unequal access to property were eliminated, would likely become the main source of fundamental class conflicts.

Machajski on State Capitalism and Cultural Capital

Jan Waclaw Machajski (1866–1926), the Polish-Ukrainian Marxist-anarchist theorist, is one of the most exciting and innovative, as well as one of the least known, figures of the prerevolutionary intellectual landscape in Russia. Some of his works have been rediscovered and published in French during the past few decades. Several decades ago, a few pages of his work were published in English, with commentary by a former student, Max Nomad,[5] but in the Anglo-Saxon world in general he has been greatly neglected.

Machajski drew on the Russian anarchist tradition. He was deeply influenced by Bakunin, but his main ambition was to create a synthesis of Marx and Bakunin. He used the Marxist method in an anarchist spirit. He practiced a "Marxism of Marxism" from the perspective of an anarchist before the "Marxism of Marxism" was formulated by Karl Korsch as an intellectual project.

Machajski's practice proved intellectually fertile. There are at least three important ideas that he was first to formulate and that had a great impact on social theory, particularly within Marxism and neo-Marxism: He was responsible for the notion of "state capitalism"; he laid the foundations of the theory of cultural capital; he was the first to develop the theory of permanent revolution. All three concepts are indeed formulated in the Marxian tradition, but they are used in his Marxism of Marxism project to offer an anarchist critique of the political implications of the Marxist scenario for socialism.

The starting point, inspired by Bakunin, for Machajski's analysis was the distinction between property and education as alternative sources of power and privilege. The elimination of private capitalists and profit would not be sufficient for the creation of a socialist society, but could only lay the foundation of an intermediary social formation that Machajski calls state capitalism.[6] There are two definitions of socialism, according to this analysis: for the workers socialism means income equality, while for intellectuals its essence is state power. But, should intellectuals succeed in acquiring state power, they would only create a new system of inequalities. While they would abolish inequality based on the ownership of capital, they would create inequalities based on differences in education.

This anarchist analysis was just the opposite of Leninism. For Lenin as early as 1903 argued that workers who gained only "trade union consciousness," who were only concerned with equality and did not desire state power, were not revolutionary. Revolutionary consciousness, according to Lenin, gives priority to the political, to the task of capturing and smashing the capitalist state, and establishing a new proletarian state in its place. For the anarchists, this was merely the ideology of the intellectual workers, who, they feared, would try to use the working-class movement as a Trojan horse to smuggle themselves into well-paid, privileged, and powerful government jobs.

Machajski operates with the scheme of historic evolution shown in Table 2. This original formulation foreshadowed Trotsky's theory of the Soviet Union as a "society in transition" or a "deformed workers state," and post-Trotskyist theorists of the Soviet Union as "state capitalism."[7] Trotsky also claimed, two decades later, that the Soviet Union was not "socialist yet," since it was ruled by a "bourgeois right"[8] or by meritocratic principles like "each according to his work." This is a bourgeois principle, since it appears egalitarian, but it is in fact inegalitarian (the right to own private property being the "bourgeois right" par excellence, the apparent right of equality upon which the fundamental inequities of capitalist society are built). Trotsky's conclusion was that the society (like postrevolutionary Russia) ruled by such a meritocratic principle is not capitalism anymore, since ownership relationships have changed fundamentally in the socialist direction from nationalization. Therefore it is not yet socialism, but rather a "society in transition."

Table 2. Machajski's scheme of historic evolution of societies from capitalism to socialism

Social formation	Private capitalism	State capitalism	Socialism
Source of inequality	Money capital: ownership of capital	Cultural capital: comparative extent of education	Equality
Character of dominant class	Private capitalists	Neobourgeoisie, intellectual workers	No classes

This view is not so different from Machajski's conception of state capitalism; Machajski also perceived state capitalism as a necessary, but intermediary, stage of social evolution between private capitalism and socialism. But there are fundamental differences between the two approaches: Trotsky offered a semi-apologia, Machajski a more critical assessment of the class character of these intermediary societies. Trotsky insisted that, with the elimination of private property, class antagonisms were overcome. Thus his society in transition was a "worker's state," albeit a "deformed" one (thus closer to socialism than to capitalism). In contrast, Machajski identified state capitalism as a New Class society, ruled by a "neobourgeoisie" (thus closer to capitalism than to socialism).

Machajski systematically explored the differences between his neobourgeoisie and the old bourgeoisie. According to Max Nomad: "In Machajski's opinion, the intellectual workers constituted a privileged neo-bourgeois class, whose interests were different from those of both the capitalist property owners and the manual workers. As owners of higher education . . . they could . . . aspire to incomes higher than those of . . . the manual workers. Members of that class who were heading the various radical anti-capitalist movements were doing so not with the view of the 'emancipation of the working class' as they claimed, but for the purposes of using the masses in the intelligentsia's struggle for a place in the Sun: first for political democracy with its job possibilities . . . later for a socialized economy under which the intellectual workers would constitute the ruling office-holding and managerial class after expropriating . . . the capitalists."[9]

But if the means of production were to be nationalized and the private capitalists expropriated, why should the new society state be considered *capitalist* and the new dominant class of state managers be regarded as a neo*bourgeoisie*? In his search for an answer, Machajski begins to explore the political economy of the New Class and makes important inroads into the theory of cultural capital.

Machajski operates with a generic notion of capitalism, which designates all economic systems in which surplus value is appropriated from manual workers and used in the interest of nonproducers, as capitalist.[10] Thus, state managers also are to be understood as a neobourgeoisie, since they similarly—though differently than the old bourgeoisie—expropriate surplus value from manual workers. It matters little, as far as the character of the social formation is concerned, whether the expropriators are private capitalists or state managers; what matters is the existence of a system of exploitation: "The expropriation of the capitalist class by no means signifies the expropriation of the entire bourgeois society. By the mere elimination of the private employers the modern working class, the modern slaves do not cease to be slaves, condemned to a life-long manual labor. The national surplus value produced by them does not disappear, but passes into the hands of the state, as a fund for the parasitic existence of all exploiters, of the entire bourgeois society."[11]

But in what way was the neobourgeoisie an exploiter; how do we know that their existence was "parasitic"? In exploring these questions, Machajski made a further contribution to the theory of cultural capital: "At a certain point complicated labor ceases to be labor of mechanical performance . . . and becomes labor engaged in directing, managing, superintending the entire labor process of society. This is the labor of the privileged employees of the capitalist system, the labor of the intellectuals, of the army of mental workers. It has a 'high value' because in its value there are contained 'higher expenditures for education' . . . . [E]very generation of privileged employees, that is, of the intellectuals during the period of its training, 'swallows' a certain amount of the national surplus value. . . . This means: for the very reason that they swallowed a certain amount of surplus value they acquire . . . the right to keep extracting . . . the unpaid product of other people's work."[12]

There is a fundamentally novel and important insight in the above quotation. Machajski makes a serious attempt to establish in a credible way that intellectual workers (today we may say "owners of cultural capital") can be understood as exploiters, analogous to owners of money capital. Investment into human capital can function as capital proper, generating profit for the possessor.

Machajski's Notion of Permanent Revolution

Max Nomad, Machajski's disciple, claimed Trotsky and his mentor shared notes and discussions while both were exiled in Siberia. In fact, in Nomad's version of the story, Trotsky took Machajski's ideas and fouled them up. The starting point was Machajski's version of historical evolution, in which capitalism, a system of inequality based on ownership, gave way to state capitalism, a system of inequality based on education and state incumbency, which would be superseded by socialism, in which there was neither private property nor a structure of educational credentials and monopoly of state offices as a source of inequality. In Machajski's analysis, state capitalist societies were ruled by a neobourgeoisie composed of intellectual workers; unlike Trotsky's analysis, this rule was not a deformation but an inevitable outcome of the elimination of property as a source of inequity before also eliminating inequities created by control of the state and of educational credentials.

For Machajski, the cultural elite was a neobourgeoisie presiding over a state capitalist regime; that they were a "bourgeoisie" and the system was "capitalist" followed from his generic notion of capitalism as a system in which surplus value is extracted from workers. In this argument, cultural capital is analogous to private capital, although the exact way this is so is never specified; Machajski had no analysis of the political economy of state capitalism, and did not identify the institutions through which surplus was appropriated. Machajski's notion of a "permanent revolution" is a call for socialists not to be naive about the "dictatorship of the proletariat"; immediately following a successful anticapitalist revolution, socialists should launch a new revolution against the educated elite that dominates the state and receives state perks. Machajski thus called for a "permanent revolution," in contradistinction to a single revolution that would smash the bourgeois state. This notion was quite close to Mao's later conception of the need for a cultural revolution against the Chinese bureaucracy (see Mao's *On the Correct Handling of Contradictions among the People* [1957]). Machajski's idea of permanent revolution is significantly different, however, from *Trotsky's* concept. For Trotsky, the permanent revolution was carried out by the proletariat of peripheral countries with significant precapitalist social relations, countries with a bourgeoisie too weak (because of its colonial nature) to carry out a bourgeois revolution. The proletariat should therefore carry out, instead, the anti-feudal revolution, simultaneously moving towards socialism.

Trotsky's theory was formulated soon after the failure of the 1905 revolution in Russia, and it attempted to draw the lesson from the relative success of the "Soviets" of Petrograd. Trotsky saw that at the heights of the 1905 uprising, which Marxists at the time primarily assessed as a bourgeois revolution, more radical, proletarian demands were formulated. Thus Trotsky believed this might be an indication that, in social conditions like the ones that existed in Russia at the start of the twentieth century, it perhaps was possible to first start a bourgeois revolution and then move directly into a socialist transformation of the society without consolidating a bourgeois social order. While Lenin was critical of Trotsky's theory for a long time, in 1917 he adapted his own position and successfully radicalized the February 1917 revolution before a capitalist social order could be established. This meant, on the other hand, that the "permanent revolution" (in Trotsky's formulation) was accomplished by October 1917—and thus the critical insights of the idea (of, that is, Machajski's version) were lost for the emerging Soviet Union. That is, Trotsky's notion of permanent revolution, like Trotsky's notion of a deformed worker's state, is far more apologetical of the Soviet system than is Machajski's concept: Machajski's version of permanent revolution would have perceived October 1917 as its beginning, while Trotsky and Lenin saw in the same event its end.

Marxist Attempts to Come to Terms with the Vanguard Role of Intellectuals

As already indicated, the anarchist challenge was ignored by Marx and Marxists for decades. They did not respond to the accusation that they promoted a scenario that might facilitate the rise of a new dominant class composed of intellectuals, technocrats, or engineers. Indeed, they did not even feel compelled to subject their own role as the revolutionary vanguard to any critical scrutiny. This began to change gradually with the emergence of what is known as critical Marxism.

Critical Marxism: Lukács, Gramsci, and Korsch

Prelude: Leninism, the Revolutionary Vanguard as a New Class?

The Marxism of Karl Marx was pregnant with two irreconcilable epistemological approaches (Alvin Gouldner referred to this as the "Two Marxisms"; Perry Anderson tried to capture the differences as those between Soviet and Western Marxism). One type of Marxism aspired to be in a science. In this respect Marx was inspired by Saint-Simon and believed a science of society, which discovers the objective laws of motion much as natural sciences describe objective reality, was necessary and possible.

At the same time, Marx was inspired by Hegel, by the project of "critical theory," and thus aimed to provide a radical critique of consciousness. In principle, no consciousness was sacred, and any could be subjected to critical scrutiny. All knowledge was *ideological* in the sense that all knowledge was intimately linked to the interests of those who created and carried this knowledge. The task of critical philosophy, or critical theory, was to unmask, demystify, and make transparent these underlying particularistic interests presented as universal. But, much as Hegel stopped short of subjecting his own system to a Hegelian critical analysis, Marx himself never attempted to use Marxist critical theory on Marxism.

During the late nineteenth and early twentieth centuries, it was the scientistic tradition of Marxism that was predominant, particularly as the Second International became a major political force. As the working-class movement in the advanced Western capitalist countries began to gain muscle, there appeared to be no real need to push toward a violent political revolution. The objective laws of economy would gradually push capitalism toward socialism. The transformation of capitalism into socialism would be an objective necessity. It could neither be done prematurely nor delayed by the bourgeoisie.

In some rather contradictory ways, the early-twentieth-century Russian Marxism of Lenin and Trotsky began to foreshadow the revival of the critical, or Hegelian, dimension of Marxist theory. Russian Marxists working in a backward country were not ready to accept that they had to wait for all the objective conditions that, according to the "scientific" theory of Marxism, would produce the revolution. They believed that the lesson of the 1905 Russian revolution was that, in a revolutionary situation, consciousness might be ahead of the "objective conditions," and thus revolutionary theory could play an active role in changing social conditions rather than just reflecting their objective realities. This pre-1917 Bolshevik theory thus was a critique of the objectivism, determinism, and scientism of the Second International, although neither in Lenin's nor in Trotsky's work can one find a hint of the application of the tools of critical analysis to Marxism or Bolshevism itself. When Perry Anderson therefore sees Lenin and Trotsky as belonging to the tradition of Western (or, in our terminology, critical) Marxism, he seems to overstate his case; Leninism was deeply entrenched in the scientistic and statist tradition of Marxism, which led inevitably to what turned out to be the most scientistic and deterministic form of Marxism, Soviet Marxism.

The reason is obvious. While Lenin was eager to subject the consciousness of the working class to critical scrutiny and find it only "trade union mentality," he had no doubt that the revolutionary consciousness that would be brought into the working class from the outside would have been arrived at scientifically by the revolutionary vanguard. He also had no doubt that the immediate task of the revolutionary transformation was to grab state power, to destroy the "bourgeois" state and replace it with a "proletarian" one. He was also certain that the time for the smashing of the bourgeois state was at hand as soon as the revolutionary vanguard was numerous enough to fill the state administrative positions with revolutionary cadres.

Lenin's message was clear: the socialist revolution did not need a society in which the majority was proletarian, with a revolutionary rather than "trade union" consciousness; what the revolution needed was a vanguard armed with the scientific tools of Marxism, and large enough to staff the state administrative positions. In September 1917, for instance, when Lenin tried to convince his fellow Bolsheviks that the party was ready to take state power, he wrote: "The proletariat, we are told, will not be able to set the state apparatus in motion. Since the 1905 Revolution, Russia has been governed by 130,000 landowners. . . . Yes we are told that the 240,000 members of the Bolshevik Party will not be able to govern Russia. . . . These 240,000 are already backed by no less than one million votes. . . . We therefore already have a 'state apparatus' of one million people devoted to the socialist state" ([1917] 1970, 413).

Thus Lenin "critiques" the consciousness of the "empirical" working class as concerned with immediate material needs rather than state power. This idea, combined with his analysis of what makes the state "proletarian" (namely, *not* that it is supported or desired by the working class, but that it is run by the cadres of the Bolshevik Party), contains all the major building blocks of Stalinism, or Soviet Marxism.

Lenin's place in the history of the idea of the New Class, and his attitude to intellectuals in general, is highly ambiguous. The above quote presents Lenin as a rather naive apologist of the rule of those who were called by Bakunin the New Class. As Trotsky astutely observed as early as 1903, when Lenin first formulated the idea of the Bolshevik vanguard party, he substituted the party for the working class.

We may want to extend, at this point, Trotsky's criticism of Lenin:

since the vanguard is composed almost exclusively of revolutionary intellectuals, Lenin substituted this intellectual vanguard for the empirical working class, for which he had neither admiration nor respect; Lenin did, on the other hand, repeatedly express his dismay with intellectuals, which is why Leninism has been perceived by many commentators as deeply anti-intellectual. The key to this contradiction is in Lenin's theory of the party. Lenin despised those whom he regarded as petty bourgeois intellectuals, those decadent, undisciplined men and women of learning who did not comprehend that history was on the side of the Bolshevik Party. These intellectuals did not join the movement, or, even if they did sympathize or actually joined, they did not subject themselves to the discipline of the party. These petty bourgeois intellectuals, who narcissistically insisted on retaining their intellectual autonomy, kept shifting ground by insisting that they were searching for the "truth." These "free thinkers" were enemies of the worse kind.

That is, intellectuals, as revolutionary theorists, had to subject themselves to the discipline of the party. Lenin had a "realist" conception of the nature of the party: the organization for him became a reality and the ultimate source of truth. The party as a collective entity was also, initially, in the process of searching for truth; therefore, at the beginning, debate among theorists was conceivable, even desirable. At one point, however, the party would arrive at the truth, which then had to be carried forth by its soldiers, the members of the vanguard.

This conception of the party, and this vision of the relationship between it and individual revolutionary theorists or members of the vanguard, moved the Marxist-Leninist socialist project one more crucial step away from its historic agent, the proletariat. As we saw in chapter 1, Marx was also tempted, in particular in *The Holy Family,* to substitute the "socialist writer" for the proletariat. However, because Marx did not have a theory of the party, he retained an external "validity test" for the truth elaborated by the revolutionary theorists. While it did not matter for Marx what the individual worker or the whole of the working class thought at any given time, since he was sure it would have to carry out the historic mission assigned to it by the radical intelligentsia, he also believed that somehow, for this theory to be true, it had to speak ad hominem to the working class. Members of the oppressed class would have to see, at some point, that this theory indeed expressed their conditions, described their misery. For revolutionary theory to take hold, it would have to help members of the working class understand their own day-to-day reality.

Lenin, because he inserted the intellectual vanguard as a collective reality between the individual theorist and the working class, no longer needed the "ad hominem" test of truth. The test of truth, for him, was whether the theory worked in the practice of the party, whether it promoted the party's aspiration to gain state power. It is in this way that Leninism forms an apologetic theory of the New Class. The essence of the Leninist theory of the Bolshevik Party is that it outlines a strategy for intellectuals, who must be ready to join the vanguard and submit to the discipline of the party, to appropriate state power in the name of the proletariat. Thus, ironically, despite his oft-expressed dismay with petty-bourgeois intellectuals, no Marxist has ever come as close to formulating socialism as a power project by the vanguard of revolutionary intellectuals organized in the Bolshevik Party than did V. I. Lenin. Lenin offers an apologetic mirror image of Bakunin's critical analysis of the "dictatorship by socialist scholars."

The critical Marxism of Lukács, Korsch, and Gramsci takes Leninism as the point of departure. These men's contribution lies in the extension of the embryonic critical theory in Leninism. Lenin saw it as the key task of revolutionary theory to change consciousness; at the same time, however, he wanted to retain the unity of the natural and social sciences. Thus he employed a "representationalist" theory of truth that posited knowledge that would exactly correspond to the "reality" of the universe, unmitigated by the activity of the knowledge producer (Rorty 1980).

Lukács moved radically beyond this "scientism," which had haunted Leninism all along. He developed a radical theory of truth that denied the existence of "social laws," but he stopped short of applying his theory either to Marxism or to revolutionary intellectuals. Thus, no matter how radical and sophisticated his theory of knowledge, the revolutionary vanguard of the early twentieth century and the Russian revolution remained untouched by his critical analysis. Korsch went one step further than Lukács by applying critical theory to Marxism, and Gramsci did the same in trying to develop a critical sociology of intellectuals. Both Korsch and Gramsci, however, as long as they remained within the framework of Marxism, fell short of answering the questions posed by the anarchists: why would the revolutionary intellectual vanguard not aspire for power of its own; why would its ideology not be self-serving when all other social actors were self-interested and their consciousness could be seen as self-serving ideologies? Critical Marxism was an important step on the road toward a critical sociology of knowledge and intellectuals, but it stopped halfway, losing its irony when it came to self-reflection.

The Critical Theory of Georg Lukács

While Georg Lukács was and remained all his life a faithful Leninist, in many respects he made a serious attempt to break away from the scientistic virus planted into Marxism, and to practice Marxism more consistently as critical theory. We are reluctant to share Perry Anderson's claim that Lenin and Trotsky were Western Marxists; we see Lukács as the founding father of modern critical Marxism, the theorist who formulated most of the major building blocks of twentieth-century critical theory (Jay 1984).

Critical Marxism is usually associated with Lukács's earliest Marxist essays, published in 1922 in his *History and Class Consciousness,* with Karl Korsch's 1923 *Marxism and Philosophy,* and with the work of Antonio Gramsci, especially his prison writings. This body of thought arose from the reaction of revolutionary intellectuals living in the advanced Western societies to the success of the revolution in Russia and its failure in the West. The question Lukács, Korsch, and Gramsci ask was the same: how could it be possible that the revolution was successful in a backward country—Russia—and failed in the advanced West, when Marxist scientific theory predicted with great certainty that socialism would be established at the core of the capitalist system, where the contradictions of capitalism would be the most mature? The answer seemed obvious: it was the politics and Marxism of the Second International that ought to be blamed. The objective conditions in the advanced West were probably ready for the revolution, but, as a result of the opportunism and revisionism of the Second International, the consciousness of the working class was not quite prepared. The problem, therefore, lay not so much with objective conditions as with consciousness. The key task of the emancipatory project became to change consciousness in order to change objective reality.

Lukács's theory of reification pushed critical Marxism in some respects—certainly in the epistemological field—to its logical conclusions. It represented the most coherent critique of positivist thought or scientism ever formulated by a Marxist, and became the natural point of departure for the Frankfurt School and for Habermas.

The problem with modern—or bourgeois—consciousness, for Lukács, was that it treated relationships among human beings as if these were relations among things. Lukács recognized that in the sphere of nature there are indeed objective laws; he resented, however, Engels's attempt to create the Marxist natural science of dialectical materialism. For Lukács, Marxism as the philosophy of social practices had nothing unique to offer to understand nature: history is made by humans; it is the product of human social practices. Only with the emergence of modernity, Lukács believed, social relations started to be seen as if part of nature. In Lukács's telling terminology, in the modern epoch[13] "second nature" is created, which means that people treat one another as objects and the appearance emerges that relationships among persons are governed by laws that seem identical to laws that govern nature.

This was an extremely influential insight. While Lukács's philosophy had, with the exception of a brief revival during the 1960s, little direct impact on modern social theory—a neglect deriving from his Leninism—the idea of "second nature" haunts critical thinking to this day. Habermas's critique of modernity as the "colonialization of the life world through the logic of system integration" is hardly more than a reformulation of the core of Lukács's theory of reification.

Reification is the process by which relationships among people are transformed into second nature, as if relationships among "things" (in German, "Ding"). It is a process through which the question of truth is reduced to the question of whether a statement corresponds to "things out there," to "things outside human practices" (see Arato and Breines 1979, 124). The English translation of the German "Verdinglichung" into "reification" is excellent. The term "rei" in Latin means at the same time a "thing" and "truth"—and it is exactly the conflation of the two that bothers Lukács the most.[14]

Lukács subscribed to a very different theory of truth. In German the word for truth is "Wirklichkeit," and "wirken" in German means "to be active, effective." As Marx argued in his theses on Feuerbach: truth is a practical question. In Lukács's formulation, as far as human history is concerned, there is no truth located outside human will and activity; only reified consciousness makes the world appear this way.

With this analysis, which culminated in his 1922 essay "Reification and the Consciousness of the Proletariat," Lukács succeeded in radicalizing the theory of knowledge. This admirable theory of knowledge had, on the other hand, some problematic political implications, and the sociology of knowledge and sociology of intellectuals undergirding the theory remained underwhelming.

Lukács's political fire was directed against Second International "revisionism," "opportunism," or "economism." The implication was that ideologues and politicians of the Second International saw the world in reified lights, and accepted that the capitalist economy was ruled by iron laws that were unchangeable. As a result, they gave up any hope of turning the trade union mentality of the workers into revolutionary consciousness. This, according to Lukács, was the ultimate reason for the failure of post–World War I revolutionary movements, which could have and should have been taken over by the revolutionary theorists capable of doing their job.

This could be seen simply as naive—the Ivory Tower philosopher suddenly turns into revolutionary activist—and Lukács himself accepted later, in his "self-criticism" (see his introduction to the 1968 edition of *History and Class Consciousness*), that he was bordering on "adventurism." In a way, his position was more than naïve; it was tragic, bordering on the criminal. Lukács, becoming one of the "commissars" of the 1919 Hungarian Soviet Republic—possibly to show to himself to what an extent he resolved the contradictions between theory and practice and overcame bourgeois reified consciousness—ordered the execution of solders whom, upon a visit to a battalion, he found not sufficiently disciplined. The weapon of criticism was turned into a criticism of weapons . . . this time, though, against ordinary soldiers of the Red Army. What a bitter irony of history, what a tragic symbol of the insanity of twentieth-century intellectuals in search of their historic mission.

It is also rather extraordinary how such an elegant, polished theory of knowledge was accompanied by such a sloppy sociology of knowledge. Although Lukács brought into the center of his Hegelian Marxist project the critical analysis of consciousness, it never occurred to him to ask himself how was it possible that he, the son of a banker, the decadent bourgeois philosopher, could suddenly turn into the socialist writer who ascribed the historic mission onto the working class. This was all the more curious since Lukács's conversion to Marxism happened overnight. Just as Saulus turned into Paulus on the road to Damascus, Lukács also saw the light and turned into a radical Marxist revolutionary within the matter of a few weeks. As late as the fall of 1918, only weeks (if not days) before his conversion, he wrote a tract on Bolshevism as an "ethical problem"; on his road to Damascus he simply *became* proletarian. There was not a shred of doubt in his mind about his authenticity as a proletarian. How such a conversion could have happened, why his own consciousness (and why the Marxist doctrine) should be immune to the kind of critical scrutiny to which he subjected other sets of ideas, are questions he would never confront.

Turning the Marxist Method on Marxism and Intellectuals: Korsch and Gramsci

While Karl Korsch and Antonio Gramsci never demonstrated the sheer brain-power at work in the essays of the young Lukács, in some ways they penetrated the problems of the intellectual vanguard and the relationship between the theorists and the working class more than Lukács ever did.

Korsch traveled an interesting intellectual trajectory. His first and major book, *Marxism and Philosophy* (1923), was politically a Leninist pamphlet. It was also, however, the first serious exercise in the Marxism of Marxism, and Korsch had the guts to follow through with his own critical insights and turn them against his own initial political project. In *Marxism and Philosophy,* Korsch made a distinction between different types, or phases, of Marxism, and, as a good Marxist, he believed that each phase should be understood as the product of the times in which it emerged. Korsch's Marxism of Marxism was born at the time of revolutionary potentials preceding the 1848 revolutions (Korsch [1923] 1971, 56); this epoch was followed by an "evolutionary stage of capitalism," and, as a result, Marxism was transformed into a scientistic ideology, the Marxism of the Second International. Korsch believed that the twentieth century brought a revolutionary crisis of capitalism and thus Russian Marxism or Leninism became a revolutionary ideology.

Korsch's political position in 1923 was basically identical with Lukács's: his critical edge was directed against the Second International and the implication was that the import of Leninism to the West might be the key to revolution. Methodologically, though,

Korsch moved beyond Lukács. Already in this politically orthodox book, he undertook a relatively radical sociological task: he treated his own religion, Marxism, as an object of study.

When Korsch faced the dilemma of choosing between his political beliefs or his epistemological commitments, he preferred the second (unlike Lukács, who for the rest of his life made a point out of remaining faithful to the Soviet Union and the Communist Party—no matter what they did). By the late 1920s–early 1930s, Korsch applied his methodology to Leninism as well (see his "The Second Party" [1928] and his "The Marxist Ideology in Russia" [1932]; see also Kellner 1977, 30–72). In these, Leninism was analyzed as an ideology that legitimated the practices of Soviet industrialization. While Korsch never turned the tools of his critical analysis on the concept of the vanguard itself, at least he subjected the ideologies of the vanguard to critical analysis.

Within the Marxist tradition, no one probed the relationship between the theorist and the class, the intellectual vanguard and the "empirical" workers, more than Antonio Gramsci did. Gramsci shared with Lukács and the young Korsch a belief in Leninism, a criticism of Second International economism, and a frustration that the revolutionary movement in the West (in his case, his native Italy) was defeated.

According to Gramsci, Bolsheviks in Russia conducted a "war of movement," a sort of frontal attack against the existing order (Buci-Gluckman 1980, 248). Such a strategy, however, was not possible in the West, where civil society and democratic institutions were too strong and only a "war of positions" was imaginable. ("War of positions" was an analogy Gramsci borrowed from the Great War, where armies often dug themselves along a long front line, faced each other for months or years, and tried to inflict casualties before attempting to break through enemy lines.) The bourgeoisie in Italy and elsewhere in Western Europe, Gramsci argued, had established a hegemonic rule that incorporated certain interests of the subordinated classes—though not their fundamental interests. The aim of the "war of positions" was to break bourgeois hegemony and establish a counterhegemony.

This analysis was already far superior, as an exercise in political theory, to Lukács's naive missionary revolutionary call. Gramsci, however, further refined the analysis. Bourgeois hegemony's great success resulted from combining diverse interests under the rule of the fundamental interest of the propertied bourgeoisie. A counterhegemony, analogously, could only be achieved if a new historic bloc was created (Buci-Glucksmann 1980, 262; Gramsci [1926] 1975, 28–51). Such an historic bloc could be the result of a politics of coalitions. The revolutionary politics would only have a chance, in countries with a strong civil society, if the working class could win as its allies other major social actors. In Italy it had to win over the peasantry, especially in the south, but it also would need the support of the intelligentsia and eventually even of civil servants or some fractions of the national bourgeoisie. This idea of the "historic bloc," the coalition among forces of labor, state workers, and domestic bourgeoisie, became the major theme during the 1970s in the so-called Eurocommunist movement, which regarded Gramsci as its guardian angel.

Gramsci's notion of hegemony and counterhegemony is of great importance. He was the first, and in many ways the only, Marxist who ever understood the importance of legitimacy. While Gramsci was hardly a polished sociologist and it is inconceivable that he had read Max Weber, it is difficult to miss the parallel between the two men's analyses.

For Marx and for most Marxists the question of why people obey orders was not a particularly interesting one: they do so because they are directly, or indirectly, coerced. Not that Marx was unaware of the problem; he just failed to appreciate its complexity. Marx believed that people do not necessarily know what their real interests are—they may have "false consciousness." Marx, however, to the best of our knowledge, never analyzed the mechanism producing false consciousness. Ruling ideas were, in his view, the ideas of the ruling class, and they misled or perhaps even brainwashed the proletariat. It was again Lukács who probed this idea further, probably under the intellectual influence of Weber, and made an interesting distinction between "false false" and "real false" consciousness. Someone's consciousness is "real false consciousness" when it serves the person's (or the class's) immediate interest but not its fundamental or long-term interest. While the difference between "immediate" and "fundamental" interests is problematic, what is crucial is that "real false consciousness" offers legitimacy to those who exercise power. It becomes incorporated into the hegemonic ideology because it creates a stake for the oppressed and/or exploited in their own oppression and exploitation. When such a stake takes hold, it creates for working people an interest to reproduce the system and to obey orders without having to be coerced.

The idea that obeying orders may happen because people accept the rules of the games as reasonable, or legitimate, was put in the center of social analysis by Weber. Gramsci arrived at a similar conclusion in his own way. The rule of the bourgeoisie was not just economically based; to a large extent, it was cultural as well. For Gramsci, social change required a cultural transformation to precede the social revolution; under such circumstances, intellectuals would play a particularly important role. At this point, Gramsci directly confronted the question that Marxists before him, from Marx to Lenin to Lukács, had avoided: is there any chance that intellectuals may articulate working-class interests? If so, why?

Gramsci made a serious attempt to develop something like a sociology of intellectuals. He made a distinction between "traditional intellectuals" of pre-modern times and the "organic intellectuals" of industrial capitalism. The traditional intellectuals had an "esprit de corps, so they [saw] themselves as autonomous and independent of the ruling social group" (Gramsci 1975, 120). While Gramsci had his doubts about how real this autonomy was, his main point was that with the arrival of capitalism even the appearance of such autonomy vanished. Under capitalism, intellectuals could only see themselves as organic intellectuals of one class or another. As for what decided which class intellectuals attached themselves to, Gramsci's rather fragmented work provides no clear answer. Undoubtedly he believed that the social origin of the intellectual played some role. Intellectuals who were the sons or daughters of the working class might be more likely to be sensitive to working-class interests, as Gramsci felt was the case with the clergy in the North (44). More important, however, was what sort of interests an intellectual articulated. Each class would "create" (118) its intelligentsia, which would articulate its own interests.

At this point, Gramsci diverged both from Lenin and from Lukács in some fundamental ways. As we have noted, both Lenin and Lukács believed that the working class was only capable of developing a practical, or trade union, consciousness; theoretical knowledge or revolutionary zeal had to be brought into the working class from the outside, as Lenin put it in his "What is do be done?" (Lenin [1902] 1960). In sharp contrast, Gramsci believed "All men are intellectuals" (Gramsci 1975, 121). The point was not that the working class did not have the appropriate knowledge, but rather that it did not have the appropriate linguistic skills. Thus intellectuals were more like the tongue of the class, articulating what the class already has at the tip of its tongue but does not know how to say. In other words, the working class had an implicit theoretical knowledge, not just a practical knowledge.

While Gramsci made great strides toward developing a Marxist sociology of intellectuals, he did not quite achieve this task. He posed the right questions but did not deliver a coherent, believable answer. If he really meant that organic intellectuals are defined by social origin, he can be easily falsified empirically. People from working-class backgrounds who make it into the professional class frequently find themselves on the conservative side. Thus, in terms of the interest they articulate, they are likely to be organic intellectuals of the bourgeoisie. Intellectuals who find themselves on the radical left frequently come from multigenerational bourgeois families and are a sort of "decadent bourgeois" who often revolt against their families by radicalizing themselves on the left. But if it is not social origin that determines what class an organic intellectual will represent, then Gramsci has no theory: there is no explanation at all why a bourgeois intellectual like Marx, Engels, or Lukács would opt to desert his or her own class and instead articulate working-class interests.

Gramsci had no solution, therefore, to the problem of the vanguard either, but it is to his credit that he at least squarely confronted the question.

"Watchman in a Pitch-Black Night": *Mannheim's Sociology of Intellectuals*

The question why, around the time of the Bolshevik revolution, so many prominent intellectuals believed their task the articulation of working-class interests fascinated not only Marxists, but their critics as well. The most prominent and most influential among these was Karl Mannheim.

Mannheim was a member of a generation of intellectuals committed to changing the world in a visionary way. This generation was particularly able and radical, and differed from the earlier generation of intellectual circles of Berlin, Vienna, Prague, and Budapest. Its members revolted against their conservative fathers and mothers, in search of a utopia. Mannheim's generation included people like Georg Lukács, Karl and Michael Polányi, and Arnold Hauser (to name just a few of the great minds that inhabited this intellectual milieu), all sharing a belief in the possibility of a utopian future. The bottom line of the following analysis of Mannheim is that his sociology of knowledge and of intellectuals can best be understood as a self-reflection of a member of this generation of the utopian vanguard. This analysis points to the same "real object" as does the anarchist critique of the "intellectual class" or the critical Marxist apologia of the intellectual vanguard of the proletariat. In Mannheim's case, however, the intellectual is portrayed as a "watchman in a pitch-black night" (Mannheim 1972, 143), neither a self-interested, power hungry New Class character nor a leader or "tongue" of an agent other than himself (or herself). He or she is just a person of ideas in search of a better future, driven in this process in part by intellectual curiosity and in part by a commitment to human emancipation.

It took some time for sociologists to realize that the key to understanding Max Weber was Karl Marx; as long as Talcott Parson's translations and interpretations dominated understandings of Weber, it was not obvious that most of Weber's work was really a dialogue with Marx. Similarly, we still have to realize that the key to understanding Mannheim is Lukács. Mannheim's essays on the sociology of knowledge and his *Ideology and Utopia* can be interpreted as an ongoing dialogue with Lukács, whom he perceived as his main intellectual competitor.

Mannheim's starting point was Lukács's critique of bourgeois reified consciousness, but he somewhat radicalized the argument. In Mannheim's view, that bourgeois consciousness reflects bourgeois reality is not unique, because all knowledge is existentially based *(Seinsverbundenheit des Wissen),* and "all knowledge" must of course include Marxism, the ideology of the proletariat. That knowledge is ideological does not bother Mannheim, for this fact does not mean knowledge is untrue, or false. Knowledge is always offered from a certain perspective; it is relational (Mannheim 1975, 253). Being relational is quite different from relativism; relativism "denies any standards of the existence of order in the world. Relationism does not signify that there are no criteria of rightness and wrongness in a discussion. It does insist, however, that . . . they cannot be formulated absolutely" (254).

Marxism, in Mannheim's view, made major contributions to a "theory of ideology," which could even be conceived as "the beginning of the sociology of knowledge" (Mannheim 1975, 248–49). It fell short, however, in fulfilling this task since "this relationship [thus the relationism or ideological character of knowledge] was perceived only in the thought of the opponent." As elaborated in chapter 1, in his "Contribution to Hegel's Philosophy of Right: Introduction," Marx tried to resolve this dilemma by claiming that the proletariat was a universal class. Thus the revolutionary theorist who takes the particularistic viewpoint of the proletariat in fact expresses universalism: proletarian ideology is science. Lukács borrowed this idea from Marx without modification—a position rather untenable since Lukács already rejected a "science" of society. The proletariat as that particularistic class that is universalistic was a dubious enough construct in Marx, but at least he still believed in the possibility of arriving at scientific truth about human existence and society, a stance rejected by Lukács. Mannheim therefore probes Lukács at the right point: to have particularism turn into universalism, an ideology turn into objective truth, when no such thing as "objective truth" exists, is unpersuasive, to say the least.

More important, Mannheim did not quite understand why a rather decadent philosopher, the son of a banker, felt obliged to take the "standpoint of the proletariat" to express the utopian vision of his generation of intellectuals. Why did Marxist intellectuals believe they had to speak for somebody else rather than courageously to speak for themselves?

In Mannheim's view, it was better to accept a distinction between "doers" and "thinkers," politicians and economic organizers, on the one hand, and the artistic, moral, religious, and scientific intelligentsia, on the other. This latter elite has a chance to develop a somewhat "detached perspective" (Mannheim 1975, 253). After all, while knowledge is always from a certain perspective, these perspectives or opposing views are far from infinite (134–35); this makes a synthesis possible. Such a synthesis is far from just the average view: the latter would only aid in the reproduction of the status quo. If a synthesis of competing paricularistic viewpoints was achieved by a relatively classless stratum, by a socially unattached intelligentsia (*freischwebende Intelligenz*, a term Mannheim borrows from Alfred Weber), then it could serve "progressive development." This, for

Mannheim, was when intellectuals were at their best, in acting as "watchman in pitch-black night."

Why, according to Mannheim, could intellectuals serve this role? "A sociology which is oriented only with reference to social-economic classes will never adequately understand this phenomenon" (Mannheim 1975, 138). The reason was that the "modern bourgeoisie had . . . a twofold root—on the one hand the owners of capital, on the other those individuals whose only capital consisted in their education" (139). This latter group could not be perceived either as a class on its own, or a social agent that would always act on behalf of others. It was recruited from "increasingly inclusive areas of social life" and therefore "subsumes in itself all those interests with which social life is permeated" (140). Mannheim accepted that intellectuals could be organic intellectuals of one class or another, but he believed that his own generation could do better: at their best, they could act as "watchmen."

While Mannheim's critique of Marxism and Lukács is well taken, his solution does not seem more persuasive; if anything, it is even more pathetic. To Mannheim's credit, he, unlike Marx or Lukács, does not walk away from the problem. In 1940, a good decade after Mannheim "solved" the problem of intellectuals as "socially unattached agents," he returned to the question in his *Man and Society in the Age of Reconstruction*: "We have progressed so far as to be able to plan society and even to plan man himself. Who plans those who are to do the planning? . . . Who plans the planners? The longer I reflect on this question, the more it haunts me" (Mannheim 1940, 74–75).

Three

A Bureaucratic Class
in Soviet-Type Society

Ever since Russia declared itself to be on the road to socialism, there have been skeptics, usually on the political left, who would argue that this experiment could not be considered *genuinely* socialist. Over the decades, the number of skeptics increased. Many of these skeptics celebrated the fall of the Soviet empire, arguing that these countries were an embarrassment to socialist politics.

We are not obsessed with definitions; the debate over what name should be used to describe those socioeconomic systems that existed in the U.S.S.R. for over seventy years and in Eastern Europe for some forty years, and that still exists (at least politically) in China does not particularly excite us. We will use the term "socialist" to describe these systems even though we recognize that these countries did not live up to some of the doctrine's key ideals—in particular, to the principles of democracy so central to the nineteenth-century theorists of socialism. Nonetheless, these countries made a serious effort to implement some of the key economic proposals of socialism: private property was outlawed, the means of production became publicly owned, and the "expropriators were expropriated"; an effort was made to implement a system in which production targets were determined by the substantive rationality of the party and its economic planners rather than by the logic of the market and the pursuit of profit.

Below, we review the most influential challenges to the argument that Soviet-type societies can be considered socialist: the "society in transition" approach, the state-capitalism thesis, and the theory of bureaucratic collectivism. As we shall see, these theories are based on differing assessments of the nature and operation of the socialist economy; nonetheless, in each the argument that Soviet-type systems should not be considered socialist has been based on an implicit comparison of existing socialism with its ideal type.

"Society in Transition" Theories

The first critics of Soviet socialism drew on Lenin's own writings, which were contested in a debate between Gregory Zinoviev and Stalin at the Fourteenth Party Congress in 1925. As early as 1918, Lenin argued that the Soviet Union was a "society in transition"; the position first appeared in *Left-Wing Childishness and the Petty-Bourgeois Mentality,* and had a significant impact on later debates regarding the Soviet economy.

Lenin's analysis began with the argument that the Soviet economy was a social formation in which many modes of production coexisted. The vast majority of the Soviet Union comprised a patriarchal/peasant sector and small-scale commodity production. The rest of the economy consisted of a private sector, a socialist sphere, and a transitional sector (that Lenin called "state capitalist").

The state capitalist mode of production consisted of firms that were publicly owned but for which the relations of production subordinated workers' power in favor of bureaucratic managers. These sectors had been confiscated or nationalized by the state, but had not been socialized. Lenin thus distinguished between legal property relations (relations of production) and social property relations (relations in production [Burawoy 1985] or social property relations [Brenner 1976]).

Because Lenin saw the state capitalist sector as a transitional mode of production, he was largely uncritical of it, despite its undemocratic (and thus seemingly nonsocialist) nature. For Lenin, the confiscation of property and the emergence of the state capitalist sector formed a step towards socialism, because these firms established public ownership, which, unlike the private sectors, did not strengthen the forces of capitalism. Unlike his left-wing critics, Lenin identified the state capitalist sector as a largely progressive force, and one consistent with the socialist project.

Lenin's distinction between legalistic conceptions of property rights (public ownership) and true socialism was a significant contribution to future understandings of socialist economies. However, his inability to identify a mechanism through which the state capitalist sector would become socialist undermined the credibility of his argument.

After Lenin, the distinction between legalistic and substantive conceptions of property rights was used in a more critical way. Within the Soviet Union, the meaning of state capitalism was debated, as noted above, by Stalin and Zinoviev at the Fourteenth Party Congress. Stalin advocated a legalistic conception of property rights, and thus collapsed Lenin's distinction between the state capitalist sector and the socialist sector. For Stalin, the existence of public ownership meant the existence of socialism. (Stalinists and neo-Stalinists subsequently used this argument when they promoted the state sector against cooperative forms of ownership.) In addition, Stalin argued that what Lenin meant by state capitalism was the participation of state-owned firms in joint ventures with primarily foreign capitalists. This position was consistent with, and provided support for, Stalin's advocacy of the New Economic Policy and its call for an expanded role of the private sector to stimulate economic growth.

Zinoviev interpreted Lenin quite differently. His argument became known as the "integral state capitalism thesis," and was expressed in the Party's minority report. Zinoviev argued that there was a capitalist and a socialist version of state capitalism. Joint ventures between state-owned firms and foreign capitalists were a capitalist version of state capitalism, and were therefore politically undesirable. Unlike Stalin, Zinoviev argued that those state-owned firms not involved in joint ventures were a socialist expression of state capitalism. Zinoviev emphasized that these firms were not yet socialist because they were linked to markets and because the state bureaucracy held control within the enterprise; this control was evidenced by the existence of the piece-rate system, used to transform labor power into labor. Although conceding that these firms were not yet socialist, Zinoviev argued that they were located in the public sector and were therefore consistent with socialism: class relations were fundamentally altered by public ownership, and served the interests of the working class.

While Zinoviev ultimately endorsed the economic system in the Soviet Union, others were not so sanguine. Karl Kautsky and Otto Bauer, for instance, were among the very first who took a strong stand against the Leninist state on the grounds that it was "state capital-ist" (Kautsky 1920; Bauer 1920; Jerome and Buick 1967, 59–60). These analysts thus anticipated much of the argument of the "state capitalism" theorists (discussed below). Both Kautsky and Bauer were disenchanted by the dictatorial nature of the early Soviet-Russian state. They had started with the assumption that a crucial feature of socialism is democracy, and therefore could not define the new dicta-torial state as socialist.

In *Terrorism and Communism* (1920), Kautsky suggested that socialism might not be viable in the Soviet Union. A Second Interna-tionalist, he argued that the attainment of a certain level of economic development was a prerequisite for socialism. According to Kautsky, the Soviet Revolution was progressive insofar as it abolished feudal-ism, but did not create the conditions for the economic and political development required for a transition to socialism.

Bauer, an Austro-Marxist, criticized the dictatorial nature of state capitalism in the Soviet Union but argued that this was a temporary stage between capitalism and socialism. Bauer believed that economic development would eventually create the social conditions for political democracy, which would then lead to the attainment of socialism in a peaceful fashion; thus the establishment of state capitalism made pos-sible the political transition to socialism in the Soviet Union.

In sum, very shortly after the Soviet Revolution, critical reflec-tions on the nature of Soviet society focused on the undemocratic na-ture of the regime and on the difference between nationalization and socialization. While all except Stalin agreed that nationalization had taken precedence over socialization, people theorizing the revolution were divided on whether this development was temporary or signified the destruction of the revolutionary project. While these theorists raised important questions and moved beyond legalistic analyses of property relations, their ideas were not integrated into a comprehen-sive theoretical framework.

A full-fledged theory of state capitalism came much later. The first concise, critical theory of Stalinism was offered by Leon Trotsky in his *Revolution Betrayed* ([1937] 1972). His argument was counterposed to the early "proto-theories" of state capitalism discussed above.

According to Trotsky, Soviet society after 1917 was a "society in transition": either capitalism would be restored (although, until the Hitler-Stalin pact, Trotsky believed that this was unlikely) or socialism would develop. The Soviet system was neither capitalist nor socialist, he suggested, because this system, like the system of petty commodity production, had its own relations of production. The "society in transition" was a mixture of plan and market, although most investment decisions and the allocation of capital goods were determined by the plan. To the extent that the market continued to exist, it was restricted to the sphere of redistribution and served bureaucratic interests.

Trotsky's analysis of class relations in the Soviet Union was based on his argument that a fundamental difference between capitalism and socialism is the difference between distribution according to "bourgeois right" and distribution according to need. Drawing on Marx, Trotsky argued that "bourgeois right"—distribution based on merit—appears egalitarian but is substantively unequal. In a socialist society characterized by the public ownership of property, goods would be allocated according to need rather than "bourgeois right"; however, in the Soviet Union, distribution was not based solely on need: bureaucrats were rewarded on the basis of their "share" (advantage accrued on the basis of position in the bureaucracy) as well as of their labor. Trotsky thus came quite close to acknowledging that bureaucrats had property rights (the term "share" clearly implied the notion of ownership) but ultimately did not do so. He also failed to recognize that workers enjoyed some property rights (i.e., access to full employment) under Soviet-type socialism: while both workers and bureaucrats collected some rewards based on property rights rather than on labor, bureaucrats collected more.

Trotsky gave several reasons that the bureaucrats were not a class: bureaucrats did not own stock and therefore could not sell their property; recruitment took place through an administrative hierarchy; their positions could not be inherited; political rather than economic power was the basis of bureaucratic privilege; bureaucrats could conceal their income; and bureaucrats were parasitic rather than productive. But while Trotsky argued that bureaucrats were not a class, he acknowledged that, as a group, they had risen above the workers and had constituted themselves as a ruling caste.

Trotsky thus rejected Kautsky's argument that Lenin had created a state capitalist formation in Russia (Trotsky [1937] 1972, 249–50). In Trotsky's view, the Bolshevik Revolution had created a society that was largely socialist in character: it eliminated private property, altered class relations, and created a workers' state by elevating bureaucratic planning over the market. The Soviet bureaucracy under Stalin's leadership, however, had deformed the political system; members of the bureaucratic stratum appropriated political power from the working class (248–49). The Soviet Union under Stalin remained a workers' state, but it was a bureaucratically deformed one.

The bureaucratic deformation of the Soviet workers' state also had an economic component. The ruling caste misused its political power for its own benefit; scarce goods were allocated unequally to benefit the bureaucracy (Trotsky [1937] 1972, 111–12). Because the Stalinist bureaucracy reintroduced market relations in the sphere of circulation, bourgeois rights dominated in that sphere. Thus it was the market allocation of consumer goods that was the source of inequality between the bureaucracy and the working class.

Trotsky's emphasis on the emancipatory potential of public ownership and planning, and his identification of the market as the source of bureaucratic privilege, meant that the restoration of capitalism was much less likely than the evolution of socialism. For the U.S.S.R. to return to capitalism, a social counterrevolution would be necessary. This would require a restoration of private property and the remaking of a propertied class. Movement toward socialism would also require revolutionary change—but a political (rather than social) revolution was all that was needed.[1] Socialist relations of production had been established.

Trotsky's "society in transition" approach is theoretically elegant and offers insights into one of the fundamental conflicts of socialism: the conflict between workers and bureaucrats.[2] However, there are both theoretical and political problems with the classical Trotskyist position.

Theoretically, the argument that the Soviet Union was neither socialist nor capitalist is highly problematic. Trotsky's analysis of the ways the deformation of the political system affected the economy is both theoretically incoherent and empirically false. First, he does not explain how capitalist relations of distribution could coexist with socialist relations of production. Second, and more important, there is ample empirical evidence that in classical socialist economies the privileges of the bureaucracy are *not* based upon the market (Nee 1989; Walder 1992a; Szelényi 1978). Rather, the bureaucracy is primarily privileged as a result of the administrative allocation of scarce resources. For example, bureaucrats receive free housing from public authorities, while workers have to build housing for themselves. David Stark's notion of "mirrored comparisons" is useful in understanding the role of markets and administrative allocation in the generation of inequalities (1986, 492–504). While, in capitalist economies, markets generate basic inequalities and the state may somewhat reduce those inequalities, under socialism the opposite is true: inequalities are created by administrative allocation, and those with low incomes and prestige must resort to the market to improve their position (Nee 1989; Szelényi 1978).

Theories of Socialism as State Capitalism

The second wave of critical theorizing about the nature of the Soviet economy—the first coherent formulation of the state capitalism thesis—came from former disciples of Trotsky. These former Trotskyites, such as Tony Cliff, found the political implications of this theory unacceptable, following the Hitler-Stalin pact of 1939.[3]

There are two versions of the state capitalism thesis, with very different assumptions about what constitutes the essence of capitalism, as well as different political implications. The first coherent state capitalist position was offered, by the mid-1940s, by Cliff (1974 [1948]). Cliff identified the bureaucracy as a new dominant class of a new statist formation, and dated the "restoration of capitalism" in Russia to the Stalinist takeover. The second state capitalist theory was formulated in the late 1960s by then-Maoist Charles Bettelheim ([1970] 1976). Bettelheim regarded enterprise management as the new bourgeoisie, and dated the restoration of capitalism to the economic reforms of Khrushchev.

Post-Trotskyist State Capitalism Theory

Cliff rejected the Trotskyist argument that the bureaucracy was not a ruling class, as well as the characterization of the Soviet Union as a workers' state. First, Cliff pointed out that the legal and formal public ownership of property did not mean that the state served the interests of the workers. Further, Cliff argued, the bureaucrats did not merely have control of the sphere of distribution, but over the means of production as well.

The Stalinist bureaucracy did more than *administer* the means of production—it became its de facto (although not de jure) proprietor. Thus, Cliff argued, the bureaucracy could not be a caste: it was much more than just a judicial/political grouping. Cliff did not consider the Stalinist bureaucracy to be identical to the classical bourgeoisie, as it lacked legal property rights over the means of production and its members were not able to exercise property rights individually. Nonetheless, Cliff suggested, insofar as the Stalinist bureaucracy exercised control of private property on behalf of the whole bureaucratic class, it was a collective private proprietor. As a result of its de jure ownership/possession of the means of production, then, the bureaucracy must be defined as the new dominant class. Workers and bureaucrats were not members of the same class, and a transition to socialism would therefore require not just a political but a social revolution.

Cliff also argued that the social formation that existed in the Soviet Union was a capitalist one. This argument rested on the assumption that the essence of capitalism was capital accumulation. In the Soviet Union, the first Five Year Plan led the country on a path of accelerated industrialization and capital accumulation. The bureaucracy performed the historic tasks (the accumulation of capital and proletarianization) normally undertaken by the bourgeoisie, and could thus be considered its equivalent. The bureaucrats' obsession with growth and with production for production's sake meant that, like the bourgeoisie, the bureaucrats would seek to diminish workers' control wherever possible. The obsession with growth also distinguished the Soviet economy from true socialism, which was aimed at the satisfaction of human need. The socialist project was thus transformed by the Stalinist bureaucracy into a strategy of economic growth and capital accumulation, and it was at this point that capitalism was restored, although in a new, statist form. For Cliff and others, it was socialism's economic efficiency and "obsession with growth" that was the object of criticism; later, critics would focus on the *inefficiency* of socialism.

Cliff's criticism of Trotsky is appropriate; indeed, it is difficult to accept the notion that the bureaucratic deformation of the Soviet system was limited to the sphere of distribution. While the Stalinist bureaucracy was not particularly privileged in terms of consumption (as compared with the conspicuous consumption of the Western bourgeoisie), the bureaucracy did exercise "despotic rule" at the point of production (Burawoy 1985, 12).

Cliff's argument regarding the class character of the bureaucracy is less persuasive. One reason for this has to do with his inadequate theorization of property rights. Without an appropriate theory of property rights, or the specification of which "bundle of rights" define a social relation as *private* property, Cliff moves from the observation that the bureaucracy acquires some property rights to the conclusion that the bureaucracy is the private proprietor of that property. This theoretical move creates a limitless concept of private property, for, if the Stalinist bureaucracy was a private proprietor, then private property and capitalism as an economic system would be universal in human history.

Cliff's proposition regarding the *capitalist* character of the Soviet economy is equally dubious. Cliff came close to calling the Soviet Union of the 1930s capitalist because it entered a growth trajectory. Economic sociologists from Marx to Weber have been much more precise about what kind of growth and capital accumulation can be considered capitalist. Both Marx and Weber agreed that, for a system to be capitalist, capital accumulation must take place on the market, and the profits used for accumulation must be generated by economic means and invested in competitive capital markets. The Soviet economy did not fulfill any of these criteria: during the 1930s coercion was the primary means by which surplus was appropriated, and the allocation of capital was not guided by purely economic criteria of profit maximization.

The Maoist Theory of State Capitalism

Bettelheim's theory of state capitalism was strongly influenced by the ideas of Mao. In the early 1940s, Mao wrote two important articles on the centrality of contradictions in the dialectical process. Mao emphasized that contradictions are never fully resolved, that with new syntheses come new sets of contradictions. Implicit in this argument is the notion that contradictions would also characterize socialist societies, as the creation of a new state would entail a new set of contradictions.

This idea is somewhat analogous to the notion of "permanent revolution" as originally formulated by Machajski. For Machajski, the notion of permanent revolution was the key to the anarchist critique of statist versions of socialism. Machajski argued that this form of socialism was inevitable: the abolition of private property would be followed by nationalization; this new society would be dominated by a technical, bureaucratic class. Machajski suggested that the establishment of statist socialism is a step forward, and that the correct strategy is to ally with the statist elements in order to break up private property. But Machajski also emphasized that this new statist elite must be opposed immediately in an effort to establish "the good society." In sum, for Machajski, nationalization meant the establishment of a new state bourgeoisie with a novel relationship to the working class.

Thus, for both Mao and Machajski, contradictions remain salient after the revolution, and are a driving force in the process of social change. Initially, Mao qualified this somewhat by arguing that, while the contradictions between rulers and the people are antagonistic, the contradictions among the people are not. By 1957, reflecting on the Hungarian experience in 1956, Mao suggested that, although contradictions among the people are not necessarily antagonistic, they may become so if mismanaged. Mao even went so far as to suggest that the relationship between the bureaucracy and the people can be permanently deformed, and can take on class characteristics.

Bettelheim's theory of state capitalism is clearly informed by this line of argument. Bettelheim suggested that the Soviet bureaucrats' mismanagement in the 1960s was so extreme that antagonistic contradictions did in fact develop, and the bureaucracy was transformed into a new bourgeoisie. The key agent of bureaucracy's transformation was the managerial technocracy.

In Bettelheim's view, the essential features of capitalism are the establishment of private ownership, the separation of the direct producers from the means of production, the commodification of goods and labor, and the separation of the units of production from each other (Bettelheim [1970] 1976, 85). The emergence of capitalism thus occurs when units of production are transformed into enterprises. Enterprises (units of production) are separated from each other economically and interact with one another through the mediation of the market. Thus, a capitalist economic system and a New Class have been established when two crucial economic activities are mediated by the market: the allocation of labor, and the allocation of capital goods. If both labor and capital are allocated on self-regulating markets (where the prices of labor power and investment goods are set by the rules of supply and demand), we can speak of a capitalist economy; this presumes that the producer, to sell his or her labor power on the marketplace, has been separated from the means of subsistence and means of production. Those nonproducers who possess capital goods are therefore private owners, or capitalists. Capitalism thus exists when enterprises compete with each other for labor and capital goods on price-regulating markets. Implicit in this argument is the notion that there is an elective affinity between forms of ownership and modes of economic coordination.

Central to this argument is Bettelheim's identification of two main types of ownership rights. "Possession" refers to who controls the process of production: managers or the direct producers may exercise control over this process. "Property ownership" refers to who appropriates the surplus: individuals may appropriate the surplus for their consumption/inheritance, or there may be collective ownership, in which case surplus is appropriated according to a plan. Under capitalism, monetary calculation—according to which single enterprises or firms emphasize short-term growth—predominates. Under collective ownership, economic calculation is longer term, and emphasizes growth for all its firms. Under state capitalism, however, managers appropriate with the short-term interests of individual firms in mind, but do not appropriate surplus for private consumption.

Bettelheim thus distinguishes between capitalism and state capitalism. The social formation in which property has been nationalized but not socialized, and in which managers possess the means of production (control the process of production) and allocate surplus not for their own individual consumption but according to a plan, is state capitalism. But what is the class character of such a society? Bettelheim suggests that the Stalinist state remains a working-class state, that the worker's enemy is the technocrat rather than the bureaucrat. It is the technocrats who seek to restore capitalism by replacing the plan with commodity production and transforming the state enterprise into the collective property of the state bourgeoisie.

Defining capitalism in terms of labor and capital markets, the separation of units of production, the emergence of enterprises, private property, and profit-maximizing behavior sounds eminently sensible. In fact, Bettelheim's argument foreshadowed Szelényi and Konrád's theorization of economic coordination and property relations in socialist societies. The problem with Bettelheim's analysis is empirical rather than theoretical. Bettelheim claims that capitalism was restored in a statist form in the Soviet Union during the late 1950s and early

1960s with Khrushchev's economic reforms. While Bettelheim was correct to note that the implementation of these reforms would send the Soviet Union on its way to capitalism, these reform proposals were not implemented, and the central planning apparatus retained power over the allocation of investment goods. Without proper capital markets, it is unlikely that labor was allocated on the market. Instead, the supply of labor, like that of capital, was politically and legally controlled. In all socialist countries, a law obliged the laborer to sell his or her labor power. Thus it was not economic necessity but legal coercion that determined the supply of labor. Under these circumstances it is not reasonable to assume the existence of a labor market.

Bettelheim's mistake, then, was that he interpreted the spirit of reform proposals as the actual practices of Soviet economic management; it was only as recently as the early 1990s that Russia made a serious effort to implement these policies. Ironically, Bettelheim's notion of state capitalism may offer a cogent means of theorizing postcommunism.

The Theory of Socialism as Bureaucratic Collectivism

During the late 1930s a rather obscure Italian author, Bruno Rizzi, published *The Bureaucratization of the World* (Rizzi [1939] 1967). This book had, for decades, a significant impact on the theoretical debate regarding the character of socialist economies.

Unlike most of the theorists we have discussed, Rizzi did not have a Marxist background or many academic credentials. *The Bureaucratization of the World* was a political pamphlet that can be read as either the ramblings of a nineteenth-century liberal against the all-pervasive penetration of government, or the statement of a fascist sympathizer predicting that the fascist way of doing business would be the future of humankind.

The crucial point of Rizzi's book was that by the late 1930s a new social formation was emerging all over the world. For Rizzi, fascism in Italy, Germany, and Japan, the New Deal in the United States, and Stalinism in Russia all seemed to have new and common features. These formations diverged from earlier more individualistic ones, promoted collectivistic values, and relied heavily on state bureaucracies. For Rizzi, this new social formation was neither capitalism nor socialism but a new kind of social organization, which Rizzi called "bureaucratic collectivism." Under this new social formation, the state bureaucracy constituted itself as a new dominant class. The power of this class was based on its collective ownership of the means of production (Carlo 1974, 45–49). Bureaucratic-collectivist societies were inegalitarian class societies based on a new property relation: bureaucratic ownership of the means of production. In 1957 Milovan Djilas expanded this idea, producing his seminal *The New Class*.

The New Class of Communist Bureaucrats

Milovan Djilas, a former high-ranking communist apparatchik in the Yugoslav Community Party, broke ranks with Tito in 1957 and shook the world of professional sociology with his book *The New Class*. The book had the most unusual history: it was not only a confession by a former communist bureaucrat (who later served long prison terms in Tito's assumedly "liberal" communist Yugoslavia for his role as a dissident), but arguably it had a greater impact on the sociological literature than did any other book, although written by a nonsociologist and without following any sociological conventions. It barely presents any data to support its large theoretical claims, and it does not cite the professional literature. Nevertheless, after Djilas's *The New Class*, one could not write about "actually existing socialism" in the same way.

The key to understanding why this book created an intellectual revolution is in the subtitle, "An Analysis of the Communist System." In many respects Djilas emerges from a long tradition of left-wing anti-bureaucratic criticism of Soviet-type societies, and restates claims made by others. We have already analyzed the intellectual tradition of "bureaucratic deformations," which can be traced from Lenin's theory of state capitalism, through Zinoviev's thesis on "integral state capitalism," to culminate in the post-Trotskyite theory of a state capitalist, new, bureaucratic class. Mao comes close to the state capitalist theory with his criticism of bureaucracy as "capitalist roaders." While Mao never went so far as to develop a theory of state capitalism and its bureaucracy as a new collective ownership class, his truest disciple, Bettelheim, certainly did. This line of analysis, however, is just an extension of the critique of Soviet-type, "bureaucratically deformed society." It only takes Trotsky one step further, and concludes: since the bureaucracy constituted itself as a New Class, it must have transformed the social formation into a capitalist one: it must have restored capitalism.

Djilas's theory of the New Class has, in addition to Lenin's and post-Trostkyite theorizing, another twin brother—the criticism of the Stalinist bureaucracy as the ruling class of a social formation that is neither socialist nor capitalist. According to this position, Soviet society is a "third way," usually referred to as bureaucratic collectivism (and what Ference Feher, Agnes Heller, and George Markus would call a system of "dictatorship over needs," three decades later).

There is one important common element in Djilas's theory, the theory of the bureaucratic class of state capitalism, and bureaucratic collectivism: all three schools of thought based their argument concerning the emergence of a bureaucratic class on the analysis of property relations. The bureaucrats constitute a New Class because they manage to attain ownership of the means of production. They have not been converted into a bourgeoisie, however, since they are not individual private owners but, rather, own the means of production "collectively." As we shall try to show later on, this in many ways is inconsistent with Djilas's major contribution to New Class theory, but he nevertheless insists on an orthodox Marxist definition of class, rooted in property relations: "The specific characteristic of this new class is its collective ownership" (Djilas 1966, 54). Later he elaborates: "Gradually material goods were nationalized, but in fact, through its right to use, enjoy and distribute these goods, they became the property of a discernible stratum of the party and the bureaucracy gathered around it" (56). Given this importance of ownership relations, Djilas develops a dichotomous class map of society. The dominant class is the bureaucracy with collective ownership of the means of production, and the dominated class consisted of farmers, workers, and the intelligentsia, those excluded from this collective ownership. "The new class maintains that ownership derives from designated social relationship. This is the relationship between monopolist of administration, who constitute a narrow and closed stratum, and the mass of producers (farmers, workers, and the intelligentsia) who have no rights. . . . Every fundamental change in the social relationship between those who monopolize administration and those who work is inevitably reflected in the ownership relationship" (45). This is all consistent with the state capitalism and bureaucratic collectivism theories, so where is the innovation? Why was the book such a splash?

We hinted at the answer in noting the subtitle of the book. Djilas is the first who claimed that the New Class of bureaucrats is a fundamentally communist phenomenon. The making of the New Class is not a deformation of the system, it is not a result of the restoration of capitalism, but follows from the very nature of communism.

Djilas astutely described why the bureaucracy is not a class under market capitalism, but is under communism: "Bureaucrats in a non-Communist state have political masters, usually elected, or owners over them, while Communists have neither masters, or owners over them. The bureaucrats in a non-Communist state are officials in modern capitalist economy, while the Communists are something different and new: a new class" (54). This statement could not have been clearer. It also distinguishes Djilas not only from other left-wing critiques of Soviet-type societies, but also from right-wing critiques of socialism. Generally, the right-wing critics rejected class analysis altogether. They saw communism as totalitarianism, in which a small political elite oppresses the passive masses (Hannah Arendt), or they accepted the self-proclaimed status of communism as being a dictatorship of the proletariat, and thus did not posit the class antagonism between the "monopolists of administration" and those who do the work.

Djilas also identified the mechanism of the emergence of this New Class, and again does not see this mechanism as a deformation but as an inevitable outcome of the deep logic of the system. While Djilas as a Marxist (or at least a former Marxist) insists on the importance of the ownership relations, he knows little about political economy, and thus, when he identifies the social mechanism that gives birth to the New Class, he draws on political analysis. For Djilas, the genesis of the New Class has to be understood in the nature of the Bolshevik party. "[T]his new class had not been formed as part of the economic and social life before it came to power, it could only be created in an organization of a special type. . . . The roots of the new class were implanted in a special party, of the Bolshevik type" (39). The idea that it is really the party—or, to be more precise, the party apparatus—that rules, though not necessarily as a class, is elaborated later, with great eloquence, by Markus in Feher, Heller, and Markus (1983).

Djilas, however, is in some pain because of his own analysis. When writing *The New Class,* he is still a great admirer of Lenin (and who was not, in Eastern Europe during the 1950s, when Stalin was the archenemy and Lenin the "good guy"?). Thus he continues: "[T]he initiators of the new class are *not* found *in the party of the Bolshevik type as a whole,* but in that stratum of professional revolutionaries who made up its core even before it attained power" (Djilas 1966, 39, our emphasis). Even this argument, however, is not enough to rehabilitate Lenin and Bolshevism and put the blame on Stalin. Djilas concedes that, "Although he did not realize it, Lenin started the organization of the new class. He established the party along Bolshevik lines" (48), but adds immediately, "This is but one aspect of his many-sided and gigantic work; it is the aspect which came about from his action rather than his wishes. It is also the aspect which led the new class to revere him" (8), and "[T]he new class was born in the revolutionary struggle in the communist Party, but was developed in the industrial revolution" (49).[4] And finally the bottom line becomes crystal clear: "The Soviet Thermidor of Stalin had . . . led to the installation of a class" (51). Thus, while Lenin is not quite innocent, this culpability follows as an unintended consequence of his actions, which contradicted his noble intentions; the New Class is fundamentally a Stalinist creation.

Professional sociologists of the 1950s hardly yearned for the apologia of Lenin. Nevertheless, they did welcome the "New Class analysis" of communism, which explains the system of domination and in fact of economic exploitation not from the restoration of capitalism but from the very logic of the "communist system," as the subtitle clearly indicates.

There is one more reason why professional sociology welcomed Djilas's book. Although it has some Trotskyite overtones, in one respect it represents a radical break with Trotsky in its assessment of the role of the working class. Here, Djilas offers an interesting class theory. On the one hand, he employs a naive Marxist class distinction between those who "work" and those who do not (those who only administer, which is not to "work"). But not only does he hesitate to locate the intelligentsia among those who do the work, but, when the chips come down, he sees the most fundamental conflict as between not the bureaucracy and the workers, but the bureaucracy and the intelligentsia. At this point, Djilas's political-economy theory of class shifts toward a theory of social closure, or a social-mobility type of class theory. "The social origin of the new class lies in the proletariat . . . [which] constitutes the raw material from which the new class arises. . . . Former sons of the working class are the most steadfast members of the new class. . . . In this case a new exploiting and governing class is born from the exploited class" (41–42). This view is consistent with the methods of stratification analysis of mainstream sociology of his time, and also was the political position of those who preferred to see the main opposition to communism come from intellectuals rather than from workers. Djilas, though he does not present statistical evidence to support his claims, is in some respects on reasonably safe grounds here. The communist parties of course recruited many members from rank-and-file workers and peasants, and even promoted some to major administrative positions. What Djilas does not mention—and how could he, without data on social stratification under socialism, which were not available at his time—is that at no point in history were workers overrepresented among members of the communist parties or among top administrators. Intellectuals and the children of intellectuals always represented a larger proportion of Communist Party (CP) members and top administrators than of the general population. Nevertheless, Djilas does have a point. Under state socialism, the chances for ordinary workers and peasants to send their children to institutions of tertiary education, and to see them become members of the ruling political party and move into top administrative/managerial positions, was of course much greater than under capitalism.

Thus it is difficult to underestimate the contributions of Djilas, the self-trained sociologist and former communist apparatchik, to the study of communism. He was the first who offered a critical class analysis of communism, without trying to find excuses for why it was still a class society or claiming that it had reverted to a class society as a result of capitalist restoration. It was a society based on a class dichotomy between exploiters and oppressed, and this system of exploitation and oppression finds its roots in the very logic of Bolshevism and the communist socioeconomic system.

Critical Comments

We would like to offer two sets of critical comments on Djilas's theory, without trying to cast doubts on his extraordinary achievements.

First, there is a logical inconsistency in the analysis. In retrospect, the attempt to identify the New Class relations from property relations is misguided. If the bureaucracy indeed becomes a propertied class, even if just collectively as a private proprietor, that can and ought to make for the "restoration of capitalism." We will return to this theme in the last section on Djilas, in what we call the aftermath of the Djilas thesis. We also elaborate, in our discussion of *The Intellectuals on the Road to Class Power,* that a class analysis of communism has to abandon a property-centered notion of class. As Konrád and the senior author claimed in that book, communism was an ideology that claimed that with the abolishment of private ownership social domination is transcended. Thus any critical class analysis of state socialism indeed has to move beyond property relations to understand that socialism is a system in which expropriation of surplus is *not* legitimated by ownership by the exploiters. This is the reason why Djilas is unable to develop a critical political economy of socialism and, in the end, had to fall back on a political explanation when he identified the mechanisms of the genesis of the New Class. But politics neither in the Marxian nor Weberian tradition is seen as the basis of class formation; Weber's notion of "political capital" privileges elites, or estates, but not classes.

This leads to our second criticism. Djilas accurately spots the nature of social domination in Stalinist societies, where the fundamental contradiction is indeed between the bureaucracy and the rest of the society. But this claim is overgeneralized, as if he presents a theory of social structure of the "communist system." Again, in *The Intellectuals on the Road to Class Power,* the authors attempted to historicize Djilas's contributions. According to this analysis, Djilas indeed was right in seeing the power monopoly of the bureaucracy under Stalinism. Nevertheless, since, under the Stalinist regime, power was primarily rooted in the political system, Djilas mislabeled the bureaucracy as a class when it rather should have been seen as an elite or as an estate. Trotsky's term "caste" is more to the point, but even the notion of caste is misleading, given the specific meanings attached, in the historical and sociological literature, to the notion "caste." More important, Djilas failed to recognize possible alliances between the bureaucracy and other strata under socialism. He did not see that the intelligentsia—especially the technocratic intellectuals—might be tempted to become the ally of the bureaucracy. Even in terms of recruitment patterns, the sons and daughters of intellectuals were always overrepresented among members of the *nomenklatura,* and, as socialism was consolidated, the influx into the elite from workers and peasants was greatly reduced. The key point, however, is that with the fall of Stalinism (and, in China, with the death of Mao) the bureaucratic "ruling estate" lost a great deal of its power monopoly.

And, in both post-Stalinist U.S.S.R. and post-Maoist China, it opened up to the technocratic intelligentsia and formed a new power block, or possibly even attempted the formation of a New Class, properly speaking.

Despite the magnitude of impact of *The New Class,* Djilas is not cited widely nowadays, although he should be. The communist bureaucracy, at least in some of the former communist countries, did manage to attain the kind of property rights Djilas attributed to it under Stalinism. For the Stalinist epoch, Djilas was obviously wrong. The Stalinist bureaucracy did not really have the right to "use, enjoy and distribute" the "material goods" (56). Certainly its rights to use and enjoy the material goods under its command were greatly restricted—this being the main reason that it is so misleading to call it a propertied class. But, ironically, with the fall of communism in Eastern Europe proper (and, to a much lesser degree, in Central Europe) a neo-patrimonial form of capitalism emerged in which the former communist bureaucracy gained property rights not only to command the production of material goods, but also to use them, enjoy them, sell them, and pass them on to the next generation. The time has come to revisit Djilas, but not so much as the theorist of the New Bureaucratic Class of socialism, but as the theorist who foreshadowed the rise of a New Class under a system of political capitalism.

The Theory of Socialism as Bureaucratic Collectivism

Bureaucratic collectivism was resuscitated by Antonio Carlo during the mid-1970s (Carlo 1974) and it had an enduring impact on Castoriadis.[5] Both Carlo and Castoriadis attempted to identify bureaucratic collectivism's unique "laws of motion."

Castoriadis suggested that the existing typology of modes of production must be replaced by a typology of social regimes, to adequately understand the Soviet system. Because of the importance of ownership for the concept "mode of production," Castorialis suggested, it fails to illuminate the nature of the Soviet system, and can be used as an apologia for socialism. Whereas in one type of social regime (traditional capitalism), state and civil society are separated, under bureaucratic capitalism, state and civil society are merged. (Castorialis used the term "bureaucratic capitalism" rather than "bureaucratic collectivism" to emphasize the similarity between this type of social regime and modern capitalism.) In the contemporary West, a "frag-mented" form of bureaucratic capitalism exists: the state intrudes on but does not dominate civil society. In contrast, in the Soviet Union, the distinction between state and civil society has disappeared. At the core of this type of regime is the commitment to the rational mastery of nature, and the unlimited expansion of the forces of production.

This argument had its roots in Carlo's analysis of the Soviet system.

Carlo emphasized that the Soviet Union had become "obsessed" with economic growth. Carlo accepted Rizzi's argument that the Soviet Union was neither capitalist nor socialist, but a "society-in-transition." Indeed, this transitional society had become an antagonistic system: bureaucratic collectivism. Like Cliff, he saw the essential feature of this formation in capital accumulation: although capitalism is char-acterized by production for profit's sake and socialism is character-ized by production to satisfy human needs, bureaucratic collectivism is driven by production for production's sake. This new economic logic is the key to the new system; the bureaucracy is a class because it operates the economy with this new logic. This logic leads to over-investment in capital as opposed to consumer goods.

This emphasis on "production for production's sake" has some parallels to Konrád and Szelényi's (1979) argument regarding the re-distributive process. Konrád and Szelényi suggest that redistributors seek to maximize their redistributive power; those who do not will lose out in the competition between bureaucracies for the state bud-get; the attempt to maximize redistributive power is thus an attempt to maximize one's organization's portion of the state budget. If the goal of each firm is maximization of its share of the state budget, less of an emphasis is placed on national wealth, and there is a tendency to overinvest in heavy industry and under-invest in infrastructure.

Carlo also suggested that, under bureaucratic collectivism, there is a conflict between the technocracy and bureaucratic managers. While the central bureaucracy controls the redistributive process and thus has an interest in sustaining the plan, technocrats are enterprise managers. Marketization offers technnocrats a means by which to become proprietors.

Like Carlo, Heller, Feher, and Markus, in *Dictatorship over Needs* (1983)[6] argued that the Soviet Union could not be called socialist—the essence of socialism is to satisfy human needs and this was certainly not the driving force of Soviet-type economies. These authors also argued that Soviet-type economies could not be considered capitalist, as capitalism manipulates needs, and generates new (and, if necessary, false) needs for growth purposes.

Instead, the Soviet Union practices a "dictatorship over needs." It suppresses needs in order to channel all resources into production for production's sake. Heller, Feher, and Markus diverge from bureaucratic collectivist theory only insofar as they do not regard the bureaucracy as a class. According to Heller, Feher, and Markus, it is the "apparatus" that holds power in Soviet-type societies, but its members exercise this "collective power" not as a class but as a group. The difference appears to us to be more terminological than substantive.

In retrospect, it is somewhat disturbing that these recent bureaucratic-collectivist theories offer a critical analysis of Soviet-type economies by emphasizing their obsession with growth and production. It is somewhat ironic that these theories appeared in print after 1974—the point at which the Soviet and East European economies entered the terminal phase of their economic decline. Like the Owl of Minerva, these theories arrived late, with the fall of dusk. While, in the 1930s and again in the 1950s and 1960s, many socialist economies did experience what appeared to be impressive economic growth, after 1975 none of these economies (with the exception of China and Vietnam) expanded.

Four

Beyond Bureaucratic Power: Humanistic Intellectuals and Technocrats under State Socialism

A new way of thinking about the structure of actually existing socialist societies began to emerge from the mid-1960s onward. A new generation of theorists focused its attention on the relations between the bureaucracy and intellectuals, in a new way. The earlier common wisdom—shared by theorists of state capitalism, bureaucratic collectivism, and the New Class theory of Milovan Djilas—that, under state socialism, the power of the bureaucracy is unchallenged and the intellectuals belong to the suppressed and exploited, was being re-thought.

The changing relationship between bureaucracy and intellectuals, and the social position of the intelligentsia in the structure of socialist societies, were approached from rather divergent perspectives. Three typical examples are Radovan Richta's *Civilization at the Crossroads,* Rudolf Bahro's *The Alternative,* and Konrád and Szelényi's *The Intellectuals on the Road to Class Power.*

Let us foreshadow briefly the analysis that follows. Richta was a reformer who recommended a renegotiation of the balance of power between the bureaucracy and the technocracy. He wanted a rationalized socialism in which reason and science would rule. Bahro, while initially attracted to the Richta type of reform scenario, became disenchanted and began to doubt the bureaucracy would ever compromise with the intelligentsia. He proposed a radical "alternative":

socialism would only be possible if everyone became an intellectual. Richta and Bahro share the view that socialism, the "good society," is one ruled by reason; thus intellectuals express the essence of this system. These two authors differ in their assessment of how to achieve the "good society": Richta, writing earlier, still had faith in a negotiated change of balance of power between the bureaucracy and intellectuals, while Bahro believed only a fundamental, "revolutionary"[1] transformation of the social order would be effective. Konrád and Szelényi also reconceptualized the relation between intellectuals and socialism, but in a way that fundamentally diverged from Richta's and Bahro's ideas. At the core of their analysis is what they—like Foucault—saw as the intimate relationship between knowledge and power. Like Richta, they also saw the rapprochement between the bureaucracy and the technocratic intelligentsia, but instead of recommending this as the coming of a "good society," they called it "the road of intellectuals to class power." If the bureaucracy could share power with the technocracy and the humanistic intelligentsia, it would lead to a new type of class domination exercised by intellectuals and legitimated by teleological knowledge. Konrád and Szelényi, following Weber and Foucault, characterize this as a step in the direction of the rationalization of the social order. They see this rational system of domination—in the case of successfully reformed socialism—as one dominated by technocratic intellectuals, thus not a classless society or an emancipated form of social life. For Konrád and Szelényi, the "rule of reason" means that reason legitimates the system of power and privilege.

While Richta and Bahro, following the intellectual traditions of Saint-Simon, believe that emancipation can be achieved through science and reason, Konrád and Szelényi were closer to the anarchist critique of socialism[2] and they certainly shared with Weber and Foucault an ironic view of rationalization as disenchantment and knowledge as the vehicle of legitimation rather than as the tool of emancipation.

Reform Technocrats and Actually Existing Socialism

Both Richta and Bahro are critical of actually existing socialism because it did not live up to its promises: it did not create a society where scientific reason rules. Further, neither are New Class theorists. They offer a critical evaluation of the bureaucratic nature of

Stalinism, and they see intellectuals as the only actors capable of correcting this deformation. Neither identifies the intellectuals as a New Class, as a social actor with self-interest. For both, intellectuals represent reason; they are the vessels that carry the interests of all, that carry universal interest. Although neither theorist uses the term, they both think of intellectuals as the real "universal class," in the Marxist sense.[3] Socialism for them is a project of rationalization and enlightenment; therefore the socialist emancipatory project cannot be carried out by the proletariat; only the intelligentsia will be able to implement it. In this respect, Saint-Simon or others in this tradition, like Veblen, Galbraith, or Bell, are more self-reflexive: they see the scientists, the engineers, the technostructure, the knowledge produc-ers, as a class, if a benevolent one—"our best card in history," to quote Gouldner (by far the most ironic among the Saint-Simonians, if he belongs to that tradition at all).

Richta, writing during the waves of the 1960s reform movements, is quite optimistic. In *Civilization at the Crossroads*, he offers a blue-print for social reform, in which science becomes the major productive force and both the anarchy of market capitalism and the counter-selective bureaucratic ossification of Stalinism will be replaced by scientific enlightenment. Richta is close to Bell or Galbraith in that he shares their belief in the coming of a new epoch in which science is the driving force of socioeconomic development, and, as a result, sees the technical intelligentsia becoming the driving force of social and economic progress. He sees the convergence of capitalism and socialism (though in his vision this is more likely to occur around the model of "scientific socialism"). Societies east and west face a new epoch, a scientific-technical revolution in which science becomes the major productive force.

Bahro's *The Alternative* is a book of dissent. Unlike Richta's work, this is not a reform blueprint prepared for the Communist Party searching for ways out of the legitimation crisis of Stalinism. Bahro comes from a similar intellectual background as Richta, and one can imagine that as a young man he must have been deeply influenced by Richta's book. He began his career as a technocratic and enthusiastic reformer (he was manager of an East German firm), but his enthusi-asm and reform spirit evaporated as the 1970s progressed and he be-came convinced that the technocratic reform promised by the Stalinist bureaucracy would not be implemented. *The Alternative* is a book written by a disenchanted technocratic reformer who no longer believes that actually existing socialism can live up to its promised rationalism and who therefore searches for some more radical alternative.

East European Intellectuals' Attraction to Rational Social Order

Civilization at the Crossroads was published in Czechoslovakia just as the winds of the Prague Spring began to blow, and it was received with great sympathy by many East European intellectuals. Before August 1968 the book was the bible of the region's reform intelligentsia. It told them exactly what they wanted to hear. During the mid-1960s the most widely accepted position among Hungarian, Czech, and Polish intellectuals, even among those who were not members of the Communist Party and were not particularly sympathetic to the regime, went something like this:

> Socialism is a beautiful idea—the problem is that it is poorly implemented. It makes sense to have a society ruled by reason, rather than dependent on the anarchy of the market. But how could socialism achieve such a noble aim? For socialism to work, one needs the right people in the right positions. Socialism as we know it, however, is highly counterselective. It has promoted ignorant working-class cadres to position of authority simply on the basis of political loyalty. Socialism can and ought to be reformed; the most essential task of such reform is to put competent professionals who know what they are doing in decision-making positions, to make the management of society really scientific. We need less bureaucracy (certainly fewer working-class cadres!) and more competence. The reward structure also ought to change accordingly. People with university degrees hardly earn more than do ordinary workers; a miner may have a higher income than a university instructor. Incomes should reflect the level of education, and education ought to be the primary criterion to select people for promotion.

During the mid-1960s East European reform thinking, while universally accepting the above premises, in other respects faced fundamental dilemmas. While the elimination of Stalinist counterselection had very broad support, and the notion of a rational social order and socialism appealed to a very broad circle of intellectuals, some heated debates still took place among them. In particular, the role of markets was a subject of much controversy. It is vitally important to understand this controversy, since it already foreshadows some of the major issues of late socialist and early postcommunist social struggles.

The common feature of 1960s intellectual reform thinking was its antibureaucratism and anti-authoritarianism.[4] The reduction of voluntaristic state intervention in the economy and a greater role for markets had an elective affinity with this stance. By the early 1960s, however, economists split into two camps; some became radicalized along the lines of market reform, while others argued that new scientific innovations, especially computer technology, made markets redundant. Markets, after all, were particularly useful for gathering and processing information. One important argument for markets instead of planning was that planners did not have sufficient information to make accurate decisions, and even if they gathered this information they processed it too slowly and thus did not respond in a timely manner to problems.[5] With computers and modern macroeconomic models, one could plan nonvoluntaristically, scientifically, and effectively. This position was particularly powerfully articulated in the Soviet Union, where a so-called mathematical revolution was taking place within economics.[6] Following the footsteps of Leontief, scholars like Nemchikov and Kantorovich (both regarded at that time as revisionists) recommended replacing Stalinist voluntaristic planning with scientific, mathematical methods. This recommendation was perceived by the bureaucracy as a major revisionist challenge, and it indeed indicated an early split between the bureaucracy firmly in power and an emergent new technocracy claiming its share of power. The "mathematical revolution" in the Soviet Union during the late 1950s and early 1960s had a major impact on scholarship in other socialist countries. Economists, like János Kornai, who later became radical critics of the socialist economic system got their first taste of revisionism by learning mathematics and doing work on the "perfection of planning methods."[7]

Already, during the early 1960s, in the Soviet Union an alternative reform scenario was formulated. Instead of perfecting the methods of planning, these reformers recommended a move away from planning toward market mechanisms. The most prominent Soviet economist who advocated such a strategy was E. G. Liberman.[8] The radical market reformers of the 1960s were not, however, advocating private ownership or capitalism. The question of property reform and especially the idea of moving toward a capitalist economy by privatizing the public sector was first formulated at the national convention of the Solidarity movement as late as the early fall of 1981, and even then and there it was a marginal position. Privatization became a serious program only during the 1980s. The early market reformers who pursued the idea of market socialism had their roots much more in Kalecki and Lange[9] than in Mises,[10] Hayek, and Friedman. Probably the most radical of them was the Hungarian Tibor Liska,[11] who in a manuscript completed during the mid-1960s, called *Oeconostat,* draws the blueprint of a society that is thoroughly commodified. His position, however, was that such a system is only imaginable under socialism, since private property is a monopoly and as such restraints the functioning of free markets. Market reformers during the 1960s intended to save socialism by turning it into an efficient market-socialist system[12] rather than by replacing it with market capitalism.

For economists, the question was how much the "good society" had to rely on market forces and how much could be achieved by the perfection of planning methods among social philosophers. For sociologists, however, the question was to what extent society had to surrender to the imperatives of the economy. András Hegedüs, the Hungarian ex-Stalinist prime minister turned revisionist sociologist, posed the question as the contradiction between the requirements of "humanization" and "optimalization." The rational social order for many East European intellectuals of the 1960s could not be the "cold" rationality of the economy. The wrong choice was to swap the iron fist of the Stalinist bureaucratic order for the iron laws of the market. The rationalization of society should produce a society with a "human face," as the most radical reformers of the time, Czech intellectuals, formulated it.

To put it simply, the dilemma was Kantorovich or Liberman, the perfection of planning or market socialism? While countries that took the reform road (Hungary, Poland, Yugoslavia, East Germany) to some extent moved on both fronts, they differed with respect to which method they emphasized. During the 1960s, Hungary and Yugoslavia, in particular, implemented significant market reforms, while East Germany moved a long way toward perfecting planning methods, especially during the last years of Walter Ulbricht's rule, in the early 1970s.

The East European intelligentsia as a whole hesitated over how to react to the choice of perfection of planning vs. marketization. They often were torn between the promise of the rational order that social-ism seemed able potentially to provide, and the values of freedom, the main promise of markets. The following stories, both set in Hungary, may be illuminating.

One of us, Iván Szelényi, had a classmate and close personal friend who was a grandson of Károly Szendi Sr., the politically con-servative mayor of Budapest during the interwar years. The father of Szelényi's friend, however, was a superb electrical engineer, whose skills were desperately needed by the regime. During Stalinist times, the elder Szendi was deported, his house was taken away, he was ha-rassed by the political police, and he died prematurely. His son's ca-reer, however, was uninterrupted: at the end of World War II, he was the chief engineer of one of the country's large electric power plants; eventually he was promoted to an even more important position in the Electric Energy Trust, an agency where usually top security clear-ance was necessary to hold a job; and by the 1960s he was elected a member of the Hungarian Academy of Sciences and received the Kossuth Prize, the most prestigious national prize awarded in the field of electricity.

Not only did Szendi Jr. not join the Communist Party, but he made a point of demonstrating his non-Communist beliefs. As a devote Roman Catholic, he went to church practically every morning, even during the 1950s, a most unusual gesture from someone in such a high position. Anyway, he certainly was as unaffected by communism as an ideology as anybody could be, and he made no secret about it.

As an academician, he served on important committees to advise the National Academy and the government on issues far beyond his field of electricity systems. During the late 1960s (or perhaps already in the early 1970s), he was asked to serve on a committee that re-viewed economic reform proposals. As a conscientious man, he want-ed to serve on the committee well, so he sought advice from Szelényi, not only the childhood friend of his son but someone whom he be-lieved knew more about economics than he himself. Szelényi visited the Szendis at their family home, at Szendi Jr.'s invitation, and had a lengthy conversation with him. The reform proposal that Szendi Jr. was supposed to review apparently proposed a far-reaching deregula-tion of foreign trade and a substantial increase in the role of markets. Szendi Jr. tried to be sympathetic, but was greatly concerned that the deregulation would create chaos. For an electrical engineer, no matter how little faith he might have in Marxism-Leninism and how pious a Catholic he might be, it made no sense to let the unpredictable forces of the market integrate the economy. Ironically, for this socially conservative, Christian engineer, Lenin's vision of the economy running like clockwork made more sense than Adam Smith's invisible hand.

The punch line of the story is that the vision of socialism as the rule of reason, as a socioeconomic system ruled by science and scientists that overcomes the irrational spontaneity and the anarchy of the market, appealed very broadly to intellectuals, well beyond the relatively narrow circle of those who thought themselves Communists or Marxists-Leninists. With the fall of Stalinism there was the cautious hope that the negative features of socialism, such as the rule by bureaucracy, the absence of individual freedom and democratic rights, the secularism, the one-sided and irrational emphasis on Marxism as the only set of body of knowledge, could be overcome.

Once these negative features were eliminated, it was believed, the positive features of socialism could finally be realized. Thus, unlike Western capitalist society, socialist societies could sustain the primacy of scientific reason over the mindless and irrational profit maximization motive (and corresponding consumerism) of market societies.[13]

Let us illustrate the strong appeal of a "rational order" to large groups of intellectuals by another story. Konrád and the senior author of this book worked, during the 1960s, in urban planning institutes. The two carried out surveys commissioned by planners and became friends with many. Many of these planners came from bourgeois families, received a degree in architecture during the interwar years, and began to work in private practice designing buildings for rich people, under their close scrutiny, before communism. Several of the planners were young and ambitious when the communists took power in 1949. They moved away from architecture and joined the rapidly expanding urban and regional planning institutes, which grew quite big by the 1960s, often employing several hundred professionals.

Konrád and Szelényi became interested in what brought these architects to urban planning and how they saw their own roles as planners, a bit of a puzzle since many had no socialist beliefs. Konrád conducted life-history interviews with many of the planners, asking them what brought them to urban planning. One striking and recurring theme in the responses was the appeal of a "rational order" versus the "anarchy of the market." Some of the planners saw their move out of the private sector as a liberation from the demands of customers whose instructions they resented; more importantly many saw a unique opportunity to create a rational regional structure with the makings of a socialist socioeconomic order: they were no longer merely serving rich customers; they were redesigning the living conditions of a society; they were instrumental in creating a new social order.

The planners had looked at the map and what they saw had made little sense. There were far too many small settlements, which looked "suboptimal." They saw in urban and regional planning, and in the system in which planners disposed resources to shape urban and regional processes, a chance to rearrange the regional structure and to replace the mess created by the spontaneous processes of the past centuries with a rational order. During the 1960s, considerable intellectual energy was spent by the country's best minds to develop the national regional development plan, which moved forcefully toward what the planners saw as an optimal system of settlements: a hierarchy of settlements, with each at an optimal size. A village with 1,000 or fewer inhabitants was suboptimal or inefficient. Even the smallest settlement should be large enough to sustain a primary school with two parallel classes at each level. This gave a figure of around 3,000 inhabitants as the minimum population for a village that could be built around urban centers large enough to house a high school and other more specialized institutions. Thus the planners wished to create cities with 25–50,000 inhabitants, arranged in a neat order around medium-sized cities, which were in turn arranged around larger cities, etc. The Hungarian regional development plan was adopted in 1971, and it basically passed a death sentence for almost one thousand of the three thousand Hungarian smaller towns and villages. (All settlements with fewer than 1,000 inhabitants were found nonviable; thus administratively they were merged with neighboring larger villages, and all funds for development were taken from them. The idea was to "starve them to death.") This monster was the brainchild of the best planners, acting with the best intention, and putting a great deal of hard intellectual labor into creating this "new order."

Around this time, Konrád and Szelényi's sociological research was taking more critical overtones, but in general they could count on the support and solidarity of their planner colleagues, who stood firm in their support of science against political intervention or control. This sociological work, however, began to question some of the assumptions upon which urban and regional planning was based. Most importantly, it began to question the rationality of a "club of planners" making decisions in planning offices and relocating people from one settlement to another, from one part of the country to the other. Sometime during the early 1970s, Konrád and Szelényi wrote a research report for one of the planning offices, and in this spirit challenged the national regional development. This report was thoroughly discussed by the planner-researchers of the institute. After the meeting one planner, an old friend and ally, came to the senior author of the current book and asked, "Are you really suggesting that we should let people live wherever they want to live?" When Szelényi answered in the affirmative, the planner was horrified: "In this case, I cannot support you any longer. What would happen with planning if you guys would have it your way?"

Both the story of Szendi Jr. and the life history of urban planners indicate the reform spirit of the 1960s. The idea of socialism as a rational order, a society superior to capitalism since it is committed to science and not dependent on the spontaneity and anarchy of market, was fairly widely shared by intellectuals, not only by those who were members of the communist parties or who accepted the ideology of Marxism-Leninism. This was the reform vision of the post-Stalinist epoch, and the frame of mind of intellectuals. They thought of themselves as people, and not simply technicians, with a responsibility for the good society. Many took Benda's advice and did not betray this responsibility and mission. Richta superbly captured this mood, which explains why *Civilization at the Crossroads* became a bestseller.

Post-Stalinist State Socialism in Search of a New Legitimacy

Because of the broad appeal of the vision of socialism as a rational social order for intellectuals, the 1960s saw the legitimacy of state socialism at its historic peak. This legitimacy emerged as the old Stalinist bureaucracy began to search for some new legitimacy, faced with the death of the "charismatic leader." This search is represented most clearly by the reform attempts of Khrushchev.

The question of the legitimacy of state socialism has been and remains an issue of great controversy. For those who define legitimacy as a positive approval of power holders by the majority of the population, socialism was never legitimate.[14] If one operates with a concept of legitimacy that is somewhat more ironic and limited, one may claim that the history of socialism is the history of shifting legitimacy claims, in which elites had varying success in achieving legitimate domination. This second approach to legitimacy, inspired by Max Weber, suggests that a system of domination is legitimate if those subjected to power are likely to obey orders without the systemic use of coercive power. Weber thought that societies tend to be legitimate, and illegitimate order is an unlikely sociopolitical phenomenon. Social order based on coercion is a limiting case, a rare event. It is simply too costly for rulers to maintain in the long run. In periods of "normal politics," most people subjected to domination will internalize the principles used by the power holders to legitimize their rule sufficiently that they will not be able to imagine an alternative way of organizing society.

If one approaches the question of the legitimacy of state socialism this way, one could argue that the first claim for legitimacy was, as in most new social orders, based on the charisma of the preeminent leader. Lenin, Mao, and Castro were charismatic leaders, like other great revolutionaries before them. Socialism, like any other system of charismatic domination, faced severe problems in "institutionalizing charisma." With the death of the charismatic leader, all socialist societies faced major legitimation crises. Stalin and his East European "deputies" made an effort to transfer Lenin's charisma onto themselves. This formidable task was not very successful but was not a complete failure, either. One can measure the difficulties of transferring Lenin's charismatic authority to the new leaders by studying the expansion of the use of coercive power. Indeed, Stalinism used coercion widely and frequently enough to approach the reality of an "illegitimate order"; still, Stalin had at least some success in transferring some charisma to his personality, and emerged during World War II as the charismatic leader. We would therefore regard Stalinist society as on the borderline between charismatic authority (with a touch of traditional domination) and the illegitimate use of power.[15]

The Post-Stalinist Order in Search of Goal-Rational Authority

With the death of Stalin, the charismatic, or quasi-charismatic, leader, state socialism entered a period of legitimation crisis. Popular reaction to the death of Stalin was a good indication that his attempt to transfer charisma of the revolutionary leader onto himself was not completely unsuccessful; a lot of grief accompanied the loss of "the Great Leader." While it is difficult to assess the sincerity of the sentiments expressed, some had to be genuine. Many tears were shed on the solemn marches held the night following the announcement of the death of Stalin, not only in the Soviet Union, but even on the streets of Budapest. Soon after the passing away of the charismatic leader, the Stalinist (and, in turn, the Maoist) bureaucracy began to scramble for some new source of legitimacy. It was judged that the institutionalization of charisma was hopeless. Rather than attempting this technique at the Twentieth Congress, Khruschev, through the demystification of the criminal character of the Stalinist regime, made sure no attempt could ever be made by any Soviet politicians to confer charisma on themselves. So what then could be the source of legitimacy? Khrushchev's project was to reach back to one important tradition of the Marxist vision of socialism and to reemphasize the "scientific" nature of this worldview and present socialism as a more rational (and thus more efficient and dynamic) order than capitalism.

This reformulation of Soviet and Eastern European socialist legitimacy was firmly rooted in Marxist social theory and also in the history of actually existing socialism. As we tried to show earlier in this book, the Marxism of Marx and, even more, the Marxism of Engels were greatly influenced by the idea of scientific thought, to such an extent that the anarchists could accuse Marxists of moving society toward the despotism of "socialist scholars." During the 1920s, it was also rather unclear which way Soviet socialism would go, whether it would take the technocratic road and produce a system of domination legitimated by scientific reason, or would keep emphasizing its revolutionary character and opt for "charismatic" authority. As Kendall Bailes (1979) masterfully documented, Soviet technocrats were indeed greatly attracted to the vision of Taylorism. Stalin's trials against the engineers were not without reason. Although there is no evidence that Soviet engineers actually conspired to overthrow the regime, they were, as Bailes documented, beyond a doubt attracted to a notion of socialism in which the major social command positions would be occupied by technocrats.

These early Soviet engineers—mainly of bourgeois social background—watched with alarm the recruitment of working-class cadres into political leadership positions. Without having read Veblen, they shared his view that a "Soviet of engineers" was a more sound idea for organizing society than were Soviets of workers or soldiers. Even Stalin himself had some mixed reactions to this technocratic project; though he was not inclined to share power with the technocracy, he did see the advantages of the technocratic legitimation of socialist power. Soviet science made important breakthroughs during the 1920s and early 1930s, from mathematical economics to aviation technology. Stalinist propaganda tried to exploit these technological achievements. As Bailes shows, success in aviation was presented as proof of the superiority of socialism.

Eventually, this early attraction of Soviet socialism to techno-cratic legitimation had to take a backseat, when Stalin launched the trials against engineers. Stalin subsequently trained a whole new generation of technocrats, recruited from working-class backgrounds and trained in accelerated courses that placed much more emphasis on ideology, at the expense of technical knowhow.

Khrushchev, therefore, had tradition to build on when, during the mid- to late 1950s, he formulated the new image of socialism—a socialism relying on science and technology. This was an attempt to create a completely new type of domination, which Rigby called *"goal-rational authority."* Rigby persuasively showed that socialist domination could not be seen as "legal-rational authority," even in its most radical reform blueprints. Legal-rational authority is based on formal or instrumental rationality; in the terminology of Marx, Lukács, and the Frankfurt School, it gives primacy to techné over telos.[16] The scientism that socialism tried to claim as its own during the reform epoch of the 1960s was instead a claim for substantive rationality, in which telos has precedence over techné. This claim is based on the belief that it is a concession to irrationalism to exclude from the sphere of rational activity the choice of values or goals, and to accept as rational only the activity that finds the most efficient means by which we can achieve the ends determined either by "irra-tional" political means, such as elections, or by personal beliefs and preferences. This is what Ferenc Fehér called "hyper-rationality," when rationality reaches beyond means and affects the sphere of goalsetting as well (Feher, Heller, and Markus 1984). The attachment of East European intellectuals to substantive rationality was so deep as to be maintained by Potocka, for instance, even when he turned openly to dissidence (1976–1977). The shift of the legitimacy claim from charisma (and in the 1960s from neotraditionalism or clientelism) to goal-rational authority had far-reaching class implications. If the bureaucrats really meant what they now claimed, they had to share power with the intelligentsia, in particular with its technocratic wing. Since the new legitimacy was meant to be based on substantive rational authority, however, that power had to be shared not just with technocrats, but also (and to some extent even more) with *teleocrats*: intellectuals, technical or humanistic in training, who believed that the historic mission of the intelligentsia was to guide and direct society through the application of scientific reasoning.

Our point is, therefore, that Richta's book achieved so much success because it expressed the interest of East European intellectuals in the offer of the bureaucracy, in a new power-sharing arrangement, to promote the ideal of a "social order with a human face in which reason rules." Let us reemphasize that this interest did not mean that the intelligentsia of the times were communists, or that most were Marxist-Leninist.[17] Indeed, Károly Szendi Jr. made no concessions to communism or Marxism, and many of the urban planners whom Konrád and Szelényi worked with did not make many concessions, either.

But there was a deeper affinity between what the planners thought the good society could be and what their role in achieving that society should be, and the new ideas about legitimacy and reform promoted by the bureaucratic ruling estate at this time. As a result, radical market reform, especially market reform that would "go all the way" and re-create private property and market capitalism, had to wait a long time. It had to wait not primarily because the intelligentsia was oppressed and prevented from expressing such radical ideas, but because first the intellectuals had to understand that the bureaucracy would never deliver on its promises concerning power sharing. The intelligentsia had to understand that its "class project" had failed: this was the precondition for its radicalization away from "socialism with a human face" toward market capitalism with its iron laws.

Knowledge and Power: Critical Self-Reflection of the Reform Intelligentsia

Konrád and Szelényi's point of departure was also the rapprochement of the bureaucracy and the intelligentsia. The empirical reality from which their book generalizes is the relatively privileged position of intellectuals under state socialism, and as the previously mentioned anecdotes indicate, what they believed to be the elective affinity between the consciousness of intellectuals and the ideals and realities of socialism.

Privileges of Intellectuals in the Socialist Distributive System

Konrád and Szelényi first began to reflect critically on the position of intellectuals in socialist society in the early 1960s, with survey research projects conducted on new housing estates. The study was ordered from them by planners who wanted to "improve planning methods" by getting sociological, or more precisely, market research, information on the product of their work. Planners were really interested in consumer satisfaction: whether they had designed the kitchen the right way, whether they had put the plugs where they ought to be, and the like. Konrád and Szelényi did not have a clear idea of what would drive their study intellectually, so they followed rather closely what the planners wanted. Just to be on the safe side, however, they asked the usual sociological survey questions about occupation and education.

They did not have well-formulated reasons for these questions, and the housing estates built by massive government housing subsidies during the 1960s were presented as major achievements of the regime. Common wisdom was that the residences were occupied by people of diverse backgrounds, although, since socialism presented itself as a dictatorship of the proletariat, it was assumed that workers were likely to have better access to these desirable and scarce goods. The researchers had no particular reason to believe this might not be the case, so they reacted with astonishment when they saw the first distribution of the class characteristics of inhabitants in the new housing estates and compared those with the urban averages. It turned out that the more educated someone was, the higher the person was in the social hierarchy, the better the person's chances of getting new housing on these estates. The two researchers conducted more surveys, focusing more and more on the question of social inequalities and the role of nonmarket, administrative allocation of goods and services in creating these inequalities. By the late 1960s, they concluded that the socialist economy operated in a curious manner. Administrative allocation systematically privileged the already privileged; those with little education, such as workers and peasant workers, had to rely on their own resourcefulness to get by. This usually meant reliance on some kind of market, as in buying the materials to build a home, or opening a small part-time repair business.

It was around this time that Konrád and Szelényi read Polányi and became familiar with his distinction between market and redistribution. They first found Polányi's distinction useful to describe a paradox: while in capitalist market economies markets generate inequalities and welfare state redistribution corrects these inequalities to a certain extent, in socialist economies redistribution creates inequalities and markets compensate for these to a certain extent. A further paradox was the class implication of this conclusion: in socialism, which presents itself as the dictatorship of the proletariat, it is the intellectuals who realize the benefits of redistribution, the uniquely socialist economic mechanism, and the workers who have to rely on market forces.[18]

Is this trivial? At the time, it did not appear trivial at all. During the late 1960s, Szelényi traveled in most East European countries to gather comparative data for a book.[19] The first surprise was that few systematic data sets existed on class position and housing tenure. There were many surveys on housing and cities, but often appropriate measures of class were not used, or the correlation between class and housing tenure was not analyzed. Szelényi also found that his and Konrád's results from Hungary generally were received with disbelief.

Most of their colleagues in other countries believed the results could only be some strange Hungarian aberration. Sometime around 1967, he spent some time at the Institute of Philosophy and Sociology of the Polish Academy of Sciences, and had lengthy conversation with the scholar who was regarded as the dean of Polish urban sociology. They discussed the Hungarian findings. The Polish sociologist shook his head and said it was very different in Poland, where the regime was anti-intellectual and gave all the privileges to the workers. True, he lived on a housing estate himself, but his next-door neighbor, for instance, was just a driver. He was not even embarrassed that this was about the hardest evidence he could produce to show the proletarian character of the Polish state. Incidentally, sporadic data from Poland from the 1960s contradicted the judgment of this Polish sociologist and showed that, in Poland, also, new housing went to the intelligentsia and members of the working class built themselves illegal housing on the outskirts of big cities. Polish peasants turned workers were not even allowed to move into the larger cities where industrialization pushed them for employment.

Such dynamics of social inequalities under socialism are not trivial even for contemporary debates. Since the fall of socialism, some critics accuse the system again of being systematically biased against intellectuals and too generous to workers. Some members of the post-communist intelligentsia believe that the past forty years belonged to the workers; postcommunism should now be their turn. Skyrocketing inequalities are justified with reference to meritocratic principles and the need to reward higher human-capital investments to correct earlier socialist counterselection. Since, with higher earnings, intellectuals no longer need state redistribution, and can afford to get those goods and services on the market that in the past they received through redistribution, they now advocate an end to redistribution altogether. The most theoretically important idea along these lines attacks socialism for having created a "premature welfare state," something postcommunist societies cannot afford. But if the earlier observation about the way social inequalities were generated under socialism was accurate, then socialism not only did not have a premature welfare state, it did not have much of a welfare state at all. Redistribution, which in a welfare state is supposed to reallocate income from the higher income groups to the poor, under state socialism was a way to complement the income of the highest income groups. While it can be argued that intellectuals under socialism were underpaid, since their incomes were lower than the incomes they could make in market economies, this does not alter the fact that socialist redistribution did not help the poor, but made the best paid better paid. (Incidentally, workers would have earned higher incomes in market economies, too. Socialism as an economic system generally operated to suppress consumption in favor of faster rates of accumulation. After all, socialism was "production for production's sake,"[20] a system that accelerated economic growth to reach its main objective of catching up with the West.)

In other words, the relatively privileged position of intellectuals under socialism when it came to the distribution of the most desirable consumer goods, and the fact that this privileged situation was created by the mechanism of redistribution, is not a trivial observation even today. It is a serious hypothesis, which should be tested and, if it proves to be correct, should have far-reaching implications for post-communist policies. For instance, it may lead to the conclusion that the welfare state has not been prematurely overgrown under socialism, but on the contrary was underdeveloped: postcommunist societies, instead of cutting back on the welfare state, should move toward creating the foundations of a welfare system and social safety net.

Toward a Theory of Socialist Redistributive Economy

The fact that intellectuals earn higher incomes and have better access to some consumer items does not turn them into a class, and it certainly does not give them class power. Konrád and Szelényi did not reach such a conclusion from the *distributional inequalities* of socialism. While the first evidence that intellectuals might not do poorly, after all, under socialism came from early research on distribution, soon their results led the researchers to begin to explore whether the same could be observed in the relations of production. The idea of intellectual class power appears in their work as they attempt to deepen the idea of "redistribution" and to develop the theory of a *state socialist redistributive economy.*

For their theory, it is crucially important to make a distinction between capitalist welfare redistribution (a phenomenon of distribution) and the *redistributive integration* of the socialist economy. The latter is considered a "relation of production," not a phenomenon of distribution (although, like all relations of production, it also has distributional consequences).

A clear understanding of Polányi is necessary to appreciate the importance of this conceptual distinction. Polányi, and his idea of a redistributively integrated economy,[21] is often misunderstood. Some commentators incorrectly interpret him as offering a theory of distribution.[22] His distinction between market and redistributive *integration* is supposed to describe two ways that surplus that can be used for extended economic reproduction is defined, appropriated, and reallocated. Market or redistributive integration of the economy does not refer, therefore, to the movement of consumer goods in the economic system; it refers to the way the factors of production are disposed with. In our mind, these are relations of production, par excellence, *not* acts of distribution. The "mode of economic integration" in Polányi's system plays an analogous role to what the "mode of production" plays in Marxist political economy; both try to capture regimes of the allocation of capital, land, and labor in the ongoing process of economic reproduction.

Konrád and Szelényi, in developing the theory of socialist redistributive economy, were aware that modes of economic integration were an alternative way to think about a phenomenon that Marxists preferred to call mode of production. The idea of replacing the concept "mode of production" with "mode of economic integration" appealed to them. The key building block of the Marxist concept of the mode of production is ownership. Approaching the theory of mode of production from a sociology-of-knowledge perspective, it is reasonable to suggest that the concept *ownership* was primarily developed to capture the unique features of a modern capitalist economy. Other modes of production can be meaningfully conceived as such only from the perspective of the *capitalist* mode of production. From an immanent analysis of feudal relations, an orthodox Weberian would not conclude that that socioeconomic system should be described as a mode of production. It makes sense to think about the feudal mode of production in order to gain a better understanding concerning the genesis and functioning of modern capitalism, but this may not be a particularly great way to proceed if one wants to understand the inner workings of relationships among people under feudalism.

For instance, it never crossed Weber's mind to try to capture the uniqueness of feudalism from the way goods necessary for the survival of members of society were produced. For him, as an historical sociologist, it was rather obvious that the best way to approach feudalism must be to start with the analysis of authority relations. Incidentally, this was no novelty to most Marxists, either: it is only in capitalism that the primacy of the economic instance over the social, political, and ideological instances is obvious. Even orthodox Marxists such as Louis Althusser argued that under feudalism it is not the economic instance that is directly determinant. In the structuralist way of reasoning, Althusser claimed that a feudal economy "picks" politics as the determinant instance, and thus the economy is determinant in the last instance (whatever that is supposed to mean).

Now this is doubly true for socialism. Even some Marxists have wondered whether it makes much sense to talk about a socialist mode of production at all. If the unique characteristic of the socialist system is that politics is in command, what is the analytical utility of the socialist "mode of production"? There is no "economic base" that determines the structure of the state and politics, but rather political structures that determine the shape of the economy. The socialist project was formulated by Marxists to transcend what has been perceived as the key problem of capitalism, private ownership. If we call socialism a mode of production, we only establish what socialism *is not:* it is not capitalism, since it has eliminated private property. But the idea of a socialist mode of production tells us next to nothing about how the socialist system actually operates; it *does not give us a positive theory of socialism* in the sense of describing how power operates in this system, who are in the command positions of the economy, how they acquire those positions, and how they legitimate the power they hold.

An Outline of the Theory of Socialist Redistributive Economy
Mechanisms of Surplus-Appropriation

The sketch of the theory of socialist redistributive economy in *The Intellectuals on the Road to Class Power* was Konrád and Szelényi's first attempt to develop a positive theory of socialist social and economic relations. As laid out there, the key questions for the purposes of comparative political economy revolve around surplus for expanded reproduction. How is surplus appropriated from the producers? How is this appropriation legitimated? And according to what logic is it allocated? With these questions, it is possible to develop a critical theory of socialism without turning into an apologist for capitalism. Once these questions are answered, a sharp contrast between the capitalist and socialist systems becomes apparent.

The answers to these questions are not simple. Capitalism is a system in which surplus is appropriated from the producers by market mechanism, and private ownership legitimates this process. The profit earned this way is then allocated according to the rules of profit maximization. Socialism, in contrast, is a system in which surplus is first centralized by the state and later is allocated by central planners, or, in Konrád and Szelényi's terminology, by the "redistributors," with the aim to maximize the future growth of state budgets.

What legitimates the power of the redistributor? In order to answer this question, one must probe whether, under the structural characteristics of a given system, an alternative way of disposing with the product of labor is imaginable. In theory, the alternative is that the "direct producers" (to use Marxian language) dispose with the product of their labor. Why then are there redistributors, and how can they claim the legitimate right to carry out their activity? The redistributors claim that some of the product, preferably as much as politically possible, should be appropriated from the direct producers, since the producers, in using the product of their labor, would pursue only their short-term, personal interests. This is incidentally not an implausible assumption, which gives credibility to the further argument that the planners, trained in economics (and thus having a monopoly of knowledge) know what is in the long-term public interest. This knowledge is called by Konrád and Szelényi teleological knowledge, which, according to them, is the basis of class power for intellectuals.

In this analysis, intellectuals are social actors who demand rewards, power, and privileges on the basis of their knowledge monopoly (hence the Foucauldian intimate link between knowledge and power). The nature of the knowledge that is accepted by society as a sufficient ground to grant to its possessors rewards, power, and privileges, varies by historical epoch. In all situations, this knowledge has both a technical and a teleological component. Those without both components give up their believable claim to be intellectuals; they become either technicians or preachers, to put it somewhat simplistically. Here again is the illuminating contrast between capitalism and socialism: while under capitalism the technical component is dominant in the knowledge of intellectuals, and thus capitalist intellectuals are defined as professionals, or technocrats; under socialism the teleological component regains its primacy, making socialist intellectuals "teleocrats."

The Social Structure of Redistributive Economies

Although the theory of a socialist redistributive economy was formulated when structuralism was at its heights, the theorists' aim was to offer a historically specific institutionalist analysis. *The Intellectuals on the Road to Class Power* tried to achieve this result at the macro level by focusing on the historical process of class formation.[23]

What can be said about the social structure of state socialism from the macro-sociological perspective? In this respect, the analysis of Konrád and Szelényi offers a somewhat eclectic combination of a Marxist and a Weberian perspective. Let us begin with the Weberian. The shift in the organization of the socioeconomic system from

Stalinism to post-Stalinism can be understood as a process of ratio-nalization. As we argued above, the Stalinist order was legitimated by a mixture of charismatic authority and neotraditionalism, while the post-Stalinist form of socialism searched for goal-rational authority.

In terms of the characteristics of its social structure, Stalinism has some "archaic" elements. In Weber's terms, it was more of a rank order than a class stratified society. The theory of socialist redis-tributive economy therefore challenges Djilas's position; the Stalinist bureaucracy should not be understood as a New Class, but rather as the "ruling estate" of state socialism.[24] After all, the essence of Stalinism is that, in this system, "politics is in command." Social rela-tions shaped this way are closer to the logic of rank order and can be more accurately described as patron-client relationships than as class relationships.

To the extent to which the base of societal legitimation changes during the post-Stalinist epoch, the quality of relations between those in position of authority and those subordinated to authority changes as well. As these relations become increasingly rationalized, one should be able to speak about a transition from a rank order to class society.

Two important theoretical issues can be posed, at this point. First, how do we approach the question of the "classness" of social relations? Second, what are the major class positions in the emergent post-Stalinist social structure?

The Question of "Classness"

As we pointed out in the introduction to this book, whether a collec-tive actor is a class actor or not may not be the right question to pose. The reality of classes is rather a process of constant formation and disintegration. Marx put this admirably in his analysis of the class character of the French peasants during the mid-nineteenth century, in *The Eighteenth Brumaire*. According to Marx, French peasants should be understood as a class "to the extent" that they break out of the isolation of their rural communities and are able to act nationally. We are not so much inspired by Marx's emphasis on class capacities in deciding whether a collective actor can be understood as a class, but by his insights that collective actors can be understood as a class to *some* extent: what the analyst should do is explore the *degree of classness,* rather than bog down in the frustrating debates so often

fought among Marxists as to whether intellectuals, the petty bourgeois, or the peasants are or are not a class. One should, rather, think
of rank and class as a continuum on which collective actors travel
back and forth.

What can be said about the classness of social relations under
post-Stalinist state socialism? To answer, we reconceptualize the
analysis of *The Intellectuals on the Road to Class Power,* with the
help of Pierre Bourdieu. The key idea of the theory of the socialist
redistributive economy is that state socialism emerges as a "class system," to the extent that politics is put in its place. During the Stalinist
epoch, the ruling bureaucratic estate forced its will voluntaristically
on actors. In the post-Stalinist system, however, economic management has ceased to be dictated by the political will of bureaucrats.
Experts armed with technical skills, technocrats, use "scientific methods" to plan the economy and indeed to plan society. The political
voluntarism of the officeholders or bureaucrats is replaced by the
knowhow of the technocrats. While in Stalinism "politics was in command," during post-Stalinism "knowledge is in command." From political voluntarism, we see, there is a shift toward hyper-rationalism.
This post-Stalinist system, however, is still strikingly different from
Western, market-capitalist societies, where "economics is in command" and power is legitimated primarily by the private ownership of
economic capital.

Now we are ready to bring Bourdieu and his distinctions among
different forms of capital into the analysis. If one can distinguish
among social (political),[25] economic, and cultural capital, one may
suggest that Stalinism is a system in which the dominant form of capital is political, complemented by cultural capital. Konrád and Szelényi
saw a trend in post-Stalinism in which cultural capital gained significance at the expense of political capital, but they believed this system
remained clearly distinct from market capitalism, where the dominant
form is economic capital.

The Weberian distinction between rank and class can be interpreted using these concepts as well. *Rank* is a system of social stratification in which power and privilege are primarily derived from *social
capital.* In contrast, class societies exist when most inequalities are
rooted in the unequal access to *economic capital.* The more successfully a party bureaucracy puts "politics in command" (or, for that
matter, the more successful the Prussian Junkers were in preserving
the patron-client relations with their former serfs), the less class-like

will be the relationship between the rulers and ruled. If politics is "put in its place," if the "economic imperative" gets the upper hand, if patronage is replaced by meritocratic, competitive, individualistic relationships based on economic capital, the greater will be the classness of collective actors.

The social character of post-Stalinist state socialism, however, is problematic. The first question is, to what extent can cultural capital be the foundation of class relations? The answer is not obvious. We would argue that a collective actor who claims successfully power and privilege primarily on the monopolistic possession of cultural capital is halfway between actors constituted by social or political capital (who are the least class-like) and actors constituted primarily by possession of economic capital (and who thus constitute by definition "classness"). Cultural capital is in many ways like economic capital: both forms need little emphasis on loyalty and solidarity; they are, rather, highly individualized, meritocratic, and competitive. In some respects, however, cultural capital has affinities with social capital: credentialing is an important mechanism by which cultural capital is accumulated. It is usually not sufficient to acquire knowledge; one also needs a degree. En route to the degree, one has to go through rituals that resemble the way social capital is accumulated: one needs mentors; one has to take hurdles, pass exams, go through initiation ceremonies.

Once accepted into the "community of saints"—once one becomes a doctor, lawyer, or professor—one is bound by some set of "professional ethics," which does not simply regulate the relationship between professionals and clients but also establishes links of solidarity among professionals. They defend each other against charlatans (those who try to practice the profession without appropriate degrees and/or without following ritualistically agreed-upon procedures),[26] and they defend each other against criticism coming from outside. If a professor criticizes the conduct of a fellow professor in front of students, if a doctor tells a patient that his or her former doctor did not prescribe the appropriate medication—irrespective of how true or accurate the criticisms—the professor or doctor violates the rules of "professionalism" or "professional ethics"; in other words, while people who belong to an economic class do not constitute a "community"—and hence the fact that they act collectively is rather unexpected—members of a profession do.

Thus, collective actors whose power and privilege are based on

possession of cultural capital in terms of classness are halfway between the ideal typical extremes of rank and class. One way to think
about this is to identify rank by social capital and economic class by
economic capital, and to call those who draw closures around themselves on the basis of cultural capital a socioeconomic class.[27]

How Technocratic Was Socialist Technocracy?

In post-Stalinist state socialism, the class character of social actors is
even more complicated, due to the unique features of cultural capital, which, according to Konrád and Szelényi, legitimates claims for
power in these societies. While we keep using the distinction between
bureaucracy and technocracy, the use of this terminology requires
justification. One crucial proposition in *The Intellectuals on the
Road to Class Power* was that socialism appealed to the intelligentsia
(as distinct from the *professionalized* intellectuals) because it rejected
the narrow definition of rationality as *instrumental* rationality. The
most ambitious project of Hegel and Marx was to bring telos back
into the center of rationality, rather than accept the "reified bourgeois consciousness" that treated only the selection of the means as
testable by the rules of reason, and treated the choice between ends
as something determined by the sphere of beliefs or, at best, by the
rather irrational political process of majority rule. In other words,
socialism insists that to retain culture in its full sense is to resist its
reduction to civilization.[28] Culture is more than the knowledge of appropriate techniques. In Weber's terms, culture is the human activity
that assigns meaning to an otherwise meaningless human existence.

The idea that socialism is an intellectual project that will transcend "formal rationality," the despotism of means over ends, and
achieve "substantive rationality" has been with us since the inception
of the Marxian project of socialism.[29] The qualitative difference between capitalist and socialist rationalities is emphasized again as the
project of "scientific socialism," the "system of scientific planning,"
is revamped during post-Stalinist reform attempts. The core of the
claim for power by a "rational redistributor" or "central planner"
is not technical but teleological. The central planners' power is not
based on technical knowhow but on their skills to arrive—by following scientific procedures—at a rational choice among goals. In this
sense, the key actors in the system of rational redistribution should
not be called technocrats, but teleocrats. This teleocratic feature of the

socialist technocracy is vitally important, since this was the base upon which an alliance among bureaucrats, technocrats, and humanistic intellectuals was conceivable. In bourgeois society, the fragmentation of intellectuals occurs to a significant extent along these lines. The humanistic intellectuals resent the technocracy, whom they perceive as not proper intellectuals but rather as mere technicians, who would use technologies irrespective of the moral implications of their actions. For Sartre, the nuclear scientist who designs the H-bomb is just a technician; he or she only becomes an intellectual in protesting against nuclear policy and joining the peace movement. The humanistic intellectuals cannot surrender their moral mission, which is primarily about goal setting. In this respect, the bureaucracy and the humanistic intelligentsia are closer to each other than to the technocrats. The post-Stalinist bureaucracy also sees the possibility to reconstitute itself as "evangelistic bureaucrats," as high priests of the teleocratic order. A technocracy that accepts the superiority of "substantive rationality" offers space for the bureaucracy to negotiate a role for itself rather than just eliminate itself in the name of efficiency.

This is ironic, since otherwise the technocrats, especially during the post-Stalinist epoch, are much closer to power than is the humanistic intelligentsia, and can even be seen as a dominated fraction of the ruling estate of late-state socialism. Humanistic intellectuals are excluded from the ruling estate; their hope of receiving their share of power depends on the formation of a broader class constituted by possession of cultural capital and taking place at the expense of the power monopoly of the dominant fraction of the ruling estate— namely, the bureaucracy.

Thus there exists a love-hate relationship, during the post-Stalinist epoch, between the bureaucracy and humanistic intellectuals; it is driven by differences in social background and lifestyles. In contrast, the relationship between the bureaucracy and technocracy is more pragmatic.

The nature of the bureaucratic estate varied across countries, the two polar examples being Russia and Hungary. In Russia, as Eyal and Townsley (1996) have demonstrated, there were clear signs for the making of a bureaucratic caste, as the high-level nomenklatura were more likely to be recruited from among the children of the nomenklatura. There is also evidence concerning the corruption and conspicuous consumption of this bureaucratic caste. The bureaucrats lived a rather luxurious life in their dachas and were in some ways above the law. Members of the bureaucratic estate in Eastern Europe, in contrast, were more likely to be recruited from among the children of peasants and workers; this was the case for Czechoslovakia, Poland, and Hungary. Although during the late socialist period the influx of working-class cadres significantly slowed down, and among the younger generation of nomenklatura the number of well-trained professionals coming from middle-class families increased, the working-class character of people in high political position remained undisputed.

The East European bureaucratic estate—and this is particularly true for the Hungarian high nomenclature during the heights of Kadarism in the 1960s and early 1970s—was far less corrupt than its Russian counterpart. According to Hungarian anecdotes, when János Kádár wanted to have a really good time, he watched bad Western movies in a private studio with his culture czar, György Aczél, while they sipped mediocre Russian cognac. The Party School swimming pool, where Kádár and other members of the politburo took their swims, reminds one of the pool of a community college in a poor American city. After Kádár's wife passed away during the early 1990s and their estate was auctioned off, the catalogue that contained the items offered to auction had several pictures of the interiors of the Kádár home. While there were a few valuable artifacts, especially paintings by major Hungarian masters, what was the most striking was the working-class character of the home. The furniture could have come from the home of a fairly well-off worker and the style of interior design was rather proletarian.

The humanistic intelligentsia, both those who were attracted to a New Class project and tried to become ideologues of socialism with a human face, and those who were the early oppositionists, were strikingly different from the bureaucracy. They were in part recruited from the old pre-Communist educated middle class. Others, especially the intellectuals in the forefront of the reforms during the 1960s, and of the opposition by the late 1970s, often came from cadre families. Unlike the first-generation high nomenklatura, they were second- or third-generation middle class and greatly bourgeoisified in their lifestyles. The East European nomenklatura took great care of their children. Many were educated in Western colleges. Their parents made sure they did not have to spend the early years of their lives struggling to find housing for themselves. They either secured for their children the best quality public housing or, by the late 1970s or so, built condos for their sons and daughters. They pulled strings to get good jobs for their children at prestigious institutions, and obtained scholarships for them at Western universities. When they got involved with opposition activities, they made sure they could keep their jobs and exit visas, and that they were kept out of jail. While the Russian nomenklatura put their children into nomenklatura positions, the East European cadres made sure their children became real professionals (and occasionally dissident intellectuals) and that they could pursue bourgeois lifestyles. They became bourgeosified early on, making it much easier for them to accept bourgeois-liberal values and worldview later on.

As a result, the contrast between the bureaucratic estate and the humanistic intellectuals could not be greater. The former were rather proletarian, or petty-bourgeois, often uneducated, and quite ascetic. They had a rough life, started in the Communist underground, often lived in working-class slums, and worked their way up slowly. Many never developed much of a taste for the luxuries of bourgeois life, or were embarrassed enough to not live particularly privileged existences. Their private lives were under the scrutiny of the party. They could not afford to have affairs, as a divorce could cost them their jobs.

The humanistic intelligentsia, in contrast, lived a much more pleasant life. They went to privileged schools and learned the value of a bourgeois lifestyle—and, with the help of their parents, could afford this. Since they opted to pursue the lives of free intellectuals rather than of party bureaucrats, they could live bohemian, eccentric lives: they could experiment with communes; no one interfered with their private lives; and no one prevented them from tasting of the life of the "flower children." These vanguard-like humanistic intellectuals had little respect for the bureaucratic estate, despised its tastes and lifestyle, and found its political conformism and pragmatism outrageous. If members of the bureaucratic estate happened to be their parents, the generational struggle—the revolt of sons and daughters against their fathers and mothers—was fought out in political terms.

Certainly, the first generation of "dissent," those who in the 1960s began to formulate a criticism of the bureaucratic estate, did not want to "restore capitalism." On the contrary, the critics accused the post-Stalinist bureaucratic estate, often their own parents, of being "traitors to the cause," of being too soft on the class enemy and not holding high enough the flame of the revolution. Stalin—or, somewhat later, Mao, Castro, or Che Guevara—were the ideals, and for them the problem with post-Stalinism was its lack of principles, its pragmatism. (In Poland, for example, Kuron and Modzelewski wrote an open letter to the central committee of the Communist Party calling for a more faithful implementation of the communist doctrine.) In Hungary, Haraszti and Dallos even participated in a Maoist conspiracy with the aim of overthrowing the revisionist bureaucratic Hungarian regime. While most humanistic intellectuals did not radicalize themselves to such an extent, they tried to work within the regime to implement reform. Eventually, for some, the new ideals were not necessarily cast in socialist terms anymore, although until the 1980s they rarely were formulated in antisocialist ways. Especially among those humanistic intellectuals who were not coming from a cadre background, social ideals either were directed towards rationalization via the reduction of bureaucratic voluntarism or were put in nationalist terms. These intellectuals called for an end of counterselection, the appointment of competent people to positions of authority, and more respect for national traditions or for the conditions of ethnic nationals living abroad.

We hope to have clarified what we called the "love-hate" relationship between the bureaucratic estate and the humanistic intellectuals. The two social groups were on a collision course: the bureaucratic estate was suspicious and feared the humanistic intellectuals of the 1960s; the humanistic intellectuals despised the bureaucratic estate for its petty bourgeois lifestyle and absence of principles in politics. Still, both groups were vanguards with a commitment to substantive rationality and both had little doubt that they knew better than "the people" what was good for society.

The relationship between the technocratic and the bureaucratic fractions of the ruling elite was rather different. In terms of their social background and lifestyles, these two groups were much closer to each other than to the humanistic intellectuals. Until the end of communism, the technocracy was typically recruited from upwardly mobile working-class or peasant families. While the technocrats were far from ascetic, some of the petty bourgeois features of the high nomenklatura lifestyle applied to theirs as well. Many of them indeed came from humble backgrounds, and the hurdle was too high to jump straight into the "grand bourgeoisie," in terms of both mentality and lifestyles. They were ready to spend money on car-phones and other gadgets, but they did not quite know what a proper bourgeois life implied, so they might be more reluctant to spend their money on a painting of a Polish or Hungarian master than on a sports car. Their language skills were often somewhat limited; their "cultural capital" (in the narrowed term in which American interpreters of Bourdieu use the concept) was not high (they were not exposed to much high culture in their childhood, might not speak foreign languages, etc). In one respect, however, the gap between the technocracy and the bureaucracy was greater than the gap between the bureaucracy and the humanistic intellectuals. The technocrats as early as the late 1960s and early 1970s seem to have been the most "professionalized" group of East European intellectuals. They valued knowhow more, and saw themselves as doers rather than people with a mission.

As a result, when the conservative counterattacks against post-Stalinism began, most technocrats did not really mind offering up a few sacrificial lambs from the critical humanistic intellectuals. In Hungary, one prime example was the purge of the Lukács school in 1973. The Lukács disciples were perceived as ideologues by the technocrats. If the price to keep continuing the economic reforms of 1968 was to see a few heads fall, the technocrats were ready to pay it; they accepted the purge of the radical philosophers of the Lukács school, who at that time still advocated the "renaissance of Marxism" and the "humanization of socialism." The technocrats could not care less about either project; they had no commitment to Marxism and they certainly preferred the rationalization of socialism to its humanization. The irony is that the project of the technocracy was much more subversive for the position of the bureaucratic estate than was the threat assumed to be coming from critical humanistic intellectuals.

Of course, eventually the bureaucracy moved against the intellectuals with a vengeance, while trying to live together with the technocracy with a series of concessions and compromises, digging its own grave along the way. In retrospect, the Communist Party ideologues in Hungary were foolish to purge the last of the true Marxists from their jobs in 1973. Those purged had offered some legitimacy to Marxism and socialism. Thus, the purge left the pragmatist technocrats in positions of real authority—to know, within a decade, all too well that the time of socialism was gone and the task was now to make capitalism out of socialism.

Class Formations under Post-Stalinism

Was there a dominant class of intellectuals in the post-Stalinist epoch of state socialism? The answer seems an obvious "no." Even in the most radically reform-oriented state socialist countries, the Communist Party retained its political hegemony; therefore power was exercised by the ruling bureaucratic estate. While members of this bureaucratic estate often were intellectuals, and some other intellectuals were co-opted as ideologues in the exercise of power, the nature of the power they exercised was not class power, in the orthodox Weberian sense, since it was primarily rooted in political structures and patron-client relations that emerged from these structures.

The more difficult question is whether there were indications of class formation, forces pointing in the direction of a transition from a socialist rank order toward a socialist system of stratification, where the major cleavages are between classes? Our answer to this question is a cautious yes. At least for awhile, there were signs of such a change in the logic of the stratification system. However, it is unclear whether forces producing this change were strong enough to create a rationalized form of socialist stratification or whether they were only capable of eroding the state socialist rank order, leading to the system collapse that took place in 1989.

There can be little doubt, however, that as socialism aged political capital kept losing its determinant role as a source of power and privilege, and both cultural and economic capital gained ground. This was far from a clear, linear trend, but rather a contested process, fought over by the social actors involved. In particular, as "politics is in command" weakened, some accumulated political capital was concentrated into personal networks. Earlier political privileges survive in the form of clientelistic networks; this change has been a traditionalization rather than a rationalization of the logic of the social structure. As paternalistic networking replaced "politics in command," the ways social and economic action were carried out appeared more and more corrupt, rather than "rational." Party bosses or domestic intelligence agents converted themselves into godfathers of mafia organizations. Ideology increasingly lost its importance; power was not legitimated anymore with references to class struggle, the dictatorship of the proletariat, or the principles of Marxism-Leninism. Either power is carried out cynically, or increasingly justified with reference to national interest as well as law and order. This appears an important trend in China and in Cuba today. The Chinese Communist Party does not justify itself any longer with Maoism; instead it appeals to people by threatening them with the prospects of a Russian-style collapse if the party is forced to give up its political power. Their principle of legitimation can be summed up by the phrase "Without us you will have chaos." Nationalism was always an important theme in Castro's striving for legitimacy, and by the mid-1990s it became the dominant theme.

Thus the transition from rank order to class society is not a simple process during mature and late socialism. Privilege and power derived from politics and ideology are to some extent converted into paternalistic, clientelistic relationships, which keep blocking forces of class formation. To the extent to which forces of class formation still exist, the would-be class agents are mostly co-opted into neotraditionalistic, clientelistic structures.

Still, some signs of class formation were clear. The more reform-oriented an East European country was, the more obvious these trends were. Within the state and party apparatus there was a shift from "red" to "expert." Proper educational credentials were required and there were more straight career trajectories, with people finishing school, getting into universities, and being recruited into the party or state bureaucracy on the basis of their university credentials. In Poland and Hungary, party membership was becoming less of a requirement to be recruited into jobs with substantial decision-making powers. Returns on education grew and returns on party membership slipped.

With the second economy gaining ground and legitimacy, market skills and economic capital also became a source of income and some prestige, although not much power. A New Class of petty bourgeois grew in size, accumulated some capital, and was very successful in earning income from market or quasi-market activities. These economic actors, especially these who were the most successful, remained often "embedded" within the clientelistic networks of party and state bureaucracies. They needed the goodwill and protection of party or state bosses to be able to operate smoothly without being harassed by the police or local party officials. In order to get a license to operate a business, one needed mentors in the party and state bureaucracy. Thus the process of class formation, even in the case of the most ideal typical instance, that of making a new petit bourgeoisie, occurred with the interaction between the logic of rank and class.

Reform socialism can be described most accurately as a dual system of social stratification in which the logics of rank order and class stratification coexist and intersect. The two logics were dependent on each other to such an extent that one began to wonder, by the later stages of reform socialism, whether this was an involutionary trap in the sense that it promoted a synergistic relation between the two strategies that simultaneously bolstered the system's legitimacy and was economically parasitic. In retrospect, it may have been an involutionary trap, which had to be shaken to its very foundation by the profound challenges of 1989.

There is substantial evidence that the logic of class stratification gained ground from the early- to mid-1960s onward, and that some rationalization did take place in the way power was exercised. It also appears that both *Civilization at the Crossroads* and *The Intellectuals on the Road to Class Power* overestimated how strong reform forces were and underestimated the resistance of the rank order. *The Alternative* offers, in this respect, the most realistic assessment. This is not surprising, since it was the last of the three books. None of these books, however, spotted the trends of the making of a petty bourgeoisie, in which class formation was driven by economic capital; thus they all missed the most prominent social process of the 1980s. If there was to be class formation, it would not be the transformation of the ruling bureaucratic estate into a new dominant class of intellectuals, but rather the making of a class of petty owners, who would not strive for political power, and thus could "peacefully coexist" with the ruling bureaucratic estate.

Five

The Fall of the Class Project of the Socialist Reform Intelligentsia

If there ever was a class project of intellectuals under East European state socialism, it certainly did not last very long, and by the time it was possible to identify this process, the transformation of the bureaucratic ruling estate into a dominant class was already in the process of disintegration.

The Counteroffensive of the Bureaucratic Ruling Estate

We associate the intellectual class project with the policies of Nikita Khrushchev. But Khrushchev was ousted from power as early as 1963; thus he lost power before the reforms he tried to implement could take off the ground in Eastern Europe. The 1960s, however, was a somewhat confusing decade in this respect. It was far from obvious, until the crackdown on the Prague Spring in August 1968, what the Brezhnev era would look like. With Leonid Brezhnev, it appeared that a group of cadres with technical training, many of them engineers, had moved into positions of power. Thus it appeared that Brezhnev's rise to power was an indicator of the ascent of the technocracy. Also during the 1960s, East European party bosses were remarkably independent from Moscow, and until August 1968 they appeared to follow independent, and usually technocratically oriented, reforms, as appeared to be the case with János Kádár, Wladyslaw

Gomulka, Nicolae Ceauşescu, and even Walter Ulbricht and Todor Zhivkov. Kádár went so far that, upon his return from a meeting in Moscow at which the dismissal of Khrushchev was explained to the East European party bosses, he announced that, no matter what happened in the Soviet Union, the reform process would continue in Hungary (and to some extent it did). There is also evidence that Zhivkov (according to Ivan Berend) and even Ulbricht (according to a dissertation of a student of Dan Chirot) tried to experiment cautiously with technocratic reforms—and the initial liberalism of the Ceauşescu regime, especially its independence from Moscow, is well-known and well documented.

Thus it appeared that until 1968 the rapprochement of the bureaucratic estate and the intellectuals continued. The peak of this process undoubtedly was the so-called Prague Spring and Hungary's adaptation of the New Economic Mechanism, the two big victories of the New Class project by reform intellectuals. These two events were so important that one almost failed to notice the first serious signs of backlash against this project, namely the confrontation between the bureaucratic ruling estate and the intellectuals and university students during the spring of 1968.

Indeed, 1968 was undoubtedly the year of the turnaround, the year when it became rather obvious that the bureaucratic ruling estate was reluctant to go as far with power sharing as the socialist reform intelligentsia wanted. Prague Spring was an important test of how far the bureaucratic estate was willing to go. During the early months of 1968, the Czechoslovak reform intelligentsia defined reasonably clearly what sort of socialism was acceptable for it, and the response of the bureaucratic estate was August 1968, the invasion of Czechoslovakia. It was also important for the Soviets that all Warsaw Pact countries participated in this action. In large part, this participation was supposed to be a message to the world that the invasion came not from the Soviet Union acting on its own, but rather the whole alliance. But the invasion had a powerful message for domestic reformers in Hungary, Poland, and Bulgaria; the Soviets clearly told them how far they could go and from what point onward they could expect military intervention.

The signal was important to the bureaucratic estates in these countries, as these estates wanted reassurances that the reform would not threaten their political monopoly. In all the East European countries, a growing proportion of the bureaucratic estate had begun to watch the reform movement with concern.

In Poland, the bureaucratic estate was anxious to crack down, itself, on reform intellectuals and students demanding an acceleration of reform in the spring of 1968. The Polish bureaucratic estate exploited the anti-intellectualism and anti-Semitism of the Polish working class to mobilize workers to demonstrate against reformist students. The expulsion of thousands of Polish intellectuals of Jewish ancestry followed, which brought the socialist reform movement virtually to a halt.

In Hungary, and to some extent in Bulgaria, however, the bureaucratic estates were not strong enough to defeat reformist forces. These estates wanted the Soviet leadership to take sides in unambiguous terms so they could use the "Soviet card" against their leaders, such as Kádár or Zhivkov, who during the 1960s were under strong reformist influence. The technocratic reform had a great deal of appeal in the German Democratic Republic (G.D.R.), and Honnecker repeatedly reported Ulbricht to the Soviets for being too soft on reformers, eventually persuading them to sack him. Kádár and Zhivkov were reported by their bureaucratic opposition to the Soviets, too; they just always outmaneuvered opponents. Usually handling opponents was accomplished, however, by offering the heads of the most prominent reformers to the Soviets to demonstrate their ideological firmness.

Rumania is probably the most interesting case. Ceauşescu in his early years was both a reformer and an anti-Soviet nationalist (as noted in Jowitt and Chirot). It turned out, however, that his nationalism was strong and genuine, while his reformism was weak and false. After he crushed his pro-Moscow opposition, he moved against the reformers. Without Soviet help, and with anti-Soviet gestures, he established a neo-Stalinist state, in which the political hegemony of the bureaucratic ruling estate was as unchallenged as in Czechoslovakia. The Romanian case is particularly insightful, since it shows that there were very strong domestic forces behind the counteroffensive of the bureaucratic estate in Eastern Europe.

Unlike what would occur in 1989, in 1968 the old bureaucratic guard still had its will to power. Thus, while the Prague Spring had massive popular support, it also met strong misgivings by the members of the bureaucratic estate. The Soviets did not have to "fake" a letter inviting themselves to invade; there were enough "old guard" types who were relieved to hear the Russian tanks rolling down the streets of Prague.

What were the reasons for the counteroffensive by the bureaucratic estate? In general terms, it was uncalled for. Before 1968 the reform intelligentsia by and large remained firmly committed to the socialist project. It appeared quite unjustified to call the Prague reformers counterrevolutionaries, compared to the participants in the 1956 Hungarian uprising, although in both instances the labeling of events as "counterrevolutionary" or "antisocialist" was fought by the reformers.

In 1956 in Hungary, preparation for the October events was done by reformer members of the Communist Party, who firmly believed, up to the last moment, that socialism would be preserved. They just wanted to make it fit better with national conditions and operate within a democratic framework. In 1956, however, it was difficult not to see genuinely counterrevolutionary elements at work. The cruel events on Köztársaság tér on 1 November 1956, in which a right-wing mob stormed a Party house, killing a Party official and members of the security forces, were carried out by nationalist forces (their critics would call them proto-fascist or even fascist), and there were strong calls for a restoration of precommunist and, in fact, prewar Hungarian social and political structures, including the restoration of precommunist property relations.

Thus while 1956 was initiated by reform communists, and in some ways was a New Class project to create a more rational and democratic socialist society, soon after the system began to break down, antisocialist elements who wanted to restore the prewar Hungarian social order took over.[1] The conflict between the reform communists and restorationists/nationalists did not yet come to the surface, since they faced a common enemy in the Soviets and the Red Army. They shared cells in the jails, went together to the gallows. It was only in 1989 that it became clear how fatal and irreconcilable their differences were. After 1989, the schism between the former reform communists (almost all of whom still alive in 1989 had shifted to a liberal, procapitalist position) and the restorationists/nationalists surfaced, spawning a major ideological battle over to whom 1956 really belongs.

The Prague Spring in 1968 was rather different from the Hungarian events. It was exclusively a reform communist movement that remained firmly committed to the idea of socialism. Some reformers emphasized the need to humanize socialism, while others emphasized the need for its rationalization, but most reformers believed that both must, and could, be done simultaneously. It is also telling that 1968 did not become an object of contestation among different political forces after 1989. The new political elite that came into power left 1968 in the cupboard of the reform communists. For the 1989 Czech and Slovak bourgeois liberals, 1968 was not a particularly attractive symbol, since it was too socialistic. Even Alexander Dubček had only a very short period of revitalized popularity before his tragic accident (in 1992), and by 1989 he was already fading into obscurity. In fact, none of the 1968 reformers played any significant role after 1989.

Socialist ideology remained hegemonic among the reform intellectuals of the 1960s. It was a movement within the intellectual elite, which stayed well within the parameters of socialist social order. This was a New Class project par excellence, an attempt by the humanistic and technical intelligentsia to reduce the political power of the bureaucratic ruling estate, and to create a more humanistic, rational, and democratic socialist system. The events of 1956 in Hungary foreshadowed this, but since they were closer in time to precommunism, they were more complex than the Prague Spring. Although initiated by the reform communists, the events were soon joined by restorationist/nationalist forces, and thus indeed had a significant counterrevolutionary component. Paradoxically, the more complex nature of 1956 makes that event a more appealing political symbol after 1989. Prague Spring was far too "socialistic" for the post-1989 new Czech political elite to identify with or use as a national symbol, but that 1956 was "not just" a reform communist event makes it more attractive for the postcommunist Hungarian political class.

If the reform movement of the 1960s was cast within the parameters of socialism, what then made the bureaucratic estate strike against it? The most obvious reason is that it represented a threat to the political monopoly of the bureaucratic ruling estate. By June 1968, it was clear that the reform communist intelligentsia wanted to see the implementation of a major political reform. While the reformers stopped just short of demanding a multiparty parliamentary democracy, for all practical purposes they wanted to eliminate the political monopoly of the Communist Party. Even without a multiparty system, it was unclear how the bureaucratic estate and the technocracy could coexist; the technocracy, whether it wanted more markets or a more rationalized system of planning, could not ask for less than the elimination of the Party's control over the economy.

This was a direct challenge to the bureaucratic estate, because the Party's role in the economy was a major source of its power. There is a telling anecdote along these lines about János Kádár. When, during the early 1980s, the Hungarian reformers called for a "second economic reform," they also suggested this could only work if the party "withdraws from the economy." Supposedly, János Kádár addressed a party meeting and told his audience, in a typical kadaresque way (a mixture of naiveté and down-to-earth realism), "Comrades, we are told to withdraw from the economy. But comrades, where are we supposed to withdraw to?" This hit the nail on the head. If the compromise of the bureaucratic estate and the technocracy was supposed to mean that the bureaucratic estate would keep politics and the technocracy would capture the economy, this would not leave much for the bureaucracy.

The level of trust between the bureaucracy and the reform intelligentsia was not particularly high. There were also important frictions between the technocracy and humanistic intellectuals, which the bureaucracy exploited for a while (though, by the 1980s, the technocratic fraction of the ruling estate, and the dissident humanistic intellectuals, began to cooperate in fighting the bureaucracy). The bureaucracy looked at the humanistic intellectuals with a great deal of suspicion, regarding them as muddle-headed, overly idealistic, and confused. During the 1960s, many members of the bureaucratic estate were of working-class origins; some had started as manual workers and been promoted to positions of authority later in life (a trajectory more likely to occur in Eastern Europe than in the Soviet Union, where, as we already noted, citing Eyal and Townsley, the working-class recruitment into the nomenklatura was substantially reduced).

These working-class cadres on the whole did not think much of the intellectual "eggheads," whether the children of their colleagues or comrades, or from bourgeois families. These cadres felt confident that they knew how to conduct the business of politics, and "these kids," who had never experienced real life, did not. The rapid changes in intellectual fashion and the tendency to radicalize ideas further fueled suspicion among the members of the bureaucratic estate, who wondered: What if these characters suddenly turn around and tomorrow they start preaching capitalism? What will we do then? The members of the bureaucratic estate were used to living with discipline. The unique feature of the 1960s intellectual dissidents was that they did not act in a disciplined manner, so how could they be trusted? Even their lifestyles, the bureaucrats felt, were disgusting: they did not dress properly, they wore bluejeans and the young men all had beards, and in their private lives they experimented with communal living, swapped husbands and wives, and did all sorts of weird things. The members of the bureaucratic estate read the reports of the domestic intelligence on the private lives of the humanistic reform communists with disbelief. They concluded these were spoiled, undisciplined, and unreliable children.

The bureaucratic estate noticed that the technocracy, too, had reservations concerning the humanistic intellectuals. As we pointed out before, the technocracy and the bureaucratic ruling estate came from a similar social milieu. Many were first-generation intellectuals, and while they were younger and better educated than the bureaucratic estate, they were also rather down-to-earth, and shared with the ruling estate a commitment to pragmatism. The humanistic intellectuals of the 1960s, however, were still attracted to the big ideological issues. They were often interested in implementing the real, original values of socialism: to make society more egalitarian, to make it conform more to what they believed its founders had wanted socialism to look like. The technocracy was not particularly attracted to these issues, and therefore it could not really care if the bureaucratic estate decided to crack down on the humanistic intellectuals.

To sum up, by the second half of the 1960s the bureaucratic ruling estate felt threatened. It believed its political hegemony was being challenged, and that it was being forced out of the economy without having anywhere to go. It also mistrusted and often despised the humanistic intellectuals, and since the humanistic intellectuals did not have the strong support of the technocracy at that time (in part, ironically, because the intellectuals were too committed to socialism and to ideology in general), the bureaucracy had also a political opportunity to crack down on the reformers, starting with the humanistic intellectuals.

This happened in the spring of 1968 in Warsaw, in August 1968 in Czechoslovakia, and during the early 1970s in Hungary (for example, the attack on the Budapest School and the Miklós Haraszti trial, to name the most notable events of this kind). The love affair between the bureaucratic ruling estate, which was searching for a post-Stalinist legitimacy, the reform-oriented humanistic intellectuals (still in search of the humanization of socialism), and the technocracy (in search of economic rationalization) was coming to an end.

The Opening to the Second Economy

The counteroffensive of the bureaucratic dominant estate culminated in what Zaslavsky called the neo-Stalinist state in many countries. The Soviet Union during the "mature" Brezhnev years, post-1968 Czechoslovakia, Rumania from the mid-1970s onward, and the G.D.R. after Honnecker consolidated his power could each be regarded as such a neo-Stalinist state. In this system, Stalinism was partially restored, although the excesses of Stalinism never reappeared. The domestic intelligence service never regained its license to hunt people down, and it especially could not touch those in the party apparatus. The neo-Stalinist state never used as much coercion as Stalinism proper. There were no show trials; there were few political prisoners and even these few were often camouflaged as "mental patients," rather than shipped off to a gulag. Most important, neo-Stalinism was a paternalistic system that guaranteed security of tenure for its staff. This was crucial for the legitimacy of the neo-Stalinist social order. The members of the bureaucratic estate, as we pointed out, felt threatened by the reform movements, and not without reason. The reforms of the 1960s called for the elimination of counterselection and for the promotion of people to position of authority on the basis of competence—a rather direct challenge to sitting officials. Brezhnev, Husak, or Honnecker boosted the loyalty of their staff by making tenure safe. The officials were safe not only from Stalinist purges, but also from possible "tenure reviews" conducted by aspiring reformers.

The neo-Stalinist state placed great emphasis on the value of security, which had an appeal well beyond the staff of the bureaucratic estate, among the broad strata of the population. In the reform communist countries of Poland, Hungary, and Yugoslavia, from the mid-1970s onward the process of socioeconomic transformation created a certain degree of insecurity; price reform fueled inflation and undermined the stability of state socialism, to some extent. The Czechoslovak and East German leaders were fast to remind their population of this. "Okay," they argued, in effect, "Hungary or Yugoslavia may show greater economic dynamism. We don't claim we are all that dynamic. But we are secure. The prices of basic consumer goods are stable; you don't have to worry about where you will find the money to buy bread and meat, to pay your rent or go on vacation. Hungarians and Yugoslavs have such worries. We may give little but you can count on that much, and we do not ask too much in return."

The second trajectory that socialist countries followed, after the counterattack by the bureaucratic estate, was a controlled process of reform. There was not simply less reform than foreseen by the reformers of the 1960s, but these reforms followed a different path. As the reform intelligentsia was by and large defeated, its reform design was not quite implemented. Most of the proposed reform of the public sector was sabotaged, and what change remained was rather cosmetic. There was, however, substantial reform by default in some East European countries—the most in Hungary and Yugoslavia but a fair amount in Poland. The essence of this reform was to open up new opportunities for what was called "the second economy." While there was much less change in the redistributively integrated public sector of the economy than foreseen by the 1960s reformers, there was an unexpectedly pragmatic and far-reaching opening to the private sector in petty commodity production.

For instance, Hungary completely deregulated small-scale family agricultural production. The authorities did not interfere at all with what families did on their private plots. They allowed them to rent more land if they wanted to cultivate it, and to sell all their production on markets for as much as they could earn. This agricultural reform was followed by far-reaching deregulation in trade and some areas of artisan-type production. Bakeries, small construction firms, television and car repair shops, gas stations, and the like opened and were allowed to operate without being harassed by the police or even by the taxation office. The urban landscapes changed quickly in Budapest and Warsaw. The mushrooming new shops, restaurants, and other small private businesses brought a major improvement in the supply of consumer goods. Substantial income was generated this way, leading to the rapid growth of a "middle class" of "socialist entrepreneurs" with solid petty-bourgeois lifestyles (Szelényi 1988). Since the entrepreneurs were operating within the framework of a not particularly competitive state sector, they earned higher incomes than they would have under a free market system. Some of their income was in fact channeled out of the public sector. The emergent new private sector firms often coexisted in a symbiotic relationship with the state firms. The public firms often sold inputs to private firms at subsidized prices, and often acted as intermediaries between the private-sector firms and the final consumers by bringing the products of the private firms to the market. Thus, at least some of these firms lived "parasitically" off the public sector and generated respectable incomes for their operators.

Such an opening toward the private sector was quite conscious, and was motivated by legitimacy considerations. As the relationship between the bureaucratic estate and the intelligentsia turned sour, the bureaucratic estate searched for an alternative system of legitimacy and an alternative social base. Reform during the 1960s was perceived primarily as an opening toward the professionals, an opening that promised them better jobs by eliminating counterselection and by implementing more rational or scientific ways of social and economic management. It also promised them liberal cultural policies. As the bureaucratic estate backtracked in these respects, it began to open towards the working class and peasant workers, offering them better life chances. Instead of searching for legitimacy in "scientific socialism," "teleological rationality," or "hyper-rationality," the late reform communist bureaucratic estate presented itself as pragmatic and uninterested in ideology, letting people alone as long as they do not question the estate's political monopoly.

Thus there were two alternative paths that socialist societies took in the late period of development. One was the neo-Stalinist state, which retained the rigid classic structure of socialist rank order but, unlike Stalinism, did not rely on coercion in securing obedience; it legitimated itself with the value of security, in particular security of tenure offered to its staff. Controlled reform socialist states entered the road to capitalism by opening up opportunities for small business, thereby making capitalism from below while retaining the political monopoly of the Communist Party and legitimating its rule with pragmatism and realpolitik.

The senior author of this book, after completing *The Intellectuals on the Road to Class Power* in 1975, was advised to emigrate and was not allowed back to his native Hungary for seven years. Upon his first visit back, in 1982, he was struck at how much change there was after this relatively brief period of time and how unanticipated, for him, was the character of those changes. What stuck him most was the dynamic growth of private activities and petty capitalism everywhere. While writing, in 1974–75, about the New Class project of intellectuals, it never occurred to him that the bureaucratic ruling estate could ever demonstrate so much flexibility toward capitalism, even in petty form. When the official in the central committee of the Hungarian Communist Party—who was already responsible for sociology during the mid-1970s and remained in the position in 1982—found out about Szelényi's visit, he arranged a meeting. The two met for a coffee in a downtown cafe. During the hour-long meeting, the party official kept talking and the sociologist listened. Embarrassed by his own silence, Szelényi finally decided he should ask at least one question. He asked, "I see all these private businesses mushrooming. You are a communist, are you not concerned that you're restoring capitalism?" It was perhaps a foolish question, but the official had the ready-made answer: "I am pleased with private business and what it does to us, the Communist Party. Where I live, there is a private bakery and I myself buy my bakery from this entrepreneur; his bread is far better than what the public bakery produced. But this is good for us. If people eat better bread, they like the regime more, so this is good politics."

This was not an overly sophisticated answer, considering it was coming from an old-timer with a Ph.D. in philosophy from Lomonosov University in Moscow, but quite telling. As another old-timer said, around the same time, in a distant land, "I don't care what the color of the cat is as long as it catches the mouse." Pragmatism is the key legitimation device of late socialism on the way to capitalism, which is being built from below. This appears true of Hungary of the 1980s (and to a lesser extent also of Poland during the same time period) and has been true in China since the rise of Deng, in 1978, to power. The legitimation with reference to pragmatism and realpolitik at the expense of ideology was particularly appealing for those Soviet satellite countries that tried to stay away from the neo-Stalinist model and keep the momentum of reform going, even if it did not follow the blueprint of the reform intellectuals of the 1960s. One important source of legitimacy for these controlled reforming countries was their dependence on the Soviet Union, and on the abilities of the political bosses of these satellites countries to navigate on a relatively independent and reasonable course. Both Kádár and Jaruzelski tried to get mileage out of the fact that they did the best that could be done under Soviet domination. While Poles remained skeptical whether Jaruzelski indeed did this, Hungarians by and large were ready, for a long time, to believe Kádár. So Hungary was thought of as the "merriest barrack in the socialist camp," or "goulash communism."

This goulash communism appealed to the ordinary people, and it sounded authentic, as one saw the number of "socialist entrepreneurs" grow by the day and their relative affluence also increase. There has been some controversy in recent sociological literature over who the real beneficiaries of this early market reform were. Indeed, who were these socialist entrepreneurs? Victor Nee (1989), in his market transition theory, suggested that "direct producers" benefited from the opening up of small private business, while Andrew Walder (1996), Ákos Róna-Tas (1994, 1998), Yanjie Bian and John Logan (1996) argued that cadres were the ones who became the new entrepreneurs. However, there is little doubt that, in late socialist states on the road to capitalism from below, there was a substantial growth in the middle of the social hierarchy: the middle class with petty bourgeois characteristics grew significantly.

Szelényi, in his *Socialist Entrepreneurs* (1988), suggested that many of these positions, especially the positions of the more dynamic entrepreneurs, may have been occupied by descendants of former petty bourgeois families. These families were on a bourgeoisification trajectory before they were interrupted by the rise of communism, and, once again given the opportunity, they resumed the project of embourgeoisement, or petty bourgeoisification. But "interrupted embourgeoisement" tells only part of the story. Socialist embourgeoisement during the 1980s in Hungary or today in China is a much broader process; it affects far more people than the descendants of former entrepreneurs or small entrepreneurs, offering a chance of upward mobility for people from ordinary working-class or peasant families. Further, as Walder and Róna-Tas point out, as small private business becomes legitimate and even respectable, and offers higher incomes than can be earned in the public sector, cadres (in particular local cadres) and the children of cadres enter such business activities.

Late socialism on its way to capitalism from below legitimated itself to a substantial degree by the success it engendered in the middle of the social hierarchy, and it indeed created a broad social base. We can see the evidence of this relatively broad social support in the return of former communist parties to power both in Poland and in Hungary. After 1989, commentators were inclined to underestimate the popular support that the late socialist regimes had. This inclination was of course reinforced by the spectacular collapse of the regimes in 1989–90 and the poor performance of the former communist parties during the first elections. But we know from public opinion polls that the communist parties before the spring of 1989 had the support of about a third of the population, which also included, beyond the party cadre, people in the "socialist middle class." In 1993–94 in the Polish and Hungarian elections, we see the return of support to these parties. It is important to note that the poorest and least educated were, still, less likely to support the successor parties (and were often attracted to the nationalistic parties of the far right). The successor parties, on the other hand, gained the support of the cadre intellectuals and those from the middle class who had done well during the 1980s.

For awhile during the mid-1980s, it was not unreasonable to assume that the major change in the social structure of reformer state socialist societies was the birth of a New Class of socialist entrepreneurs, an event that transformed the nature of state socialism in some important ways, although it did not challenge either the political monopoly of the ruling estate or the hegemonic role of redistributive integration and public ownership.

The Intellectuals on the Road to Dissent

By the mid- to late-1970s, intellectuals got the message. The bureaucratic estate was not willing to go far enough with reforms. It above all wanted to retain its political monopoly; it would not move out of the economy; and therefore it had very little to offer the intelligentsia. If there was to be a New Class of mature socialism, it would not be a New Class of enlightened technocrats and their intellectual allies, but rather the class of new socialist entrepreneurs, a new petty bourgeoisie willing to leave political power to the party, and to accept a complementary role in a second, subordinated sector of the economy, in exchange for higher incomes.

Intellectuals in the former socialist societies began to travel the road of dissent from leftist or socialist or plebeian critiques of "actually existing socialism" to eventually become the theorists of liberal capitalism. The most important milestones along this road were: the invention of the theory of civil society; the idea of antipolitics; the idea of embourgeoisement without a propertied bourgeoisie; the questioning of the usefulness of the distinction between socialism and capitalism; and the consideration of the possibility of a Third Way between the latter two. These developments culminated in intellectuals constituting themselves as a new *Bildungsbürgertum* whose historic mission was to lead the nation, whether to an authentic national life and/or to liberal market capitalism.

As we have pointed out, the idea of socialism was hegemonic among intellectuals during most of the 1960s. This hegemony did not imply a positive belief or approval among all professionals, but rather a passive acceptance of the socialist system of domination, with the understanding that under the given circumstances there was no viable alternative and, with gradual reform, it could be improved and made livable. For sure, the coercive apparatus was also in place to support this hegemony. While Khrushchev shut down the gulag system, by the standards of Western democratic systems even 1960s reform socialism was rather oppressive. Domestic intelligence had been active, and while for most of the 1960s the most prominent intellectuals usually could feel fairly secure from police prosecution, there were always enough rank-and-file intellectuals and ordinary people in jail, under observation, or being interrogated for political and ideological reasons to remind everyone what the ultimate realities were. By the late 1960s and early 1970s, the bureaucratic ruling estate went on the counteroffensive, and the coercive features of the regimes became more visible. Thus, socialism was never free of dissent, even during the reform epoch when, we claim, the ideals of socialism were hegemonic, at least among intellectuals. During this time, dissent was likely to be nationalistic and religious. Political dissent, be it bourgeois-liberal or conservative-right-wing, was not completely absent, but basically it was dormant.

Shortly after the fall of the 1956 uprising in Hungary, József Antall, who in 1990 became the first Hungarian postcommunist prime minister, told his old school friend Ferenc Fehér, at that time a devote socialist and a disciple of Georg Lukács, "Now I take a deep dive and stay under water" ("Most alámerülök"). Indeed, Antall remained invisible for thirty years. He locked himself up in the Library of Medical History as a historian and researcher (and eventually became the director of the institution), and was known as a jovial man with a taste for good wine. According to his acquaintants, Antall, the son of a high-ranking official in the Ministry of Interior of Admiral Horthy, had prepared himself for a political role his whole life. He may have had the dream to be the prime minister eventually, but he kept this dream to himself and appeared on the surface as nonpolitical. To "take a dive and stay under water" is a wonderfully precise way to describe a major strategy of survival of anticommunist intellectuals during the epoch of socialism.

What we began to perceive first as dissent typically came from intellectuals who were part of the hegemony of socialist ideology of the 1960s. Our main hypothesis is that at least one main component of dissent was constituted by the vanguard of the New Class project, who turned toward dissent as the project disintegrated.

Political dissent under socialism was a very complex phenomenon. There were of course bourgeois liberals or conservative patriots who always felt alienated under communism. There were also nationalists and religious oppositionists who were persecuted all along, and some of whom courageously fought against communism all their life.

This reformer-dissident trajectory addresses, it is important to note, the central theme of this book: was there a "class project" by intellectuals, and, if there was one, how did it fail and to what extent did its failure contribute to the eventual breakdown of the socialist system?

Krzysztof and Janina Zagorski (1989) suggested that intellectuals, rather than being on the road to class power, were on the "road to dissent." We believe the question is not either/or, but is rather an issue of sequencing. Many, probably most, East European intellectuals entered the road to dissent as their road to class power was blocked, as their hope to achieve a compromise and power sharing with the bureaucracy withered. During the 1960s, the predominant view was that reform and change were necessary but ought to be carried out from within. Some prominent dissidents of the 1970s and 1980s, such as Kuron and Modzelewski in Poland, and Kis, Bence, Haraszti, and many others in Hungary, first became active within the Communist Youth League, or even in the Communist Party. They began to formulate their critique within the framework of Marxism (even Marxism-Leninism) and within the horizons of socialism. From there, it took a long time and a difficult road to arrive at the ideal of liberal capitalism.

The first milestone on this road was possibly the idea of civil society. The theory of civil society gained prominence during the second half of the 1970s, and it served as a halfway house between a socialist critique of "actually existing socialism" and an affirmation of the ideals of liberal capitalism. The term "civil" was suitable to begin this slow process of intellectual transformation. "Civil" did not carry the baggage that "bourgeois" did, but at the same time was useful to critique state socialist clientelistic-paternalistic relations from the perspective of a "social contract among free individuals." Much like the theory of civil society during the eighteenth century, which facilitated a critical analysis of feudal structures and values without offering much of an idea about the nature and internal contradictions of the society to follow feudalism, the East European version of the theory of civil society could be used to dissect the realities of actually existing socialism from an ideal point of departure, in which social relations were based on contract. Some (e.g., Szelényi 1977) went so far as to coin the term "socialist civil society." Some radical market reformers, such as Tibor Liska, entertained the idea that the free operation of the market assumed elimination of all monopolies; since private ownership could be perceived as a type of monopoly, Liska argued, a real market economy could only be "socialist." If "civil" did not imply "bourgeois," why could it not coexist with socialism?

The simple explanation could be that "civil society" was simply a code to say "capitalism" when this idea was still taboo. Some may have used it this way; however, we believe, many if not most of the dissent came from the socialist camp, and we assume that the theory was not designed to hide the project of capitalist transformation. Rather, it was one step along the road of radicalization. When the idea of civil society was first formulated, we think, theorists interested in civil society tried to express as clearly and as radically as they could their understanding of the world, rather than hide their position under a label more acceptable to those in power.[2]

The trajectory that the concept of civil society traveled in Germany is particularly telling. During the eighteenth and nineteenth centuries, the term civil society was translated into German as "bürgerliche Gesellschaft" ("bourgeois society"); this is how Hegel and Marx used it, although, to avoid misunderstanding, Marx eventually shifted from "bürgerliche Gesellschaft" to the concept "capitalist society." When, in the 1970s and 1980s, the idea of civil society was revived, some left theorists in Germany avoided "bürgerliche Gesell-schaft" and used instead "Zivilgesellschaft"—the German way of saying bourgeois without actually saying bourgeois.

The next terrain on which the theoretical-ideological transition from socialism to capitalism was fought was around the idea of "Bürger" or "bourgeois." In English or French, the distinction between those who are defined by their property ("bourgeois") or by their citizenship ("citoyen") is sharply drawn, and as a result the question of the relation between property and citizenship can be posed in a sharp analytical way. The German "Bürger" does not allow separation of these meanings, since it means at the same time "bourgeois" and "citizen," and as a result one can skate across the two ideas with ease.

During the 1980s—especially after 1989—the process of making "Bürgers" ("Verbürgerlichung" in German, "polgárosodás" in Hungarian) became a major theoretical and ideological issue. Stemming from the initial dual meaning of the concept "Bürger," "Verbürgerlichung" implied the transition from subject to citizen as much as the making of a propertied class. On which element of this process the emphasis is placed, and how the two components of this process are interlinked, remains unexplored.

Bill Lomax (1995), in his vehement critique of the way Hungarian ideologues used the ideas "civil society," "Bürger," and "Verbürgerlichung," is justified in expressing frustration with the absence of lucidity in this tradition of theorizing. One should not assume devious motives, though. The concept "Verbürgerlichung" is fuzzy for sure, but the phenomenon it tries to capture was rather fuzzy in Central Europe during the nineteenth century, and remains fuzzy in non-German Central Europe still.

Jürgen Kocka makes an instructive distinction between two types of Bürgers: a "Wirtschaftsbürgertum" (propertied bourgeoisie) and a "Bildungsbürgertum" (educated middle class). His theory for nineteenth-century European social history suggests that the two components of the bourgeoisie developed differently in different parts of Europe. In Western Europe, in particular in England and the Netherlands, it was the growth of Wirtschaftsbürgertum that led the growth of capitalism and the bourgeois class. In Central Europe, primarily in Germany and its cultural sphere of influence to the east during the nineteenth century, the Bildungsbürgertum was at least as well developed as the Wirtschaftsbürgertum and as a result played a particularly important role in the process of modernization. Finally, Kocka suggests that in Russia there was not much of a Wirtschafts-bürgertum at all; thus the process of modernization had to be carried out by the educated middle class.

Kocka's approach helps us to recast aspects of the central hypothesis of this book. We take Kocka's point that, during the nineteenth century in the less advanced, semiperipheral regions of Europe, given the relative weakness of the propertied bourgeoisie, the educated middle class found itself in the position of having to act as a vanguard of modernization. During the nineteenth century the middle class's first response to this challenge was to constitute itself as a Bildungsbürgertum and try to act on behalf of a propertied class—which in Russia hardly existed, and which was relatively weak in Germany and among its eastern neighbors.

The transition to capitalism led by the Bildungsbürgertum was, though, a difficult, frustrating process. Thus, by the late nineteenth and early twentieth centuries, a growing proportion of the educated middle class was attracted to left-wing and right-wing radicalism. Instead of carrying out the task of making capitalism without capitalists, it began to search for an alternative to capitalism. The attraction of the intelligentsia to the communist project can be seen as an expression of such frustration.

The educated middle class eventually finds that the making of the propertied class is neither as viable nor as attractive as it appeared for awhile. Indeed the intelligentsia always has a somewhat schizoid attitude toward the propertied bourgeoisie: it admires it as the force of revolutionary change, and despises it for not having the proper lifestyles, cultural values, and tastes. Thus, it looks for another historic actor it can act for, and finds the proletariat. What we try to capture in this chapter is this cyclical movement of intellectuals in Eastern Europe: during the mid-nineteenth century, they constitute themselves as a Bildungsbürgertum, the force to promote capitalist modernization and the making of a propertied class; during most of the twentieth century, they define themselves as the vanguard of the communist modernization process; finally by the end of the century—after the project to reach a compromise with the socialist bureaucratic estate fails—they reconstitute themselves one more time as a Bildungsbürgertum.

It takes some time for this late socialist or early post-communist Bildungsbürgertum to define what social role it is supposed to perform, how it shall relate to various social actors, and where the center of action is in the embourgeoisement process. The recent history of the idea "Bürger" is instructive. For a short while, the theorists of civil society and embourgeoisement consider the actors of the second economy, the emergent state socialist petty bourgeoisie, as Bürgers. Soon, they realize that these socialist entrepreneurs have been coopted into state socialist clientelistic networks. So the Bürgers of late state socialism are perceived as members of a Bildungsbürgertum. Civil society, as a society of intellectuals, thus arrives in 1989 at the radical conclusion: their task is to carry out a bourgeois revolution in order to create a bourgeoisie.

One may suggest that intellectuals on the road to dissent not only abandon their project to act as a universal class, but constitute themselves as the "universal estate" of state socialism. They are the estate of state socialism that eliminates all estate forms of rule and creates the foundations of a class society. Unlike the third estate of feudalism, however, they do this not to create their own class rule, but to pave the way for the class rule of a still nonexistent class, the propertied bourgeoisie. On their way from a (badly flawed) "universal class of state socialism" to the "universal estate" of communism, they become the postcommunist Bildungsbürgertum, which takes upon itself the historic mission of dismantling socialism and creating capitalism.

However, there is one last halfway house, which during the 1980s is variably called the "Third Way" or the "mixed economy." As formerly socialist intellectuals radicalize themselves and turn into dissidents, for a long while they want to dismiss the accusation that they are "restoring capitalism." Even to suggest, for example, that Hungarian reforms were leading to the restoration of capitalism would garner the label of Stalinist.

For most of the 1980s, the response of most dissidents was that the distinction between capitalism and socialism was outdated, anyway. All "actually existing systems" were "mixed economies." In Eastern Europe in particular, given its unique historic heritage, it made little sense to recommend a capitalist transformation. If anything, Eastern Europe was a likely candidate for the Third Way, something between Western capitalism and Soviet-style socialism. There is no way capitalism could be "restored" in Eastern Europe, since there had never been much capitalism in that part of the world. In the later stages of ideological struggle, during the second half of the 1980s, the dissidents' response was formulated in terms of realpolitik. The point, they argued, was not to bash capitalism. Whatever its merits as an idea, it was not really viable in Eastern Europe. The actually existing Eastern Europe, if not forced to follow the Soviet model, was likely to take a road in between Soviet authoritarianism and Western capitalism. This might not be for the better; it was just the reality of this part of the world.

By the late 1980s, the ideas of the Third Way or the mixed economy were dismissed as populist utopias, leaving only the hard reality of capitalism. It is important, however, to remember that the intellectual ideologues-turned-neoliberals by 1989–90 had been pushing strongly for the idea of mixed economy, the irrelevance of the distinction between socialism and capitalism, and the feasibility and realism of the Third Way for quite some time. They dismissed those who accused them of wanting to establish a capitalist order as neo-Stalinist. So it may be reasonable that they could not have it both ways: they either had to concede they were wrong in accusing their critics of neo-Stalinism (for accusing *them* of capitalist restoration), or they had to concede that they indeed had wanted to restore capitalism, for quite some time, and that their so-called neo-Stalinist critics had caught them red-handed. Why would the latter be that embarrassing when the ideals of capitalism were ruling supreme, anyway?

Our point here is that during the 1980s it was not obvious who stood for socialism, who for a mixed economy. It is time to clarify this, at least retroactively.

The Bureaucracy and the Technocracy on Collision Course

As the socialist countries approached system breakdown, intra-elite struggles began to play an increasing role in the dynamics of social change. From the mid-1960s onward, the bureaucratic ruling estate was gradually transformed into an internally differentiated power elite in which the power of the bureaucratic estate was increasingly challenged by the new technocracy. Erzsébet Szalai's work since the mid-1980s offers the most penetrating analysis of these intra-elite conflicts.

The divide between "bureaucracy" and "technocracy," between

"red" and "expert," has been a long-standing characteristic of communist power. This divide gained increased significance with the reforms of the 1960s and with the recruitment of a new generation of cadres, who were not only younger than the old guard but were better educated (mainly in economics and engineering). Members of the new technocratic elite often came through the education system directly; they rarely started their occupational career as manual workers (a fairly common background for the old guard). The old guard was also baptized in fire. In Eastern Europe many members of the old guard had joined the Communist Party before communism took power, and so had an exposure to underground communist politics, and in the Soviet Union they had fought during the Second World War.

The Hungarian old guard, for instance, came to power after 1956. Many members were on the receiving end of Stalinist purges, but after the 1956 uprising they decided to side with the Soviets. Somewhat reluctant and guilt-ridden, they still managed the violent oppression of the revolutionaries of 1956 and established the new order, which during its first years had some of the features of neo-Stalinism. There was blood on their hands, and their relationship to their Soviet masters and KGB was complex, to put it mildly.

Over the decades, members of the bureaucratic estate may have grown cynical, but they usually joined the movement out of idealistic considerations. They were the faithful ones.

The new technocracy grew up under communism, and joining the communist youth league of the party was part of a normal career; it did not require much reflection or ideological commitment. Members of the new technocracy often had traveled to the West, usually spoke foreign languages, or even had Western educations.

Thus, the distinction between the bureaucracy or the old guard, and the technocracy or the new elite, is not merely a distinction among the character of their positions (although there is an elective affinity between what kind of people are recruited into what sort of positions); it is a distinction between different habitus. The new technocracy first moved into major economic command positions. They became CEOs, joined the staff of the planning office, worked in the ministry of finance and the banking system, occupied positions in international economic and financial institutions and foreign trade companies. Subsequently they were recruited even into the central committee apparatus and began to transform the party from within.

The Intellectuals on the Road to Class Power noted the emergence of this new technocracy and saw in it the core of the New Class of intellectuals in formation. The possible alliance between this new technocracy and humanistic intellectuals was also considered. It is in the works of Erzsébet Szalai, however, that the focus of attention shifts from the relationship between intellectuals and the bureaucratic ruling estate to intra-elite conflict.

As Szalai documented in Hungary, by the late 1970s and early 1980s the struggle between the old guard and the new technocratic elite had intensified. The new technocratic elite was becoming impatient with the reluctance of the old guard to move ahead with economic reforms. It was indeed the new technocratic elite rather than the dissident intellectuals who began to call for the second economic reform, and in particular for the reform of property relations (though eventually many of the technocratic elite joined the dissidents and early on created good working relations with them).

Some reformers proposed a transformation of property rights along the lines of self-management (Tamas Bauer was the most outspoken theorist of this school of thought). Others proposed changes that would have directly enhanced the decision-making power of managers or technocrats. Marton Tardos, for instance, advocated a system of holdings; according to his scenario, public firms would be converted into joint stockholding companies and the stocks would be owned by a number of investment banks, which would be publicly owned but would compete with one another. The most radical proposal was elaborated by Tibor Liska, who can be seen as an early dissident even though he never joined any dissident group; he is actually the "godfather" of voucher privatization. Liska's scheme was to divide the whole national wealth into stocks and distribute them equally "by birthright" among the citizenry. Each citizen would deal with these stocks. Those who invested them well would earn profits; those who invested poorly would make losses. Still, Liska, a good socialist for most of his life, tried to invent a system that would prohibit the inheritance of wealth accumulated this way and would also make it impossible for anyone to lose all his or her stocks. Enough stock would remain unalienable so that a minimum guaranteed income would be assured for all.

It is interesting that none of these blueprints created identifiable owners of firms; they all tried to create market-conforming but diffuse property relations. In retrospect we know that, while this result was not necessarily intended by the economists who elaborated these schemes, such schemes would have shifted the power of control to managers and technocrats. In particular, the holding or voucher system would have transferred economic power from "redistributors" to finance managers. While, after 1989, the rhetoric changed radically and the professed aim of property reform was the creation of private ownership, in the reform scenarios of the early 1980s private property was exactly what the reformers did not want to create. One might argue, of course, that they did not do so because private property was still ideologically taboo, or because they believed the Soviet empire would not allow it.

Although this argument might very well have been the case for some individuals, during the early 1980s, we believe, the idea that individual private property might not be the most desirable, and certainly was not the most viable way to reform socialism, was still hegemonic. It was only the youngest generation of economists, then in their twenties, who already believed capitalism was the only alternative to socialism. Certainly those engaged in the reform discourse shared this view—that socialism could be reformed without creating capitalist personal property—either from tactical consideration or, as we are inclined to believe, mainly for genuine theoretical reasons. This statement is not intended to cast doubt on the intellectual integrity of reform economists—far from it. One cannot expect a theorist to see beyond the horizons of the social realities he or she is operating within. As late as the early 1980s, socialism was still conceived as one economic system, with its own unique contradictions. It was not assumed that the only economically rational way to act was on the marketplace with private property.

From the early 1980s, when the idea of property reform entered the political agenda, managers and technocrats began to reshuffle property rights to increase their own power, and if possible to acquire ownership rights in their enterprises. However, the bureaucratic fraction of the elite was dragging its feet. It had misgivings on ideological grounds; indeed, the bureaucratic estate had difficulty to join in with technocrats and management in this gradual transformation of ownership relations. Children of the members of the bureaucratic ruling estate were more likely to take advantage of the new opportunities. Many became "experts" and thus members of the technocracy, and took advantage of the transformation, under the protection of their parents. Still, the dominant trend was a deterioration of the relation between the old guard and the new technocratic estate.

Social transformations in Russia under Gorbachev fit into this picture rather well. Gorbachev tried to continue the technocratic reform where it was interrupted with the fall of Khrushchev, but he also tried not to alienate the bureaucratic estate. As a result, the Gorbachev years were full of compromises between the two fractions of the elite. Arguably the deadlock of intra-elite struggles resulted in the disintegration of the Soviet Union, culminating first in the August 1991 coup d'état, and later in Yeltsin's takeover, in which experts and specialists played a crucial role (see Garcelon 1997).

It appears that, as the 1980s unfolded, the new technocratic elite, confronted with the footdragging and sabotage of the bureaucracy, eventually came to the conclusion that it did not want to rule in the old ways. The technocracy began to build bridges to the dissident intellectuals, who began to grow in numbers and influence, especially in Hungary and Poland.

Six

Intellectuals under Postcommunism

1989: A Successful Revolution of Socialist Technocrats?

In retrospect, it appears that 1989 can be seen as a successful revolution by the socialist technocrats and managers. After two decades of intra-elite struggles, the technocrats were finally able to defeat the bureaucratic fraction of the elite. This happened first in Hungary and Poland, and two years later in the Soviet Union. In the other state socialist countries, the domestic processes may not have been enough to culminate in a system breakdown. In countries like Czechoslovakia, East Germany, Rumania, or Bulgaria, the old guard had to be forced out with the help of Soviet reformers. In the whole region, however, the trend of declining bureaucratic power and increasing influence of the technocracy was visible.

The most clear-cut change took place in Hungary, where, at the February 1989 meeting of the Central Committee of the Communist Party, the old guard lost power and the technocratic reformers finally took charge of the party. Both the Hungarian and Polish technocratic elite at this point wanted a negotiated transition from communism in which a transition to a capitalist economy would take place under the conditions of the cautious expansion of democratic rights and institutions.

The new technocracy did not want to rule as the bureaucratic estate had; thus the separation of economic and political power was foreseen. Unlike the bureaucratic estate, the new technocratic elite's power base was not in politics, but in the economy. Thus the essence of the strategy was to retain the command positions in the economy and gradually transfer political power to some new political elite, which was supposed to come from the younger generation of Communist Party politicians and from a mixture of liberal and nationalist dissidents. The roundtable negotiations between the technocracy and the dissident intellectuals were supposed to figure out how this transition could be stage-managed without a political break (Bruszt and Stark 1991). The new technocratic elite accepted the principles of a relatively autonomous sphere of democratic politics and a move toward a multiparty system. Initially, however, it wanted to manage this change in a way that kept the process under the control of the politicians of the Communist Party. According to public opinion polls of early 1989, the Communist Parties in Hungary and Poland had the support of about one-third of the electorate; thus, with a carefully designed electoral system, it was not unrealistic that some sharing of political power between former dissidents and reform communist politicians could be achieved.

How and in what capacity the new technocratic elite could retain economic power became a struggle. As early as 1988, the project of privatization began to enter the political agenda. Both in Poland and Hungary, policies were implemented that were supposed to serve what was then called "spontaneous privatization," which really was a strategy of management buyouts. Judwiga Staniszkis (1991) and Elemér Hankiss (1990) developed their theory of political capitalism and formulated their hypothesis concerning the conversion of political capital into private wealth, after being inspired by these practices.

The 1989–90 period, however, had its own, unforeseen dynamics. Instead of there being a gradualist, negotiated transition to capitalism and democracy, the socialist systems began to collapse, a development that fueled a strong anticommunist mood. Around 1990, it appeared that the former socialist technocracy and managerial strata might not be able to retain power. Everywhere in Central Europe, the former Communist Parties, even though they made an attempt to recast themselves as social democratic parties, were wiped out of power. In the Eastern part of the region, however, this did not happen. Former Communists were able to retain political power in Rumania, Bulgaria, and Serbia, though they had to open to the nationalist right wing to do so. The first democratic elections in Czechoslovakia, Hungary, and Poland were won by conservative, patriotic, occasionally religions parties that pursued a strong anticommunist campaign. In all of these countries, suddenly a new political elite appeared on the scene, which made an effort to implement radical change in the composition of the cultural and economic elite. Legislation was considered, in both Czechoslovakia and Poland, to exclude former members of the nomenklatura from the privatization process and possibly also from public office. The mood shifted from reform to revolution and a call for radical circulation of elites. The hegemonic ideology was to implement capitalism by design, to use shock therapy to manage the transition to a West European style of capitalism within a short period of time, and to cleanse society from communism and communists.

There has been, indeed, a major change at the top of these societies. We conducted a survey among members of elites in 1988 and 1993 in five East European countries (Poland, Czech Republic, Slovakia, Hungary, Bulgaria) and in Russia. Our survey indicates that about half of those in elite position in 1988 were downwardly mobile. This change affected not only the political but also the cultural and economic elite.

Indeed, as Erzsébet Szalai pointed out in several of her essays after 1989, there was an intense struggle within the elite. The new incumbents of political power, who, particularly in Hungary, tried to establish themselves as, in Szalai's terms, a new political ruling estate, and were recruited in substantial proportion from the precommunist genteel middle and upper-middle class, clashed with the former communist technocratic new elite. Szalai uses the term "new political estate" for good reasons—good, at least, in the case of Hungary. In 1990 the Hungarian Democratic Forum won the first postcommunist elections. This party did not have a clear profile at that time; it appealed to both right-wing and left-wing plebeian, or populist, constituencies. Its lead politicians, especially Prime Minister Antall and his close circle, were traditional conservatives; they came from the genteel upper-middle class, the gentry, and some members of the former aristocracy, and they had a great deal of nostalgia for prewar Hungarian values and lifestyles. From state socialist paternalism, society was, with the new party's ascendancy, sliding back to social relations that were reminiscent of prewar Hungarian patron-client relations. Postcommunism produced in other countries as well some interesting mixtures of socialist and presocialist clientelism; Slovaks make reference to this shift probably the most frequently.

It is not surprising under these circumstances that there was considerable mutual distrust and suspicion between the new political estate and the late state socialist technocracy and managerial strata. There were a few spectacular attempts to remove some key figures in public life and in the economy who were perceived as having a communist past or who did not fully cooperate with the new political estate, and to replace them with reliable clients. The symbolically most interesting such action was the sacking of the president of the Hungarian National Bank under the Antall administration. This man was a highly competent, late state socialist technocrat, one of the prototypical figures of what Szalai called the "late kadarist technocracy" or the "new technocratic elite." (Not surprisingly, one of the first acts of the government led by the ex–Communist Party, which won the 1994 elections, was to restitute this person to the old position.)

In the Czech Republic and Poland, those who won political power in 1990 were not so strongly affected with the spirit of prewar rank order as were those in Hungary; they were either liberals, like Tadeusz Mazowiecki, or modern, rather than traditional conservatives, like Václav Klaus or Hanna Suchowska. Nevertheless, in these countries too there was pressure to purge personnel—to remove faces from the past, including the communist technocrats. Walesa got much mileage in his 1991 presidential campaign, waged against Mazowiecki, with attacks against the liberals who were too soft on former Communists and allowed them to take advantage of privatization to keep their positions.

Eventually the new political ruling estates realized that these countries were too small to have a second set of elites. They had to compromise and let the late socialist technocratic and managerial elite occupy key positions in the new society. They were also forced eventually to do so by the elections after 1994, though even before these elections the purges came to an end—and even during the purges, typically the new political elite had little choice but to promote second-tier cadres to top positions. The electorate grew tired of the anticommunist rhetoric of the new political estate, a rhetoric aggravated by that estate's incompetence in managing politics, culture, and, in particular, the economy. Thus, in many countries, most spectacularly in Hungary and Poland, the ex–Communist Parties won elections, primarily by persuading the electorate that, in contrast to the amateurish anticommunist political estate, they would run the countries like professionals.

Thus the change in elites after 1989 offers a complex picture. There was a great deal of outward and downward mobility from the former nomenklatura. In particular, the members of the old bureaucratic ruling estate lost power and most privileges, but some members of the new technocratic elite, also, in the shift from reform to revolution, suffered. People who were in politically exposed positions were squeezed out, but when the new political estate looked for clients to fill these positions they had a hard time finding appropriate personnel. As a result, they had little choice but to replace top cadres with their deputies. Tamas Kolosi joked that 1989 was the "revolution by deputy department heads," reflecting the surge in upward mobility for people in the middle ranges of the nomenklatura, who were elevated into top positions.

This mobility was particularly present in the economic field. Somewhere between 70 percent and 90 percent of those in major command positions of the economy in 1993 were already in management, or at least on a trajectory to become managers, in 1988. In this respect, 1989 was an accelerated promotion of middle managers to top managerial position.

There are two points we would like to make concerning the nature of social struggles that shook the socialist systems around 1989. First, it would be difficult to overestimate the role that the late state socialist technocracy played in bringing these systems down. While the system breakdown had been facilitated by popular struggles, resistance either by ordinary people or by the socialist entrepreneurs, and by intellectual dissent, the single most important factor that brought the system down was intra-elite conflict. The technocratic fraction of the elite decided it did not rule in the old ways, and after a long period of struggle defeated the bureaucratic estate (between 1988 and 1991). Reform communists have a point when they tell former dissidents, in effect, "you guys better appreciate that we brought the system down, not you." Second, there was an attempt to purge the system of former communists, including technocrats. It was not due to the lack of will that this did not work. The former Communist technocracy was able to resist the purges and mastermind a comeback of ex-communist parties because they were the only ones who had the knowhow, the human and social capital, necessary to run these societies and in particular to manage their economies.

We do not want to sound overly deterministic or structuralist. We do not want to imply that there was no alternative whatsoever to postcommunism as a system in which the core of the new power elite consisted of the former communist technocracy. In chapter 5, we demonstrated that the one or two decades preceding the fall of communism can be understood as shaped by a complex set of historically contingent struggles. By the 1980s, we began to believe that the New Class making history with the decay of state socialism was that of "socialist entrepreneurs." During the early 1980s it was unclear how alliances would be formed in Hungary or in Poland among the major social actors of the epoch: the bureaucratic estate, the new technocracy, the new socialist entrepreneurs, and the dissident intellectuals.

The Making of the New Intellectual Power Elite

The victory of the late socialist technocracy could be interpreted in at least three ways. First, one may see in this a victory of the New Class. Second, one can claim that this victory is the sign of political capitalism, and that the nomenklatura, or at least its technocratic fraction, established itself as a new propertied bourgeoisie by converting its political influence into private wealth. Third, in the fall of communism, one can see the making of a new Bildungsbürgertum. The late socialist technocracy, according to this last interpretation, can neither consolidate its power as a self-reproducing elite nor transform itself into a grand bourgeoisie. Instead, it reaches out to other intellectual strata and forms an alliance with the new politocracy and with opinion-making intellectuals to carry out a capitalist modernization project—to complete a bourgeois revolution without a bourgeoisie, in order to create a propertied dominant class. Whether or not elements of the intellectual power elite will make it into this new propertied class remains to be seen.

The Victory of the Technocracy: The Victory of the New Class?

If, as we suggested in chapter 4, there was a New Class project at the peak of reform communism, then the vanguard of the New Class was the technocracy. The test of its success was whether it would be able to force the bureaucracy into major concessions and carry with itself other strata of intellectuals into power. So is the victory of the technocracy not a sign that the New Class was successful, after all?

It is unlikely that this argument could be a persuasive interpretation of the events following 1989. In the introduction to this book, we suggested that the formation of any class, and the formation of the New Class in particular, depends on whether the right actors are occupying the appropriate social positions and have an adequate ideology.

One key hypothesis of this book is that reform communism of the 1960s may have brought the New Class closer to formation than at any time before or after in history. The technocracy, in alliance with the humanistic intellectuals, was indeed a modern agent. Unlike modern professionals in the West, its members were not too fragmented to have acted as one class. There was also a structural position, namely, socialist redistribution, around which this class could have been formed. Finally, the technocracy's ideology, teleological rationality, was beyond the formal rationality of capitalist modernity but was still cast in rational terms, as one would expect from a class ideology.

This class formation could not advance too far, however, because, to win its struggle against the bureaucratic ruling estate, the technocracy had to destroy the social position and give up the ideology upon which its class power could have been based. In the struggles against the bureaucratic ruling elite, the dissident intelligentsia adopted bourgeois ideology and the idea of civil society. The technocracy readily accepted these ideological underpinnings, which they complemented with neoliberalism, neoclassical economics, and monetarism. This consciousness was no longer the ideology of a New Class; rather, it was the ideology of the late state socialist, early postcommunist, Bildungsbürgertum. Most important, the late state socialist technocracy moved against the redistributive institutions. Instead of pursuing the strategy of the rationalization of redistribution—the main aim of the reform communist New Class—it aspired to privatization and market integration.

The major question that remains is whether the former communist technocracy or its intellectual allies, who with the fall of communism established themselves as a new politocracy, will be able to establish themselves as a new propertied bourgeoisie. It is beyond doubt, however, the technocracy and intellectuals will never again strive for a dominant class position as redistributors.

The Transformation of the Nomenklatura: Political Capitalism

The most provocative hypothesis concerning the change in class structure of postcommunism was formulated as early as 1989 by Elemér Hankiss (1990) and Jadwiga Staniszkis (1991). They both suggested that the policy of privatization, especially so-called spontaneous privatization, transforms the former nomenklatura into a new propertied grand bourgeoisie: postcommunism should be understood as a system of political capitalism in which political office is used to convert political power into private individual property. In light of evidence available to us (especially from the study of elite circulation directed by Iván Szelényi and Donald Treiman in five East European countries—Poland, the Czech Republic, Slovakia, Hungary, Bulgaria—and in Russia), this hypothesis requires major modifications.

There are very significant differences across countries in to what extent former communists were able to retain their power. In Russia and in Eastern Europe "proper" (i.e., countries where "Eastern Christianity" is dominant, such as Serbia, Bulgaria, Rumania, and the Ukraine), there has been much more of a reproduction of the former communist elites than in Central Europe. Thus, in Poland, the Czech Republic, Hungary, and probably also in the Baltic states, there has been a substantial change in the composition of people in command positions. While there has been considerable continuity of personnel throughout Central Europe, this has been accompanied by substantial downward mobility of certain types of former cadres from certain positions and by substantial upward mobility from the ranks of former rank-and-file intellectuals and former dissidents.

There is strong evidence that the dynamics of reproduction and change affected very differently the political and cultural spheres, on the one hand, and the economy, on the other hand. In Eastern Europe proper, there has been much more change in the personnel of politics and cultural elites than of economic elites; this trend is even more striking in Central Europe. In all postcommunist countries, therefore, some of the Communist "old guard" lost out. Some former nationalist and liberal dissidents gained not only freedom but also some power, at least in the cultural sphere, and often in politics as well. Even in rather extreme cases, such as Russia or Serbia, former dissidents who were exiled or in and out of jail in communist times are not only free today; they can write and publish basically what they want. Indeed, they often lead legal opposition movements, are heard by the broader public, and in the longer run may have a shot at political power. In Poland, Hungary, and the Czech Republic, this is even more obvious, although some of the humanistic intellectuals or dissidents who were so prominent right after 1989 in politics occasionally dropped from power (either at their own will, like Miklos Tamás Gáspár or Miklós Haraszti, who became bored with politics, or, like Mazowiecki or Suchowska, by being voted out of office) and were replaced by former communist "wheeler-dealer" politicians or other political operators. These professional politicians do not share their predecessors' moral commitments to high idealism, but they know how to get votes and win election. Still, many of the humanistic intellectuals are (or were until recently) in parliament, or even in civil service bureaucracies; Vaclav Havel (former president, Czech Republic), Árpád Göncz (former president of Hungary), and Gábor Demszky (current mayor of Budapest) are good examples.

To put this strongly: it was not the former nomenklatura that won in 1989, but the reform communist technocracy. And even this former socialist technocracy had to make an effort to co-opt some of those who had negative political capital before the fall of communism, some former dissidents and independent intellectuals, into the new power elite.

So far, we have argued that the political capitalism thesis held greater insight for the analysis of Russia and Eastern Europe than for Central Europe.[1] It also needs specification: the winners were not the members of the nomenklatura full stop, but rather its technocratic fraction. Some of the old political guard lost out badly, while some of the former dissidents and other humanistic intellectuals benefited and were co-opted into the new power elite. Thus, one could propose a more sophisticated version of the political capitalism thesis; Erzsébet Szalai essentially does this. She argues that it is not the former nomenklatura that converted political capital into private wealth, but the former technocratic-managerial elite and their clients, and (some members of) the postcommunist politocracy, or what Szalai called the new postcommunist political ruling estate. This narrower version of the political capitalism thesis is much closer to the target.

We believe, however, that even this narrower theory of political capitalism overstates how successful the former technocratic-managerial elite and its new political allies were in becoming a new propertied grand bourgeoisie. First, there are strict limits under which the technocratic and managerial elite and the new political establishment can operate when it tries to "enclose the commons" and convert it into individual property. These limits are stricter in Central Europe than in Eastern Europe or Russia, but they are also present in Eastern Europe. All postcommunist countries operate within the framework of multiparty parliamentary democracy, with some degree of freedom guaranteed to the press. In Central Europe the freedom of the press is substantial and comparable to the freedom of the media in the West. Thus the enclosure movement has to take place under the watchful eyes of journalists and is subject to parliamentary scrutiny. Many "dirty deals" are caught this way, stopped, or even reversed. The very fact that in Russia or Slovakia journalists are murdered is an indication of how dangerous and how powerful they are.

The power of the media may not be equal to the power of the technocratic-managerial elites, or the politocracy, but it is difficult to doubt that there is a powerful mediacracy in postcommunist countries and that, no matter how hard postcommunist economic and political elites have tried to subdue this media and turn it into their obedient tools, they have never been completely successful. In Hungary the first postcommunist government staged a "war" for four years to colonize the major radio and television stations, with little success. Even in Slovakia or Serbia, where television is basically under the control of the politocracy, there is a reasonably free press.

Further, the postcommunist elite is far from homogeneous. There is vivid competition between the former communist technocratic-managerial elite and the politocracy. Members of the political class have to play a different game: they have to confront, every fourth year, the electorate in reasonably—or, in the case of Central Europe, genuinely—free elections. This sets some limits on how much corruption or robbing of the common good transpires. As we pointed out before, many members of the politocracy—again, *more* in Central Europe, but at least *some* in Eastern Europe—are former dissidents or former rank-and-file intellectuals. These members of the politocracy dislike the former communist technocratic managerial elite. They do not trust them, are envious of them, and would like to replace them with their own clients. In other words, the relations between the technocratic-managerial elite and the politocracy, and the former dissident intellectuals, is one of competition.

The ex-Communist technocratic-managerial elite will not be allowed to get away with murder. Not that the former technocratic-managerial elite is completely unified: some try to acquire property in legal ways; others become members of "mafias" (especially in Russia), who use their links with former KGB and other forces of the underground. However, the vision of a unified, well-organized, former nomenklatura appropriating former public wealth under the table in a conspiratorial way seems utterly false; this is not (by and large) the way postcommunism works. Further, postcommunist transformation occurs in front of the eyes of the Western public. These countries are open to the Western media as well as to Western social scientists who can do research and reporting virtually without limitations. Western political and economic organizations such as the Organization for Economic Cooperation and Development (OECD), European Union (EU), World Bank, and International Monetary Fund (IMF) follow closely what is happening in the economy, and, in particular, they monitor closely the privatization process. Western business wants to grab whatever is really valuable in the process of privatization. Especially in countries that are deeply in debt, the World Bank and IMF have a great deal of influence, which they use to stop former communists from pinching the more valuable assets away from them. Of course, some of the technocratic elite amassed enormous wealth, especially in Russia, but this grand bourgeoisie, commonly referred to as oligarchs, is remarkably small compared to the bourgeoisie in the West.

Our key point is that even Szalai's much more realistic, narrower version of political capitalism theory is likely to exaggerate the extent to which the technocratic-managerial elite turned into a propertied grand bourgeoisie. While this maneuver worked for some of them, most, so far, have failed to accumulate enough private property to control major businesses.

Of course, in any capitalist economy the major owners will be far less numerous than the pool of technocrats or managers from which they are drawn. And while it is true that former managers could not easily gain ownership of large enterprises, there is, at least in Hungary, significant ownership by former managers of small and medium enterprises (King 2001a). The majority of larger businesses are still state owned, were sold to foreign investors, or were privatized by a uniquely state socialist system of institutional cross-ownership (called by David Stark recombinant property [1996]). Even in Hungary, the country where capitalist transformation progressed the furthest and where management buyouts were most common, as of 1993 only half of the technocratic-managerial elite owned business property. They typically owned less than 10 percent of the assets of the firms they had stakes in, and at least half of the managers-owners had ownership in firms other than ones they managed. As a rule, the smaller the firms, the more widespread the technocratic-managerial ownership. In other words, as Eric Hanley pointed out, a lot (though of course not all) of technocratic-managerial ownership, or private acquisition of public wealth, has been petty bourgeoisification rather than the making of a grand bourgeoisie.

We are not suggesting that there is no political capitalism under postcommunism. There is a great deal, especially in Eastern Europe. However, according to all the evidence available to us, it is a gross simplification to call the postcommunist system political capitalism and assume—even within the narrower version of political capitalism theory—that the technocratic-managerial elite, or even its majority, has became a propertied grand bourgeoisie. We believe this hypothesis is just false. Some did become big proprietors, but most did not. Privatization is a much more complex process than just an elite appropriating private wealth.

As King (2001a, 2001b) documented, there are many ways that firms have transformed themselves. A small percentage come to resemble "recombinant property" as described by Stark (1996). Others result in various types of "self-ownership" schemes, in which ownership rights rest neither with the state nor with private individuals but with the institutions themselves. For example, the second largest firm in the Czech Republic in 1996, the giant Chemapol Holding Company, which owned a group of about sixty firms in the chemical, pharmaceutical, and petrochemical industries, was itself owned by these very same sixty firms. This process was called "privatization by incest" in the Czech Republic, because during privatization Chemapol managed to buy controlling shares in about sixty enterprises that had been "given" very small amounts of Chemapol shares as a result of economic reforms implemented in 1969. Thus, Chemapol, with over ten thousand employees, was essentially self-owned. This means that the top managers of Chemapol had the de facto, but not the legal, ownership rights.

One reason why the hypothesis of political capitalism survives so stubbornly can be attributed to the fact that indeed the overwhelming majority of those in postcommunist economic command positions were in managerial positions before the fall of communism. But these members of the technocratic-managerial elite, especially its most powerful fraction, the financial and banking elite, did not come to hold power because they converted their political power into private wealth, but simply because they managed to keep these command positions without acquiring property.

This leads us to our final criticism of the political capitalism hypothesis. The theory suggests that it is political power or office that is converted into private wealth. Both sides of the equation are misspecified. So far, we have pointed out that what the majority gained was, typically, not sufficient private wealth to qualify its members as grand bourgeoisie. But the left side of the equation is false too. It is not typically political capital that has been converted but, in most cases, a mix of cultural/human and social capital. It is undoubtedly true that the core of the postcommunist power elite is constituted by former technocratic-managerial personnel. These persons kept their positions, however, in part because they were the only ones who knew how to run firms, in part because they have sufficient knowhow, and in part because they have the proper connections to get things done. Paul Windolf[2] in a 1995 survey of 288 randomly selected East German managers found that almost 90 percent were already in managerial positions in 1989 in East German communist firms. While today these managers own virtually none of the East German economy—it is almost completely owned by West German businesses, often through institutional cross-ownership—these former communist managers are often employed by the new Western business owners, since such managers are the only ones who know how to operate the firms in this part of the country. If this is true in East Germany, it certainly is more true in Hungary, Poland, and the Czech Republic. Thus, our final comment on the political capitalism thesis is that the new postcommunist power elite converted personal networks and managerial human capital into economic power, occasionally though not typically into private wealth.

Postcommunist Intellectuals: A New Bildungsbürgertum

The punch line of our analysis is that with the fall of communism a new power elite occupies the top of the social hierarchy, but not as the New Class of technocrats, managers, or intellectuals. Nor do they occupy it as former nomenklatura, managers or intellectuals turned into a grand bourgeoisie. The new power elite can be understood most precisely as a new Bildungsbürgertum, as a loose coalition of many kinds of intellectuals who together take upon themselves the task of carrying out what they see as a "modernization project." They believe that their task is to conduct a bourgeois revolution without a bourgeoisie. They want to build capitalism without capitalists by making a propertied bourgeoisie, which under the given circumstances does not quite exist yet.

The emergence of this new Bildungsbürgertum can be seen as a "negation of negation." Jürgen Kocka, in his brilliant analysis of nineteenth-century Central European social history, makes the crucial distinction between Wirtschaftsbürgertum and Bildungsbürgertum, a propertied bourgeoisie and an educated middle class (the latter defined by him as a bourgeoisie whose power and privilege is based on education, or, to use our terminology, on possession of cultural rather than economic capital). Kocka suggests that this distinction is particularly useful for a comparative analysis of nineteenth-century European history and the quite different dynamics of making a modern society in this part of the world. In England or in the Netherlands, capitalism emerged under the leadership of a strong Wirtschaftsbürgertum and the Bildungsbürgertum was formed at a later stage. In Russia, in contrast, there was virtually no propertied bourgeoisie to speak of, and thus capitalist transformation had to be attempted by the intelligentsia, the educated middle class, or Bildungsbürgertum. In Germany and in the nineteenth-century German sphere of influence, there was a reasonable balance between the propertied and educated middle classes in the formation of capitalist society and institutions.

In our, somewhat more ironic interpretation, intellectuals took upon themselves the task of creating a propertied bourgeoisie in Central and Eastern Europe during the nineteenth century. Often these intellectuals were of gentry origins. Mannheim called them "socially unattached intellectuals," since they were pro-modernization agents, and both lived off their feudal privileges and were at the forefront of

anti-feudal struggles. They were the major agents of embourgeoisement, or "bourgeoisification." We may add that the "anti-thesis" to
this thesis was the radicalization of the intellectual elites. By the late
nineteenth and early twentieth century, many of them lost faith in
the viability or even in the desirability of a bourgeois transformation
of society. They became attracted to left-wing (and occasionally to
right-wing) radicalism, and turned anticapitalist. They took on a new
task: to carry out a proletarian revolution in countries with a very
small working class. Historically, therefore, we may suggest that the
nineteenth-century Central European Bildungsbürgertum abandoned
the classical Bildungsbürgertum project, turned often violently anti-
Bürger and antibourgeois, and constituted itself as the "vanguard of
the proletariat," but in reality pursued its own power aspirations (as
described in *The Intellectuals on the Road to Class Power*). During
the late 1970s, early 1980s, and most clearly after 1989, the Central
European intelligentsia saw its New Class project disintegrating under
the leadership of the former communist technocratic-managerial elite
reconstituting itself as a new Bildungsbürgertum.

The nineteenth-century classical Central European Bildungsbürgertum and the late socialist, early postcommunist East European
Bildungsbürgertum are analogous, though not identical, phenomena.
The composition of the two Bildungsbürgertum is rather different.
The first was mainly constituted by gentries-turned-intellectuals and
by humanistic intellectuals who came from former artisan or mer-
chant Jewish or German minorities, whose economic existence was
gradually undermined with the decay of the guild system and by petty
commodity production. The classical Central European Bildungsbürgertum was also primarily humanistic, and it had strong allies in
an emergent bourgeoisie. The postcommunist Bildungsbürgertum, on
the other hand, has at its core a technocratic-managerial elite. Ironically the historic agent that now takes upon itself the making of capitalism and the formation of the propertied bourgeoisie comes from
former communists, who ally themselves with former anticommunist,
dissident intellectuals. Despite these differences, the common feature
of the two Bildungsbürgertum is in their historic project: both are
modernizers, and present themselves as altruistic social agents
who act on behalf of some group other than themselves.

So, the social history of Central East European intellectuals came
full circle from the nineteenth-century intelligentsia Westernizers—

who struggled for bourgeoisification, then constituted themselves as a New Class (the vanguard of a nonexistent proletariat), only to reconstitute themselves once again as a new Bildungsbürgertum at the end of the twentieth century—as the New Class project faded away.

Where Is the New Wirtschaftsbürgertum Likely to Come From?

We know that the classical Central European Bildungsbürgertum failed in its modernization attempt. The late nineteenth, early twentieth century may not have been a favorable time for this modernization project, and intellectuals as Bildungsbürgers may also have had limited enthusiasm for the propertied bourgeoisie they were supposed to foster. After all, intellectuals have a long history of suspicion and resentment against the nouveau riche and against material wealth in general. As Vera Zasulich put so eloquently to Marx in her famous letter: why do we have to create the bourgeoisie first, when we know we don't like them and want to overthrow them anyway? Can't we find a shortcut? And Marx was sympathetic; he thought hard whether it was indeed absolutely necessary to make a bourgeois revolution first rather than to proceed to the real and final revolution right away. The real revolution, of course, was believed to be the proletarian one. But since the revolution at issue was in a country with not much of a proletariat, then, as is not that difficult to see in retrospect, what were being considered were attempts by radical intellectuals to appropriate power for themselves as a "vanguard."

The big question of postcommunism is what is likely to happen with the project of this new Bildungsbürgertum. Are intellectuals any more committed now to the making of a bourgeoisie and capitalism than a century ago? Are the chances any better that they can pull it off if they really want to?

As Dan Chirot pointed out, the unique opportunity for the new Bildungsbürgertum project can be seen in global perspective. Intellectuals opting for left- and right-wing anticapitalist radicalism at the turn of the nineteenth century or during the interwar years did so when forces of liberalism were weak, but now liberalism is hegemonic and possibly the strongest it has ever been in history. Also, although earlier in the twentieth century, economic and political nationalism was not only widespread but arguably was viable, by the beginning of the twenty-first century the economy is increasingly globally organized. There is indeed one capitalist world system, which to a significant extent tightly organizes most of the globe. Finally, it is also important that, at the core of the postcommunist Bildungsbürgertum, one finds the technocratic-managerial elite, which is not adverse at all to wealth and private property. Indeed, as we have just pointed out, the managerial elite is likely to be greatly attracted to such wealth and, if it has not turned itself into a propertied bourgeoisie yet, this did not happen through lack of will; it happened because other social forces blocked the conversion of networks, political office, and cultural capital into individual private property.

One important reason, therefore, why the project of the postcommunist Bildungsbürgertum may work is that this very Bildungsbürgertum, or at least its technocratic-managerial fraction, may eventually succeed in transforming its members into owners. Some already have succeeded. Others have accumulated enough capital (in the form of valuable real estate, bank accounts held abroad, small but profitable subcontracting firms) that, even if they have not been able to use privatization as a vehicle to become propertied bourgeoisie, since privatization is mostly over and the postcommunist economy is stabilized, they may go the back way by starting relatively small businesses. If there ever is a major postcommunist economic boom, they may grow very rich very fast. In previous work, the junior author (King 2001a, 2001b) documents several instances of managers "privatizing" not the shares of the firm they worked in, but the social networks of human capital and market contacts that were embedded in the firm. Thus, managers have started private legal businesses in the same line as the old state company, utilizing their old business contacts, and often employing their old employees. Some of the nontechnocratic types, particularly the politocracy, also have become new owners. Further, it is very likely that the children of both the former nomenklatura and the new politocracy will be in a very advantageous position when the economy experiences growth.

When we stated that, so far, the formation of the propertied bourgeoisie—and in particular the transformation of the former nomenklatura, technocratic-managerial elite—into a grand bourgeoisie was relatively slow, we implied that this took place under the conditions of the postcommunist transformational crisis, when acquiring property, especially productive assets, was a very risky proposition.

Possibly some of the future members of the propertied bourgeoisie are likely to lay low, and wait for insecurities to be reduced before they really get moving. On the other hand, at least in Russia, it was precisely the period of postcommunist transformation crisis when hyperinflation combined with destitute employee owners to make it possible for those with access to some wealth to acquire the assets of major firms incredibly cheap.

Having said this, we still would like to point out that the formation of the propertied bourgeoisie is likely to be a highly contested process. We already pointed out that foreign capital is likely to play a crucial role. Again, this varies substantially from country to country, and, as of the most recent data, Hungary has the largest inflow of foreign capital, closely followed by the Czech Republic, Estonia, and the rest of Central Europe. In Hungary, by 1995 almost half of the largest three thousand firms had some foreign investment. If we compare the ownership structure of firms with more than fifty employees in 1992 with that for 1995, we see that firms with majority state ownership shrink from 43.9 percent of all firms to only 13.7 percent. Foreign majority ownership increased from 13.6 percent to 18.1 percent, while private domestic firms exploded from 28.8 percent of all firms to 52.2 percent (King 2001b, 39). Many of the domestically owned firms are small- and medium-size enterprises, and many of the industrial giants are foreign-owned. It is increasingly clear that foreign investors have gained the "commanding heights" of the economy, and therefore the emergent postcommunist propertied class will not be dominated by domestic owners at all.

It is also important that selling formerly public firms to foreign investors can serve well the interest of domestic managers. In cases where managers do not have sufficient capital to buy a public firm, let alone to invest in the firm and make it internationally competitive, it may be a good idea for management to use its former foreign business contacts and negotiate a good deal for them with the state privatization agency. The foreign owners will be inclined under any circumstances to keep the old management in place, and they will do so especially if they were acquainted with the management in the past, and if that management helped them negotiate a good deal, or even helped them acquire accurate information to judge under what circumstances it would be worthwhile to invest in the firm. Managers can in this way serve as bridges to facilitate the intrusion of foreign capital into the domestic market.

Of course, it is far from clear that such a prominent role for foreign investment is undesirable. Foreign direct investment, in the majority of the cases, is advantageous for the postcommunist economy, since it brings in new technology, capital, managerial skills, and foreign markets.

Foreign capital, of course, is not necessarily good. One complaint is that foreign capital buys Eastern European firms to capture their markets (i.e., to shut down local production and sell goods made elsewhere). This seems to have happened in supermarkets, where Hungarians still need to bring a German dictionary if they want to read the labels of the foodstuffs. Foreign firms can also create monopolies by buying all the firms in one sector, as seems to have happened in the Hungarian plant oil industry. The point is, whether foreign investment is good for the country as a whole or not, it is still an attractive strategy for the former socialist technocracy.

The technocracy, management, the politocracy, and their clients have competition not only from foreign capital for the position of the new grand bourgeoisie; they also have to compete with domestically grown small business. On the whole, 1988–89 represented a sharp change in the making of capitalism in Eastern Europe. In Hungary and Poland, as pointed out in chapter 5, there was substantial growth of capitalism "from below" as private business was growing out of the second economy (out of small ventures). The period 1988–89 on the whole was a sharp turnaround: the victorious technocracy made sure that economic policy did not unduly promote "garage capitalism." Post-1989 policies focused on the changes of property rights in the former state sector. The main purpose of economic policy was not to promote the growth of domestic capital, not to encourage small private business, but to privatize public property. Thus what followed 1989 was "capitalism from above": economic policies favorable for corporate managers, technocrats, the politocracy, and their clients. Small businessmen could hardly survive. As a result, even in Hungary and Poland, where a great deal of second economy and small private business existed already during the 1980s, in 1993 less than 2 percent of the managers of the three thousand or so largest firms were private entrepreneurs before 1989. There have been of course a few very successful individuals who were private businesspersons before the collapse of communism. In Hungary the most well-known personalities are Janos Palotas, who even tried to start his own party and was a Member of Parliament (MP) in the first free Hungarian parliament, and Gabor Széles, who was, like Palotas, close to the first-postcommunist, patriotic-Christian Hungarian government. Both own substantial property and may belong to what can be called a grand bourgeoisie. But these persons are the exception. To make it to the top of the business world under postcommunism, one was, at least until 1995–96, much better served to come from a socialist managerial background than the competitive business world.

This is not, however, the end of the story. There is much dynamism in the small private sector, which is greatly diversified. Some of the self-employed are very successful; others barely survive. The most successful grow fast and can give hard competition to privatized firms run by the former socialist managers. If we can believe Bourdieu, habitus matters. The former socialist managers are so successful exactly because they carry with themselves their socialist habitus. They are well-networked; they understand the way clientelism works; and they are linked to one another in a complex web of reciprocal relationships. It is exactly their networks and their skills that enable them to navigate successfully in a world in which personal connections matter even more than in the Western business world. This is one major reason why foreign investors keep them employed, as even West German investors in East Germany rely on them. But no matter how useful this knowledge of how to get things done under socialism and postcommunism may be, it can turn out to be a limitation too. Proper markets may reward more genuine entrepreneurship and readiness for risk-taking than the former socialist managers are likely to have. Only time will tell.

So far we have considered three types of candidates for the position of grand bourgeoisie: former socialist managers and their allies in politics; foreign investors; and small businesspersons whose firms are growing larger. Let us conclude by adding that a postcommunist capitalism in which the class of individual proprietors may not be as important as in Western capitalism is not unimaginable. Postcommunist capitalism began with pretty ill-defined property relations. Public ownership—as Pavel Campeanu put it (1980)—created a property vacuum that was not easy to fill. Voucher privatization spread ownership among a great many actors. The state retained a great deal of ownership, via state banks, investment funds, and the state's privatization agency. There is no conclusive way to tell how much real individual private property will emerge from this; statistics telling us what proportion of capital is "privately owned" can be very misleading. David Stark has gone so far as to argue that postcommunist capitalism may produce a property form that is different both from classical socialist public ownership and from individual private property as we know it in the West. He has called this a system of "recombinant property" (Stark 1996).

In the case of Hungary, Stark seems to have been proved empirically incorrect. Stark jumped the gun by identifying this "recombinant property" pattern as the dominant type of property in postcommunism. Many very large, high-capital–intensive industries underwent a prolonged period of reorganization and privatization during which time their formal ownership structure could be mistaken for "recombinant property." During this period (typically 1993–95), there was indeed a good deal of cross-ownership and mixed public and private property. However, over the next several years, ownership rights were clarified and "real" private owners emerged. These were either multinationals or domestic ownership groups (see Hanley, King, and Tóth 2000).

However, various types of recombinant-property-like schemes involving cross-ownership and a blurring of state and private ownership may be prevalent elsewhere in the postcommunist world. These can be described as types of "managerial" capitalism. Thus far, there is no cross-national firm-level data set that would allow us to speak to this possibility.

The last scenario is of course far from irrelevant to the major theme of this book. To the extent to which the postcommunist economies turn into market capitalist ones, without creating a substantial class of domestic propertied bourgeois, they create space for the postcommunist power elite to retain more of its power and deliver less on its promises to act as the "universal estate of state socialism," a Bildungsbürgertum that makes the new propertied class and then leaves the stage as soon as the New Class has been formed. As long as the new social class does not appear on the scene, the postcommunist Bildungsbürgertum will stay center stage. While it can be hardly called a new dominant class, the postcommunist Bildungsbürgertum has been more than just a "supporting actor."

Postcommunist economy and social structure is still in flux. It seems certain that the New Class project of reform communism is dead. Intellectuals, technocrats, managers, or other possible New Class actors, or any combination of these, can hardly make a claim for class power. Still, these actors make history and we do not quite know yet what kind of history they are making.

Seven

Bourgeois and Post-Marxist Theories of the New Class in the West

The most significant contributions to New Class theory came in the East, where the weakness of capitalism and the success of communism gave these theoretical debates far more gravity than in the West. They were developed in response to the hegemony of a party guided by Marxism, and thus struck at the very heart of the legitimacy of the existing order, the notion that the "vanguard" ruled for the people. Further, the state socialist society that emerged in these countries endowed these ideas with much greater power than they would generate in the advanced capitalist West. It is the lack of the separation of the "political" from the "economic" under state socialism that was responsible for this. Where politics dominates, political loyalty is the primary attribute for social mobility; one of the most important ways to demonstrate this political loyalty is the ritual espousal of the dominant ideology. Thus, ideas that directly challenge this dominant ideology are far more important and potentially dangerous than under a capitalist system. Under capitalism, the economy functions (relatively) independently from the political and ideological spheres. Political elites will remain "structurally dependent" on the capitalist economy, creating much greater personal freedom of expression for elites in these spheres.

Thus, New Class theory in the West was developed in the shadow of the much more consequential New Class debate in the East. Western New Class theories were influenced not only by the debate in the East but also by the existence and evolution of the communist states—above all, the Soviet Union and then China. Nonetheless, Western New Class theories were still about Western society, and thus reflected the evolution of the position of intellectuals under Western capitalism; only, these theoretical constructs were often shaped in important ways by the towering example of the apparently successful anticapitalist regimes of the East. This is true for Marxist, bourgeois, and post-Marxist theories.

Theories of the Technostructure in the West

The shadow of the New Class in the East can easily be seen in analyzing the work of the first major Western theorist of the New Class, Thorstein Veblen. Shortly after World War I, Veblen put forward a theory about the class potential of engineers in the United States. Veblen expressed some of the experiences of the Progressive Era: scientific management, Taylorism, and the early power aspirations of the emergent American technical intelligentsia. In the wake of the Russian Revolution of 1919, he suggested that in the United States the engineers and not the proletariat would be the class that could and would carry out the socialist transformation. Veblen was an early-twentieth-century version of the Saint-Simonian New Class theory; he was the apologetical theorist of the emergent American technical intelligentsia, which had not yet been fully integrated (or co-opted) into the structure of capitalist society.

Veblen's most provocative work, *The Engineers and the Price System*, in many ways was a sophisticated sociological comment on the ideas propounded by the scientific management movement, led by Frederick W. Taylor. Taylor's work arose in the context of the growth of corporations and the incorporation of electrical and chemical technologies into the production process, two decades before the turn of the century. (See Chandler 1962 for the classic account of the corporate revolution.)

The rise of large, complex organizations meant that the owners of corporations, now often dispersed stockholders, became increasingly removed from the direct control of their businesses. In their place, an army of accountants, engineers, managers, and other New Class actors arose. From the 1890s forward, engineers no longer were primarily shop stewards with only practical knowledge of the production process, but instead were educated in college, where they learned theoretical knowledge and the discourse of scientific reason (Stabile 1984).

With intense and widespread labor militancy[1] in the recent past, and the reform era under way, the theoretically trained engineers sought to reconcile what they saw as the contradiction between profit maximization and productive efficiency. Taylor and those in his camp believed that scientific principles could be applied to the organization of production, replacing the profit-maximizing behavior of bankers and financiers that engineers perceived as the cause of industrial strife and economic crises. Scientific management, in classic New Class style, vastly enhanced the power of intellectuals (in this case, engineers) while claiming to serve the interests of all society. Taylor wrote, "Scientific management will mean, for the employees and workmen who adopt it, the elimination of almost all causes for disputes and disagreements between them" (Taylor [1911] 1947, 71). This feat would be accomplished by replacing the workers' and managers' informal knowledge and practices with scientifically generated rules of behavior.

Thus, Taylor undertook his famous time-motion studies at Bethlehem Steel—in which he attempted to measure the exact amount of motion necessary to perform certain tasks. Once tasks were delineated in minute detail, it would take all the guesswork out of production, resulting in much higher efficiency. Also, armed with the exact amount of labor necessary to do a task, a "fair" wage would be easy to agree upon, a result that, in Taylor's view, would ameliorate the cause of industrial conflict. Not only would labor essentially lose all control over the organization of production, but managers too would be disciplined by scientific rationality. Because the organization of production would be scientifically determined by the experts, there would be no need for managerial discretion. Taylor envisioned the creation of planning departments, staffed by ultraspecialized clerks, who would each oversee some narrow aspect of production.

The scientific managers, although seemingly securing for themselves control over the organization of production and distribution, were in Taylor's eyes altruistic social actors. In *The Principles of Scientific Management,* Taylor declares "those companies are indeed fortunate who can secure the services of experts who have had the necessary practical experience in introducing scientific management and who have made a special study of its principles" (Taylor [1911] 1947, 122). Nor were the theoretically trained engineers to restrict their benevolence to the industrial arena. Taylor, speaking at the American Society for Mechanical Engineers, posited, "It should take but few years of active help and cooperation with the public for us to become the accepted authority to which both the legislative and administrative branches of our municipal, state and national governments would turn . . . for general advice" (quoted in Stabile 1984, 54).

Despite the generosity of the scientific managers' offer to plan the production process, both workers and managers rejected it. Workers had little trouble seeing through the supposed universalism of the Taylorites' activities, and loudly protested the de-skilling that scientific management proposed. Nor was existing management much impressed with Taylor's plans to routinize (bureaucratize) their work. Taylor complained that both financiers and managers stubbornly resisted the introduction of scientific principles into the organization of business. By 1915, only 140 enterprises, employing sixty-three thousand workers, had adopted scientific management practices. A study by Robert F. Hoxie found that the programs were partially implemented at best, and were mostly an excuse to weaken worker unity (Stabile 1984).

Veblen, far more sophisticated and erudite than Taylor, was nonetheless greatly influenced by the scientific management movement.[2] Veblen's point of departure was the transformation of the economy that occurred with the rise of the corporation and with, especially, the application of electrical and chemical science to production, which he conceptualized as a move away from entrepreneurial capitalism to an "industrial system."

The industrial system, he wrote, increasingly replaces entrepreneurial activity centered on an open market with "a close-knit, interwoven, systematic whole; a delicately balanced moving equilibrium of working parts, no one of which can do its share of the work well except in close correlation with all the rest. . . . [T]he foundation and driving force of it all is a massive body of technological knowledge . . . running in close contact with the material sciences, on which it draws freely at every turn—exactingly specialized, endlessly detailed, reaching out into all domains of empirical fact" (Veblen [1921] 1983, 119, 126–27).

The indispensable agents in this system are the engineers, whom

Veblen contrasts with the parasitic "Vested Interests" (his euphemism for the capitalist class). The financiers, running these corporations for "absentee owners" for the purposes of profit maximization, induce waste and economic crises. These inefficiencies include restricting production, squandering resources, producing unnecessary items, and predatory business strategies.

In an argument reminiscent of the "forces of production" outstripping the "relations of production," Veblen contends that "[t]wentieth-century technology has outgrown the eighteenth-century of vested rights. The experience of the past few years teaches that the usual management of industry by business methods has become highly inefficient and wasteful, and the indications are many and obvious that any businesslike control of production and distribution is bound to run more and more consistently at cross purposes with the community's livelihood, the farther the industrial arts advance and the wider the industrial system extends" (Veblen [1922] 1983, 104). Much as this argument resembles an orthodox Marxist analysis, Veblen never for a moment entertains such determinism.

Although Veblen believed that the continuing growth of the industrial system reduced the ability of the system to withstand economic crises, he did not surmise that even a depression of unprecedented proportions would eliminate the capitalists' control of the economy, "not so long as there is no competent organization ready to take their place and administer the country's industry on a more reasonable plan" (Veblen [1922] 1983, 121). Rather, a revolution would depend on the activity of social actors, whose consciousness was to a large part inscribed by the "Vested Interests." Indeed, Veblen's most famous work, *The Theory of the Leisure Class,* details how capitalists mold the consciousness of other social groups.

Veblen's implicit theory of class formation is actually quite close to the tripartite theory propounded in the introduction: there must be the proper agents, with the proper structure, and a proper consciousness. The working class, for Veblen, was not the agent of progressive change. It is true that in his earlier work, specifically *The Theory of Business Enterprise,* Veblen identified the working class as the carriers of socialism. However, Veblen's definition of the working class foreshadowed the "New Working Class" theories (discussed in the next chapter). That is, Veblen defined the working class as "[t]he civil engineer, the mechanical engineer, the navigator, the mining expert, the industrial chemist and mineralogist, the electrician—the work of all [of whom] falls within the lines of the modern machine process as well as the work of the inventor who devises the process and that of the mechanician who puts the inventions into place and oversees their working" (quoted in Stabile 1984, 208). The traditional proletariat was not part of this picture.

By the time Veblen wrote *The Engineer and the Price System*, the unionized workers were clearly not the potential agents of a revolution. Rather, for Veblen, they were no better than capitalists in seeking to restrict the labor market, or to disrupt production via strikes, to increase their own privilege and wealth. They were as far from the engineers' "production" rationality as were bankers. Moreover, since they did not have technical training, they could not possibly run the industrial system.

For Veblen, only "those gifted, trained, and experienced technicians who now are in possession of the requisite technological information and experience are the first and instantly indispensable factor in the everyday work of carrying on the country's productive industry. . . . Therefore, any question of a revolutionary overturn, in America or in any other of the advanced industrial countries, resolves itself in practical fact into a question of what the guild of technicians will do" (Veblen [1922] 1983, 127). Veblen did not believe that this New Class had anything close to the requisite consciousness to be a revolutionary force. However, he did not feel the situation was hopeless. To this end, Veblen started the Technical Alliance during his tenure at the New School for the purposes of organizing engineers (Layton Jr. 1986, 225). Veblen soon gave up this effort, however, as the conservative backlash of the 1920s swept through the nation.

Veblen's argument that the rise of the modern corporation could potentially transform the class structure of modern capitalism would be picked up by subsequent theorists, although the particular New Class agents that might form the heart of a postcapitalist class structure differ. James Burnham, a former Trotskyist, was one of the first to do this, with his notion of a "managerial society." As with Veblen, Burnham's theory was inspired by events in the Soviet Union. According to Burnham, the Russian revolution replaced the bourgeoisie with managers as a dominant class. However, he also believed that the managerialist revolution was a worldwide phenomenon, with fascist Japan and Germany also examples of managerialism. Even the

United States with the New Deal, Burnham argued, might be heading in this direction.

During the 1930s, the idea of a technocratic-managerial transformation of modern capitalism was emphasized both with apologetical and critical overtones by many theorists. Berle and Means reported approvingly the advance of managerial power in the United States. They argued that the rise of the giant corporation was a change in the economic organization of society on a par with the transition from feudalism to capitalism: "the dissolution of the atom of property destroys the very foundation on which the economic order of the past three centuries has rested" (Berle and Means 1967, 8). As modern businesses grow larger and larger, they argued, no capitalist family is wealthy enough to supply all the capital necessary for their expansion and functioning. As a result, owners are forced to sell shares to other owners. In time, as the size of the enterprises continues to increase, the ownership stakes get smaller and smaller. Eventually, once ownership is dispersed enough, the managers of the corporations end up with their real control. As a result, the economy is no longer organized on the capitalist principle of competition on the marketplace to maximize production. Many took "the separation of ownership and control" to mean that managers, no longer forced to worry about what owners want, are free to pursue organizational goals other than simply maximizing profits.

Several theorists of the Frankfurt School, and even Habermas in his early works, have an analogous, though critical, analysis of modern capitalism, fascism, and Stalinism. Frankfurt School authors regard all these societies as technocratically deformed. Frankfurt School theorists are inclined to picture early capitalist development as liberal-democratic. They critique advanced, technocratic capitalism as worse than the earlier liberal epoch. Technology intrudes increasingly on all spheres of life, even culture and politics. Fascism and Stalinism are extreme expressions of this scientistic, technocratic development. Marcuse for instance rejects the idea of the "innocence" of technology. Where orthodox Marxists attack "relations of production" for producing alienation, Marcuse believes that technological evolution per se may have alienating implications. Frankfurt School authors, and Habermas in his early work, critiques Marxism also for being the prisoner of positivist scientism. The theorists of the Frankfurt School in such writings come close to a theory of a postcapitalist, or state capitalist, society in which the technocracy and scientists constitute a new dominant class (although in the last instance none of these theorists accept a New Class theory).

Echoes of Veblen, Burnham, Berle and Means, and the Frank-furt School are to be found in John Kenneth Galbraith's seminal work *The New Industrial State*. Like Burnham, and like Berle and Means, Galbraith believes that the rise of the modern corporation enormously diminishes the role of the owners of capital in organiz-ing production. Like the Frankfurt School theorists and like Veblen, Galbraith believes that technology and knowledge have dramatically transformed capitalism. Galbraith, in addition, incorporates the dra-matically increased role of the state in the economy, creating a power-ful theory of postcapitalism that elevates several groups of New Class actors to positions of social preeminence.

Galbraith's point of departure is the triple transformation of the economy in the twentieth century. Like Veblen, Galbraith bases his analysis on the massive concentration of industry that resulted from the rise of the giant corporations, and the expanded role of scientific knowledge and organization in the production process. In addition, however, he emphasizes the dramatic postwar increase in state spend-ing from roughly 5 percent of the gross national product to approxi-mately 25 to 30 percent. While Galbraith believes that part of the economy still consists of competitive, entrepreneurial businesses, he argues that the most important sector of the economy, consisting of giant corporations, can no longer be accurately depicted as competi-tive enterprises.

For Galbraith, the most important part of the economy is essen-tially planned, what he calls the "planning system." This system con-sists of three components—the giant corporations, the state, and the universities—that operate so closely that they start to blend into one another. The lion's share of production in this system no longer pro-ceeds in the anarchic manner characteristic of capitalist economies. Thus, for example, the economy is no longer plagued by business cycles resulting from crises of overproduction. In the 1985 edition of *The New Industrial State*, after there having been fifteen steady years of a falling rate of profit in the advanced economies, Galbraith main-tains that only one recession had hit the West, in 1975, and this "was the result of a deliberate act of policy to arrest inflation" (Galbraith

1985, 3). Indeed, the planning system is so efficient, Galbraith contends, "that big corporations almost never lose money" (87).

The basic units of production, the giant corporations like Exxon and IBM, bear little resemblance to the capitalist enterprises of old. First—Galbraith cites Berle and Mean's analysis—individual shareholders are too small and dispersed to exercise any power over the employees of the corporation. "In the past," Galbraith writes, "leadership in business organization was identified with the entrepreneur— the individual who united ownership or control of capital with the capacity for organizing the other factors of production and, in most contexts, with a further capacity for innovation. With the rise of the modern corporation, the emergence of the organization required by modern technology and planning and the divorce of the owner of the capital from control of the enterprise, the entrepreneur no longer exists as an individual person in the mature industrial enterprise" (73–74). Similarly, the great size of these corporations eliminates the influence of bankers and financiers, by "providing it with a source of capital, derived from its own earnings, which is wholly under its own control" (85).

How then do these corporations operate—if, as Galbraith, relying on Berle and Means, claims, they are "no longer subordinate to the market, [and] those who run [them] no longer depend on property ownership for their authority" (406)? According to Galbraith, these corporations are so big that they are often simultaneously monopolists and monopsonists, that is, they are often the only buyer of some range of products and the only seller of some other group of products. They are not market dependent, rather, they dominate, and in some cases create, markets. Market creation occurs when these corporations make extensive use of advertising to shape consumer preferences, creating needs that never before existed.

In fact, he argues, modern production cannot be effectively organized by the market. The increasing scale of production, utilizing high technology, has a major consequence for how the modern corporation functions: "The large commitment of capital and organization well in advance of result requires that there be foresight and also that all feasible steps be taken to ensure that what is foreseen will transpire" (4–5). The amount of information that goes into these decisions is so great that no single entrepreneur could possibly make them. Thus, groups and committees, consisting of people with highly specialized and technical knowledge, make all the decisions in the corporation and thus exercise decisive power over the production process. The scale and scope of the modern enterprise, the long-term time horizon of product development, the complexity of the production and marketing mean that production is essentially planned.

The planning system creates a powerful group of New Class actors that run these corporations on the basis of the possession of specialized knowledge and technical expertise, so that "organized intelligence is the decisive factor of production" (73). Unlike Berle and Means, Galbraith believes the group with decisive power in the modern corporation is not merely the management, nor (as Veblen held) are its members the production engineers. Rather, it consists of all "those who, as participants, contribute information to group decisions. This latter group is very large; it extends from the most senior officials of the corporation to where it meets, at the outer perimeter, the white- and blue-collar workers whose function is to conform more or less mechanically to instruction or routine. It embraces all who bring specialized knowledge, talent, or experience to group decision-making. This, not the narrow management group, is the guiding intelligence—the brain—of the enterprise. There is no name for all who participate in group decision-making or the organization which they form. I propose to call this organization the technostructure" (74).

The technostructure and the corporation, although insulated from interference by owners and financiers, are not completely self-sufficient. Whereas in the past the entrepreneurial firm depended on an outside force for the key factor of production, namely capital provided by bankers, the modern corporation is dependent on the "complex of educational institutions" to provide the "qualified talent" that is now the key factor of production. In addition, the universities provide much of the basic research that is too costly for any single corporation to underwrite yet still essential for the development of the high technology upon which modern manufacturing relies.

Thus, Galbraith has identified another group of intellectuals that has gained in strength and numbers with the rise of the modern corporation. Galbraith points out that college and university professors have ballooned from 24,000 in 1900 to 907,000 in 1972 (294). Galbraith does not call these intellectuals a class, but rather—more precisely, we believe—an "educational and scientific estate," which has gained enormous influence and potentially enormous power.

The educational and scientific estate, Galbraith points out, is no longer primarily funded by private capital, but rather by the state; thus, the planning system and the technocracy depend on state support for education to provide educated employees, the key factor of production. However, the planning system relies on the state for far more than this. Modern corporations must make decisions about investing capital far in advance of any possible payoff. They can only do this if they have a reasonable expectation of a stable economic environment and adequate demand for their products. The state provides the stable economic environment through wage and price controls, and through Keynesian deficit spending, as well as through direct purchases, particularly of military items: "[t]he state regulates the aggregate demand for the products of the planning system." The relation between the state and the planning system is so close that, "[i]n notable respects, the mature corporation is an arm of the state. And the state, in important matters, is an instrument of the planning system" (307).

In relating the growth of the technostructure, the trivialization of capitalists and financiers, the shrinking of the working-class proper, and the marginalization of market dependent firms, Galbraith essentially describes the emergence of a postcapitalist mode of production. Although he does not use this terminology—he does not refer to a "new class" in formation—his message is clear. A new type of society is emerging, one that is leading the West beyond capitalism (and thus beyond the leadership of the owners of capital) toward convergence with the planned economies of the East: "The American business liturgy has long intoned that this is a profit-and-loss economy. . . . This may be so. But it is not true of that organized part of the economy in which a developed technostructure is able to protect its profits by planning" (88). As a result, "we have an economic system which, whatever its formal ideological billing, is, in substantial part, a planned economy" (6–7). Again, Western New Class theory, while meant to describe the advanced capitalist countries, nonetheless reflects the perceived realities of postcapitalism in the East.

Galbraith's description of the emergence of a planned economy does not in itself quite qualify him for inclusion as a New Class theorist. However, he does not stop with this economic analysis. His book winds up a call to arms for the intellectuals of the educational and scientific estate.

While Galbraith argues that the economic cycles that have always plagued capitalist society have ended, and that economic scarcity is essentially a thing of the past, he is no Pangloss. Galbraith identifies many areas of market failure—mass transit, urban and suburban housing, commercial property development, conservation of the environment, and especially health industries—that urgently need planning. Galbraith laments, "[S]ince the market is assumed generally to be a success, the planning in these areas of failure is conceived to be abnormal. It is approached halfheartedly and with a sense of being unfaithful to principle. Nor are all of the requisites of effective planning identified and provided. In consequence, these tasks are badly performed to the general public's discomfort or worse. Were it recognized that they require planning, and in the context of a largely planned economy have been left unplanned, there would be no hesitation or apology in the use of all the necessary instruments for planning. Performance would be much better" (367).

Not only are there market failures in important areas, Galbraith points out, but the planning system as it currently exists relies heavily on military production, justified with an aggressive foreign policy. Thus, the United States desperately needs "a safer basis for underwriting technology," lest a nuclear catastrophe result (392). But where will this change in the goals of society, where will the *teleological* or *substantive* rationality, come from? Galbraith makes it clear that "[t]he initiative cannot come from the planning system, although support can be recruited from individuals therein. Nor will it come from the trade unions" (393). The technocracy has been molded by the needs of the planning system; its members' outlook is too narrow and specialized to allow them to break free from the confines of the corporations' emphasis on profits. Labor no longer has the power to transform society, and "they are under no compulsion to question the goals of the planning system," anyway (393).

In keeping with the tradition of New Class theorizing, Galbraith assigns the role of society's savior to his own kind, university professors. "Yet it is safe to say that the future of what is called modern society depends on how willingly, rationally and effectively the intellectual community in general, and the educational and scientific estate in particular, assume responsibilities for political action and leadership" (393–94). For "[t]he needed changes, including those in the images by which military and foreign policy are shaped, all involve the sensibilities and concerns of the mind. Their natural, although by no means exclusive, interest therefore is to those who are called intellectuals. The largest number of intellectuals with an occupational identification are those in the educational and scientific estate. It is to the educational and scientific estate, accordingly, that we must turn for the requisite political initiative" (393).

Knowledge-Based Theories of the New Class in the West

The theories about power aspirations of the highly educated during the 1970s are quite different from the earlier "waves" of New Class theorizing. The first wave of theories about the rise of the New Class in the West was based on claims that the structure of the economy changed as ownership and control were separated with the rise of the modern corporation, and with the increase of the state's role in the economy, thereby creating a new *structural position* from which power must be exercised (thus, managers or the technostructure perform the role that owners did, before); in the last wave of theories, the emphasis is on the *importance and character of knowledge.*

In this "third wave," the key—and, in comparison with earlier New Class approaches, new—argument is that the highly educated have a claim for power based on the changed status of knowledge as a principle that structures society. Daniel Bell argues that knowledge has increased in importance because of the supposed transformation of the modern Western economy from an "industrial society" to an "information" or "knowledge" society. Others argue that knowledge takes on new characteristics: it is "adversarial," "cybernetic," "context-free," "teleological." These new qualities of knowledge, appropriated by intellectuals, challenge the existing system of authority, and make the knows/knows-nots relations analogous to the haves/have-nots relations.

Thus, the knowledge-class theories of the 1970s are diverse, especially as far as their political implications are concerned. Many of the theorists are on the neoconservative or neoliberal side (Schelsky is the best example). There are also genuine liberals among knowledge-class theorists (such as Daniel Bell). Finally, the left-liberal, left-anarchist tradition is also represented (in Alvin Gouldner). Depending on the theorists' political attitudes, their assessment of the knowledge class varies. For the neoconservatives/neoliberals, the adversary-culture intelligentsia is the main enemy, a threat to liberal democracy; the liberals quite like it; the left has the usual mixed attitudes (such as Gouldner's comment: the New Class is badly flawed and still it is our best card in history).[3]

Some of the neoconservative or neoliberal authors get substantial mileage out of Lionel Trilling's concept "adversary culture."[4] Here, the key argument is that left intellectuals developed a culture that undermines middle-class values and the democratic process. For instance, these intellectuals support quota systems against individual merit; reject individualism from the perspective of collectivism; moralize politics, thereby preventing rational political discourse (a charge levied against the anti-Vietnam War movement by neoliberals). While Gouldner disagreed politically with most of these criticisms, his notion of the "Culture of Critical Discourse" is influenced by the adversary-culture idea. This culture is the foundation upon which New Class power aspirations can be built, since it challenges the legitimacy of power based either on ownership or on office and it claims that only intellectuals can serve as judges of what is right and what is wrong.

Finally, knowledge-class theorists believe that what makes intellectuals and their claim for power believable is not simply that they know *more* than nonintellectuals, but that they know *something else*: they monopolize a *different kind of knowledge*. Bell, for instance, notes that it is theoreticity that makes the knowledge of the knowledge class unique. This theoretic, rather than practical-empirical, knowledge is particularly important in the emergent information society since it is the dynamic force behind technological development.[5] Gouldner also emphasizes that the context-free character made such knowledge the foundation of power claims by intellectuals. (Konrád and Szelényi use the term "cross-contextual" in a similar way.)[6] Unlike Bell, Gouldner does not imply that such context-free discourse has productivity gains or that it is more necessary or useful, but that it is directly related to domination. If one can make the claim that one's knowledge is theoretic, then one will be able to define the situation for those who concede in the language game that they only have practical knowledge. Here we are back at the knowledge/power concept, and the claim that struggles about knowledge are struggles about power.

Bell's *The Coming of Post-Industrial Society* was the most prominent work of this last wave of New Class theorizing in the West.

Following the contemporary wave of theorizing in the East, this new wave emphasized the new character of knowledge in a "postindustrial" society. In many ways, this analysis is similar to Galbraith's argument—and it reflects the same basic shifts in American capitalism. These are the rise of corporations and the (supposed) separation of ownership and control, the increasing centrality of the state in economic activity, and the growth of higher education along with the increasingly technical production process.

If Bell builds much on the foundation laid by Galbraith, he nonetheless rejects Galbraith's claim that the major corporations have become both monopolists and monopsonists, arguing that there is less concentration of industry than after the mergers that accompanied the corporate revolution at the beginning of the twentieth century (1976, 271). Instead, Bell emphasizes the change in the *character* of knowledge in modern society, and the consequences that this new type of knowledge has for the social structure.

Where Galbraith saw a new industrial system emerging, in which giant corporations plan production with the aid of the technostructure, Bell sees the coming of a "post-industrial" society. Preindustrial society was premised on extractive activities like agriculture, fishing, and mining. Industrial society was premised on mass production using powered machines. Postindustrial society is based on "an intellectual technology" (Bell 1976, xiii). The economy is now dominated by "science-based industries (computers, electronics, optics, polymers) which increasingly dominate the manufacturing sector of the society and which provide the lead, in product cycles, for the advanced industrial societies. But these science-based industries, unlike industries which arose in the nineteenth century, are primarily dependent on theoretical work prior to production" (25).

What distinguishes the knowledge utilized in this type of production from previous forms is that it is based on "the codification of theoretical knowledge" (Bell 1976, 44). Because many great inventions of the past were produced by tinkerers working outside of scientific paradigms, the knowledge involved was not theoretical (defined as "the codification of knowledge into abstract systems of symbols that, as in any axiomatic system, can be used to illuminate many different and varied areas of experience") (20). Such knowledge allows for the "substitution of algorithms (problem-solving rules) for intuitive judgments" (29). The computer, of course, is the ultimate tool for utilizing this theoretical knowledge.

The importance of theoretical knowledge is not limited to the corporate sphere. Because society in general (and the government in particular) needs to control social change, it must engage in planning and forecasting. As a result, the old conceptualization of politics as the push and pull of various social interests and forces "is astonishingly out of date for an understanding of politics in the second half of the twentieth century, for it fails to take into account the three most decisive characteristics, or shaping elements, of national policy today: the influence of foreign policy, the 'future orientation' of society, and the increasing role of 'technical' decision making" (Bell 1976, 310–11). Military goods are created by scientists, and the management of the economy relies "increasingly [on] technical decisions" (312). As a result, "The shaping of conscious policy, be it in foreign policy, defense or economics, calls to the fore men with the skills necessary to outline the constraints ahead, to work out in detail the management and policy procedures, and to asses the consequences of choices" (311).

Thus, the new society is based on the production of knowledge. However, the production of knowledge is a *public* good, except where the knowledge gets copyrighted or patented. Because it is very difficult to enforce such protection of knowledge, "some social unit, be it university or government, [must] underwrite the costs" (xiv).

Given the rise of the importance of theoretical knowledge for both production and politics, we are entering, Bell argues, a new type of society with a new social structure. The organization of the old industrial society, in which the private corporation was the most important institution, and the most important type of conflict was among "horizontal" social classes and statuses, has been transformed: "And if capital and labor are the major structural features of industrial society, information and knowledge are those of post-industrial society" (xiii).

Because of the application of theoretical knowledge to the production process, the traditional working class is disappearing. "In fact, by the end of the century the proportion of factory workers in the labor force may be as small as the proportion of farmers today; indeed, the entire area of blue-collar work may have diminished so greatly that the term will lose its sociological meaning" (125). The notion of a class of private owners with control over society's productive forces—that is, a capitalist class—is also outdated. The separation of ownership and control, first noticed by Berle and Means, is responsible for this: "The point is that today ownership is merely a legal fiction" (295). Individual ownership is further attenuated by mutual funds, pensions, and trust funds, and corporations have increased autonomy because they are mostly self-financing (294).

Further, as Galbraith observed, the government becomes an increasingly important player in the economy. This results from the auxiliary activities that support postindustrial production. Whereas industrial production required supporting activities like transportation and restaurants, postindustrial society requires a growth in human services, such as health and education. Indeed, "The major problem for post-industrial society will be adequate numbers of trained persons of professional and technical caliber. . . . The expansion of science-based industries will required more engineers, chemists and mathematicians. The needs of social planning—in education, medicine, and urban affairs—will require large amounts of persons trained in the social and biological sciences" (232).

To provide this knowledge-based manpower, the government becomes more and more prominent in the economy. This prominence is accompanied by the rise of the nonprofit sector. As a result, the entire character of our economy has been transformed: "[W]hat is public and what is private, and what is profit and what is not-for-profit is no longer an easy distinction" (Bell 1976, 322). Because of these changes, "we in America are moving away from a society based on a private-enterprise market system toward one in which the most important decisions will be made at the political level, in terms of consciously defined 'goals' and 'priorities'" (297–98). This postindustrial society "is increasingly a communal society wherein public mechanisms rather than the market become the allocator of goods, and public choice, rather than individual demand, becomes the arbiter of services" (159).

As capitalism transforms itself, the working class disappears, and capitalists lose their function. As a consequence, "the class of knowledge class workers is becoming predominant" (343). Indeed, Bell seems to mirror Marx's logic for the inevitability of the formation of the proletariat, as famously laid out in the *Communist Manifesto*. Capitalism did indeed "create its own gravediggers"; only, they were not the manual workers. Postindustrial society is based on key services. These are the jobs "that represent the expansion of a new intelligentsia—in the universities, research organizations, professions, and government" (Bell 1976, 15). The corporation loses out in importance, "[a]nd the university, research organizations, and intellectual institutions, where theoretical knowledge is codified and enriched, become the axial structures of the emergent society" (26). Following Marx's logic, "If the struggle between capitalist and worker, in the locus of the factory, was the hallmark of industrial society, the clash between the professional and the populace, in the organization and in the community, is the hallmark of conflict in the post-industrial society" (129).

Not only will this "class in itself" of knowledge workers come into being, but it seems likely that it will eventually form a class-consciousness, and become, to use Marx's term, a "class for-itself." Bell writes, "Since the post-industrial society increases the importance of the technical component of knowledge, it forces the hierophants of the new society—the scientists, engineers, and technocrats—either to compete with politicians or become their allies" (13). Indeed, he elaborates on the steps leading to class formation and conflict. For Bell, postindustrial society will generate its own economic crises. The core of the logic, with him as with Marx, is a decreasing rate of profit. The rise of service industries means that society will not make the huge productivity gains of manufacturing (155). This will be combined with an "inflation which has been built into the structure of the economy itself by the *secondary* effects of bilateral actions of strong unions and oligopolistic industries" (155). In effect, unions get wage increases, and oligopolies pass these, as prices, on to the public (156). Demands on the government create a fiscal crisis of the state since it cannot just raise prices like oligopolies. "This may well be an intractable problem of post-industrial society" (158).

The nature of likely fiscal crises, and the very nature of post-industrial society, as a "communal" society that satisfies public goods, will draw interest groups, such as members of the New Class, into the political arena at a much higher level of participation than under industrial capitalism. "But a decision to allocate money to one scientific project rather than another is made by a political center as against a market decision. Since politics is a compound of interests and values, and these are often diverse, an increased degree of conflict and tension is probably unavoidable in the post-industrial society" (263). This participation will initially be based not on horizontal class groups, however, so much as on vertical interest groups, or "situses," corresponding to the major institutional areas of society (377). Intellectuals will be divided according to their major type of activity, since they will have different commitments. For instance, pure scientists will differ from technocrats, administrators, and cultural/expressive intellectuals (376). These differences, as well as crosscutting interests, will hinder the formation of a class consciousness.

However, Bell also emphasizes the long-run pressures for the emergence of a class of knowledge workers, able to apply a "sociologizing" mode of rationality, in contrast to the "economizing" mode dominant in the private economy. The sociologizing mode here refers to what we have been calling "teleological" rationality (a rationality over ends), and "economizing" mode refers to what we have been calling "technical knowledge" (a rationality over means to a given end). For Bell, the legal institution of (corporate) capitalism has indeed been outstripped by the forces of production. Bell writes, "The problems confronting the modern corporation—how to deal with women, minorities, community responsibility, environment increasingly are ones of the sociologizing mode" (291). Indeed, "The modern business corporation has lost many of the historic features of traditional capitalism, yet it has, for lack of a new rationale, retained the old ideology—and finds itself trapped by it" (295).

Indeed, Bell believes "The private enterprise system has been the primary institution of Western society not because of its coercive power but because its values—economizing and increasing output of material goods—were congruent with the major consumer values of the society. . . . Today, however, those values are themselves being questioned, not in the way socialists and radicals questioned them a generation ago—that they were achieved at the cost of exploiting the worker—but at the very core, the creation of more private goods at the expense of other social values" (297).

And, while Bell goes to some pains, at places, to acknowledge an indeterminateness to politics in postindustrial society, he argues there is a logic pushing the men and women of the knowledge class into self-organization. Here Bell strikes the same theme that Veblen sounded a half century earlier. "Science itself is ruled by an ethos which is different from the ethos of other major social groups (e.g., business, the military), and this ethos will *predispose* scientists to act in a different fashion, politically, from other groups" (359). He specifies that knowledge workers are "the products of a new system in the recruitment for power (just as property and inheritance were the essence of the old system). The norms of the new intelligentsia—the norms of professionalism—are a departure from the hitherto prevailing norms of economic self-interest which have guided business civilization. In the upper reaches of this new elite—that is, in the scientific community—men hold significantly different values, which could become the foundation of the new ethos for such a class" (362).

Indeed, Bell can ultimately be read as an ideologist of the New Class, which must move to impose a "sociologizing" logic on private corporations. In effect, he calls for a formal "socialization" of corporate property: "[I]f ownership is largely a legal fiction, then one ought to adopt a more realistic attitude to it. One can treat stockholders not as 'owners' but as legitimate claimants to some fixed share of the profits of a corporation—and nothing more" (295). Indeed, the owners must be thought of as "not just the stockholders, but workers and consumers too—and with due regard to the interests of society as a whole" (296). And while Bell wisely refuses to predict the imminent decline of the capitalist mode of production, we are left with little doubt about the eventual revolutionary rupture. "At some point, the major social groups in society become conscious of the underlying social transformation and have to decide, politically, whether to accept the drift, accelerate it, impede it, or change its direction" (481).

Postmodern Critiques of the New Class

While Bell's work was widely influential, the most theoretically innovative contribution to New Class theorizing, among the knowledge-based theories, is Alvin Gouldner's last project.[7] Unlike Bell, *Gouldner radicalizes the sociology of knowledge.* Gouldner subjects critical theorists themselves to self-reflexive, self-critical scrutiny. His main point is that, if knowledge is indeed implicated in power, so are intellectuals, who produce or disseminate this knowledge. Habermas argued the case for the possibility of knowing on the grounds of the *quasi-transcendental interests* of humankind *in cognition* in general, and in emancipation in particular. Gouldner explores the *existential interests* that knowledge producers as knowledge producers may have. He argues that intellectuals use their possession of the "culture of critical discourse" (CCD), the new hegemonic discourse, to establish their own class domination. Through CCD, they undermine the authority of the old classes, the moneyed bourgeoisie in the West and the old-line bureaucracy in the East. They are the New Class, a new dominant class.

Gouldner's theory of the New Class of intellectuals is the culmination of a decade of sociological and journalistic work on middle-class radicalism, on challenges which come to the existing economic, political, and cultural order from the highly educated. Many of these theories are far less radical than is Gouldner's. Some simply note that the highly educated may be (and possibly always have been) more radical, more anticapitalist or antibureaucratic, than blue-collar workers, the traditional working class.[8] Others foreshadowed Gouldner's conclusion, in claiming that this anticapitalism or anti-bureaucratism of intellectuals in, respectively, the West or communist societies might not be altruistic, but could be self-serving and pave the road to a new social order dominated by a new priesthood of intelligentsia,[9] or a New Class of technocrats, scholars, or planners-redistributors.

Gouldner radicalized the sociology of knowledge, beginning a movement towards reflexive analysis that would culminate in the work of Jürgen Habermas and Michel Foucault. These three authors set the agenda for the *critical (or reflexive) sociology of intellectuals*. The twin questions such a critical sociology of intellectuals asks are these: (a) do intellectuals have power aspirations, and, if so, in what ways can they use knowledge to attain power of their own? (b) to what extent (if at all) do self-interest (and specifically power aspirations) of intellectuals affect the nature of knowledge that is being produced, processed, and disseminated by intellectuals?

The critical sociology of intellectuals represents a radicalization of the sociology of knowledge. It aims at a higher degree of self-reflexivity: in exploring the knowledge/power or knowledge/interest link it wants to subject the knowledge producer himself of herself to critical scrutiny. Such a critical sociology of intellectuals intends to move beyond the assumption that the knowledge producers *as* knowledge producers are neutral (think of Mannheim's sociology of knowledge and his notion of socially unattached intellectuals),[10] or that they have only cognitive, or emancipatory, interests (think of Habermas's radical theory of knowledge)[11] in the process of knowledge production.

The critical sociology of intellectuals posits instead that knowledge producers *as* knowledge producers pursue self-interest and have power aspirations that intrinsically affect the way they produce discourse. As Gouldner, the most powerful theorist of this reflexive sociology of intellectuals, puts it: in this approach, the camera is focused on the "cameraman" himself.[12]

This emphasis on the camera operator does not imply that the whole story about knowledge and power—the politics of knowledge—can be told in this way. There are at least two reasons. First, knowledge is not the *only,* and in most historical circumstances not even the most *important,* source of power. Second, intellectuals pursue cognitive, or emancipatory, interests in the process of the production, processing, and dissemination of knowledge. All that a reflexive sociology of intellectuals can do is to complement other approaches in investigating the power/knowledge link by focusing on a previously underemphasized dimension, on the "missing link" in critical theory, on intellectuals—ourselves—with an ironic view, self-reflexively.

During the 1970s, in the West many social theorists—of different persuasions—were fascinated by the knowledge/power link. One interesting feature of social theory during the last decade was the reformulation by some theorists of the relation between these two phenomena. Theorists are often inclined to treat knowledge as somewhat epiphenomenal in relationship to power. Knowledge is frequently regarded as a dependent or, in more sophisticated formulations, an intervening, variable, while power or interests (more narrowly, economic, more broadly, social structural, institutional, or existential) are defined as the independent variable. During the 1970s, some theories reversed this relation, or at least emphasized the terms' interrelationship.

To illuminate this controversy we will illustrate the first position with a somewhat simplistic neo-Marxist view[13] and contrast it with the second position, which we label the "knowledge/power approach" (see Figure 1). There are many varieties of the knowledge/power approach. The New Class approaches discussed above use the triad intellectuals/knowledge/power instead of the dyad knowledge/power, and identify intellectuals as the agents whose claims for power are based on knowledge monopoly. During the 1970s many of these theorists claimed that a new knowledge class was in the making, but of course one can have an agency-centered knowledge/power approach without necessarily calling the agents a *class.* What to call the structural position that intellectuals may occupy in a society in which knowledge can be the base of domination is a question to be

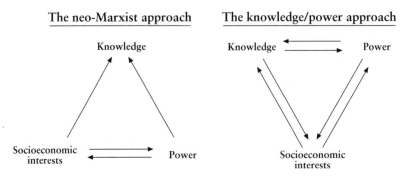

Figure 1. Competing hypotheses about the interrelations among knowledge, power, and social structure.

explored. It may be "class," or some other name may be more appropriate to describe the space intellectuals would try to conquer.

A second approach, propounded by the likes of Foucault and Habermas, seeks to *de-center* the relation between knowledge and power. While knowledge or discourse is identified as a source of domination, no particular group or class of individuals is named as exercising power. We briefly review here this second version of the knowledge/power approach.

Discourse as an Act of Domination

Foucault and Habermas, in sharply contrasting ways, provide examples of decentered theorizing at the most abstract, philosophical level. Foucault is—at least from this point of view—probably the most radical of all critical theorists. For him knowledge/power are twin, inseparable concepts.[14] Knowledge for Foucault is deeply implicated in power; whenever he says knowledge he means power, too. Discourse is intimately linked to social domination. The construction of discourse is an act of domination, an act of violence. The task of social analysis therefore is not to aim at emancipatory discourse, which is by definition impossible, but to try to produce instruments of analysis, and to let people use them for the deconstruction of the discourses within which they have to operate.[15] Foucault wants his theory to be a set of such critical instruments. In order to break the vicious power/knowledge circle, Foucault makes a desperate attempt not to create his own discourse, his own theory, or any conceptual apparatus in the conventional sense of the term. Foucault, in this way, by implicating any discourse formation in the exercise of power, pushes critical theory to its most radical, logical conclusions.

Habermas, while—as we will try to show below—disagreeing with the "postmodernist" implications of Foucault's approach, basically agrees with Foucault as far as the diagnosis of the nature of domination in modern society is concerned. Habermas also emphasizes the importance of discourse, rather than economic interests, as a source of social domination in contemporary societies. In this respect, he follows Frankfurt School tradition.

Max Horkheimer, Theodor Adorno, and Herbert Marcuse moved away from an economic reductionist critique of capitalism to a culturalist critique of modernity, away from the critique of the mode of production toward a critique of consciousness. As a result, the critique of instrumental reason and the resulting "disenchantment of the world" becomes, particularly for Horkheimer and Adorno,[16] the center of their analysis.

Although Habermas accepts this emphasis on the critique of consciousness, he abandons the overall rejection of instrumental reason. Within his revisionist Frankfurt School approach, instrumental reason has its legitimate place: there is nothing particularly wrong with instrumental reason in the natural sciences, or even in "system integration" (the organization of production and distribution). The problem for Habermas is posed by what he calls the "colonization of life-world by the logic of system integration,"[17] the projection of instrumental rationality into the domain of human interaction. This results in strategic action, in asymmetrical relations in communication, and in distorted communication.

Modern society learned how to deal with system integration; thus the major source of domination is this distortion of communication. The main aim of critical theory, the main task of emancipation, is to create a domination-free discourse, to create symmetrical relationships in communication.

Habermas is often perceived as a theorist who is less radical than Horkheimer and Adorno, since he does not reject instrumental reason per se, just limits it to man-nature relationships. But, in another sense, Habermas is actually more radical than the core of the Frankfurt School: he moves one more step away from the Marxist heritage of economic reductionism. Adorno's and Horkheimer's global rejection of instrumental reason is after all analogous to Lukács's critique of reified consciousness. Both for Lukács and for the Frankfurt School (particularly Marcuse), the final ontological foundation of instrumental reason or reified consciousness is in commodity production. Thus, despite their insistence on a culturalist critique, *in the last instance* they relate it to market-capitalist economy, while Habermas radically cuts this cord and, for him, the causal arrow points without qualification from knowledge to power, rather than the other way around.

But there are limits to Habermas's radicalism, too. Habermas, unlike Foucault, believes in the possibility of a discourse that transcends the knowledge/power link. This transcendence is not necessarily an empirically identifiable reality; indeed (Habermas can be interpreted in different ways in this respect), it may only be the vantage point from which criticism of distorted speech can be conducted. In other words, Habermas does not think that discourse with perfectly symmetrical relationships is ever achievable, but the *idea* of such speech still will enable us to discover what is wrong with any given distorted communication—where and how communication is distorted. For Habermas, Foucault's radical agnosticism is unacceptable. If one gives up hope in the existence of a domination-free discourse, then one has to reject the Enlightenment altogether and fall into postmodern irrationalism (such as that of Bataille, foreshadowed by the "impossible heritage"[18] of such thinkers as the Marquis de Sade and Nietzsche).

Despite their fundamental disagreements, at least in one important respect Foucault and Habermas converge. Both their theories are de-centered;[19] both theories are without an addressee.[20] Foucault insists that domination is within us; to project it into a group or class of people is itself a repressive discursive practice. For Habermas, emancipatory interests are quasi-transcendental; human beings *have* emancipatory interest. There is no particular agent that can be pointed to as being the carrier of, or for that matter the main barrier to, the cause of emancipation.

Was There Ever a Knowledge-Class Project?

Foucault and Habermas retain their influence, in part because they used reflexivity to move beyond New Class theorizing. The knowledge-class theories that preceded theirs, however, disappeared as fast as they came. What explains the rapid rise and fall of these knowledge-class theories? We have argued that all waves of New Class theories reflect real, but failed, power projects by groups of the highly educated. It is our contention that the knowledge-class theories of the 1960s and 1970s were theoretical overgeneralizations of the "1968 phenomenon." However, the social process that Gouldner and the others identify was not so radical as they thought—and was already defeated by the time they discovered it!

We have already discussed the rise of intellectuals in Eastern Europe in the late 1960s, a rise based on a rationalization of redistribution. In the West, there was an analogous movement, but it was linked to the rapid expansion of tertiary education and research activities, to the radicalization of college graduates around issues such as civil rights and the Vietnam War, and to the increasing role of the government in the economy, and in particular as an employer of university-trained cadre. In the socialist countries, the antibureaucratic struggles of intellectuals culminated in the reform movements of the 1960s; these movements were much more "technocratic" than countercultural. In the West, radicalized intellectuals were advocating planning, praising the public and knocking the private, even as their "socialist counterparts" in the East were advocating markets and rediscovering the values of the private sphere. In spite of these striking differences, the two movements were somewhat analogous, and indeed coincided in time: the timing of the events of May 1968 in Paris and the Prague Spring are no coincidence.

The most reliable evidence of a New Class project in the West, *in the Gouldnerian sense of the term,* is the political radicalization of the educated middle class, particularly of the young college graduates, during the late 1960s and early 1970s. This radicalization in itself is a subject of controversy: did such a radicalization take place, and was it followed by a de-radicalization of the educated middle class?

Two sociology dissertations have addressed these issues, and their authors have arrived at rather different conclusions. Steven Brint argued that the radicalization–de-radicalization process over the past thirty or so years was not class-specific, but happened across the board. Bill Martin used Brint's work as his starting point, and he tried to show that, if one analyzes data by cohorts, one finds significant differences among strata.

To put it quite bluntly, according to Martin the radicalization of the highly educated was a short-term phenomenon. If one looks at political attitudes in the United States over several decades, starting with the 1950s and reaching into the 1980s, one finds that the curve of political opinions of workers vs. those of college-educated people in the same cohorts cross-cut. Although, before the mid-1960s, workers typically show more liberal attitudes than college-educated people, this changes quite dramatically for the younger cohorts during the late 1960s. The liberalism of the educated middle class peaked around 1974–75, the college-educated young being far more liberal, or radical, than any other group of the population around that time. Following that peak, a new conservative trend is reported, and by the mid-1980s things have returned to normal, the college educated being more conservative than workers. The "hippies" of the 1960s and 1970s give way to a "yuppies" of the 1980s. Thus it appears that Parkin's notion of middle-class radicalism in which the university educated are more radical than blue-collar workers, or Gouldner's idea of the New Class project of radically anticapitalist and/or anti-bureaucratic intellectuals, may have been an overgeneralization of a rather exceptional decade fueled in large part by contingent events, such as the Civil Rights Movement and the Vietnam War.

One of the interesting features of middle-class radicalism of the late 1960s and early 1970s is that it reaches beyond social-ethical issues into the sphere of the economy. Measured by certain items, there is indeed relatively little change across strata and over time. Thus, higher educated and younger people are, were, and probably always will be more liberal on certain social issues. But the unique feature of the radicalism of the "1968 phenomenon" is the expression of anti-business, pro-government, pro-planning views among the highly educated.

Bill Martin measured the changing political attitudes through the use of attitudinal survey data. These included questions like: should the government help with medical care; should the government guarantee jobs and a decent standard of living; should national spending on welfare be increased; should the government help blacks get fair treatment; should the government help minorities improve their social and economic position; should the government support busing to achieve racial integration of schools; should there be federal government funding of public schools; should there be national spending to improve and protect the environment? It also included questions on feelings toward big business; confidence in leaders of major companies; confidence in leaders of banks and financial institutions; attitudes towards civil rights, abortion rights, and equal rights for women in industry, business, and government; attitudes toward premarital sex; and opinions about capital punishment.

Martin found different trends for different items. Generally, on social and ethical issues such as views about abortion, premarital sex, and civil rights, more educated and younger people were more liberal than the rest of the population. But on questions on the economy, he found major fluctuations. Views about the role of government in guaranteeing jobs and decent living standards, and attitudes toward big business changed dramatically. The young college graduates during the 1950s and early 1960s were quite conservative—more conservative, or as conservative as, any other group—but by 1972–74 they began to take the most radical stands, only to return to conservatism by the 1980s. Thus there is some support here for Gouldner's idea of a New Class project: there is some evidence of a certain degree of pro-government, pro-public, more collectivistic attitudes, with some anticapitalism, antibusiness, and anti-private-enterprise feelings.

Bill Martin identified some structural changes that point in this direction, too. For example, by the late 1960s: a greater proportion of university graduates find jobs with the government; young people turn away from business schools and go in greater numbers to graduate schools to study social sciences; young lawyers move away from corporate law and express interest in legal aid. By the mid-1970s a new change occurs: government job opportunities sharply decline; enrollment in business schools jump; corporate law rides high again. We are not sure what is the cause and what is the effect between attitudes and these structural characteristics: is it the radicalizing cohort that is looking for different types of vocations, or is it the change in the labor market, the temporary shifts towards the public sector, that is reflected in public opinions?

Thus, there is some evidence that a "project" of the highly educated existed. It affected them broadly, cutting across different professions that we call the technical intelligentsia and the humanistic intellectuals. "Class" may be a misnomer, though, for this project. We do not know if the motives were particularly selfish, or self-serving; they may have been quite altruistic. Further, there was no real blueprint for a new social order. However, many involved were quite radical, antiestablishment, even anticapitalist, and believed in the need and possibility of fundamental social change. They believed that intellectuals would have to play a key role in that change. "Professionalism" was widely rejected. The radicalization of this cohort began with a revolt against overspecialization. The ideal was the Renaissance person, the person of ideas—who is committed, who is an activist, who, unlike professionals, does not separate personal beliefs about political commitments from professional judgement.

In a dissertation that parallels Bill Martin's work, Kojiro Miyahara looked at changing value orientations from the early 1970s onwards. He also was interested in spotting the trends toward and away from "instrumental rationality" among the highly educated. On the basis of data from public opinion polls, he persuasively demonstrated that around 1972–74 (these seem the crucial years in middle-class radicalism) there is a clear trend away from "instrumental rationality" toward "substantive rationality" or "value rationality" (this corroborates Martin's finding of pro-government and antibusiness feelings). One of the most interesting findings of Miyahara is that during the 1980s the "instrumental rationality" of the 1950s and early 1960s does not return. While the "substantive rationality" of the earlier radical cohort decays, it gives room for more affectual orientation (with this point, Miyahara captures the importance attached to consumption, style, or form by the "yuppies," captures elements of a "postmodern" value system). As in Martin's work, in Miyahara's study the young college graduates are strategically important in capturing the changing moods of the 1970s and 1980s because theirs is the social group where the changes are the most pronounced.

The relationship of these social movements to the economy is complicated. It is suggestive, for example, that the changes in the ideology of these intellectuals follows the long-term business cycle. The 1960s saw the continuation of the long expansion of the U.S., Western European, and the Japanese economies that began in the 1950s (although the U.S. boom started in the late 1930s).[21] By 1966 in the United States, over-competition among manufacturers in the new post–World War II economy had led to a radical decline in profitability. By 1973, this massive turnaround in profitability had affected all of the advanced capitalist nations, including Germany and Japan. It was this fall in profitability that led to a fall in productive investment, and eventually to a fall in growth and thus tax revenues. This led to the fiscal crisis of the state, and the trimming back of money spent on social programs that employed university-trained social scientists, social workers, etc. At the same time, speculation and finance flourished, creating super-high-paying jobs for various forms of "finance capitalists," a fact that was a major factor "pulling" intellectuals into the professions (Arrighi 1991; Brenner 1998).

Of course, the student movement could not have simply been a response to these economic trends. For it started before the economic downturn affected state budgets. Japanese students toppled a government in the midst of one of the most spectacular economic expansions the world has ever seen. Obviously there were numerous contingent factors, like the Vietnam War and the Civil Rights Movement, that produced the social movements and political crisis of the 1960s, which was fundamentally a legitimacy crisis.

Some analysts, such as Piven and Cloward, have suggested that the economic downturn was actually a result of this political crisis. According to this view, the economic recession of the 1970s was the result of a counterattack by business. Can this possibility be accepted as fact and thus as indirect evidence of a "power project" by intellectuals? Did indeed radicalization present a serious enough threat that business wanted to respond with a recession to create cutbacks where it hurt the most to intellectuals? Was there indeed a project of a knowledge class, where claims for power, challenges to the existing order, and dimensions of a future order would come from knowledge?

While one may debate the degree of "classness" among the rebellious intellectuals of the 1960s and 1970s, it is undeniable that this project has essentially died. Indeed, by the time Gouldner published his book in 1979, it was over. The counterattack by business (waged on the ideological and economic levels) was successful. One may argue that the radical middle class was taught a lesson. Through the stick-and-carrot method, the young highly educated began to accept again the professionalized roles, to withdraw from substantive rationality, to learn how to live with business and how to like it. The age of the yuppies had arrived.

Eight

The Neo-Marxist Response to Bourgeois Theories of the New Class

Marxist class theory was slow in responding to the challenge (to the Marxist scenario for the transition to socialism) provided by the bourgeois theories of the New Class discussed in the last chapter. There were several possible lines of defense. The first was to expand the definition of the working class to include intellectuals, or at least the possessors of technical knowledge. Serge Mallet was among the first who attempted to reformulate Marxian theory to acknowledge the increasing significance of technocratic skills.

According to Mallet, in advanced capitalism a "new working class" is being constituted by the highly skilled technicians and engineers. Working-class party politics, self-limited in the second half of the twentieth century to the blue-collar, traditional working class, is self-defeating. Left parties have to appeal also to technicians and engineers, who should be considered not only as part of the proletariat, but as its most advanced, most revolutionary vanguard. André Gorz expands Mallet's argument by including civil servants as members of the new working class.

Another possible Marxist response to bourgeois and post-Marxist theories of the New Class was provided by Barbara and John Ehrenreich. They stirred quite a controversy by suggesting that the professional-managerial strata may have been transformed into a New Class. While, in his earlier work, Erik O. Wright was highly critical of the Ehrenreichs' work, under the impact of John Roemer's "general theory of exploitation," Wright began to consider that capitalist domination might be first replaced by the domination of a managerial-bureaucratic class, and in a later epoch by a professional-technocratic class. Wright based his new theory on the concept of organizational and skill assets.

Socialization of the means of production does not eliminate class divisions, according to Wright's general theory of property and exploitation, as long as bureaucratic position or skill—two major forms of productive assets—remain monopolistically controlled by certain groups. Wright conceptualizes bureaucratic state socialism as a formation ruled by a bureaucratic class, the monopolistic owners of organizational assets; he also regards socialism as a class society in which professionals, the monopolistic owners of skill assets, constitute the dominant class. In Wright's view, only communism—a social form that will emerge in the distant future—will be classless.

A neo-Marxist alternative to the professional-managerial class rests on the analysis of a "state mode of production." First elaborated by Henri Lefebvre, this concept captures the qualitatively new role that the state plays in the regulation of the economy in late capitalist societies. We will consider how this concept can be used for theorizing the emergence of a New Class whose power is based on the structural positions created by the "state mode of production."

A final theoretical response, provided by Nicos Poulantzas's theory of the New Petty Bourgeoisie and his complementary definition of the "working class," was never very successful. There were no social agents in the contemporary capitalist world attracted to the term, no agents who wanted to use it to identify themselves. The theoretical/political/ideological left was at first confused by the concept, experimented with the idea, then quickly discarded it. Bourgeois sociologists naturally ignored the concept, since they found the Marxian conception of class useless. They agreed with Poulantzas that the Marxist proletarianization thesis, in which all of society increasingly became either capitalists or proletarians, was wrong. Unlike Poulantzas, however, they saw this issue resolved by stratification analysis. For them, both "capital" and "labor" had experienced a decomposition (Dahrendorf 1976, 41–51), leaving a society with a huge middle class stratified by many gradations of authority, income, occupational prestige, gender, race, ethnicity, etc.

Poulantzas kept an "orthodox" Marxist definition of the working class, running against the current of the New Working Class wave of theorizing that emerged hegemonic in the New Left. Poulantzas insisted that a narrow definition of the working class was useful in analyzing the emergence of the new kind of "bureaucratic intellectuals" in late capitalist social formation, and their formation into a new middle class occupying structures opened up by the state mode of production. Poulantzas seems the only orthodox Marxist who honestly (and with great courage) tried to come to terms with the problem posed by Gouldner: what is the class basis of intellectuals?

Marxists, when they systematically avoid confronting this issue, are following the example of their founding fathers. As noted in chapter 2, Bakunin quite clearly told Marx that his communism was likely to lead to the dictatorship of intellectuals. The First International broke up around this clash, but Marx never took up this challenge theoretically. Marx merely dismissed Bakunin's criticisms with a few ironic comments. His own writings on intellectuals, however, are fairly pathetic, and mark a huge lacuna in his work. His few scattered remarks completely contradict his own materialist emphasis, suggesting that this was the one area where Marx desisted from his "Ruthless Criticism of Everything Existing." For example, in the *Communist Manifesto* Marx writes, "[I]n times when the class struggle nears the decisive hour . . . a small section of the ruling class . . . joins the revolutionary class . . . in particular, a portion of the bourgeois ideologists, who have raised themselves to the level of comprehending theoretically the historical movement as a whole" (*Marx-Engels Reader* 1978, 481). While all other classes and actors are motivated by material interests, bourgeois ideologists, such as Marx himself, are free of such motivations.

Lenin similarly pretends to be a deaf-mute when confronted by such criticisms. Even the most brilliant and entertaining authors, like Berdayev, rarely receive a footnote in the Marxist literature on class. While the explosive analysis of Berdyayev is virtually ignored, the few, scattered, and imprecise comments about intellectuals by Gramsci generated a plethora of Marxist commentary, enough to virtually fill a library. When one follows Poulantzas's scholarly struggle to re-think theoretically the consequences of the emergence of a New

Class for Marxism and socialist political strategies, one can sense an almost unbearable tension that builds up between Poulantzas the scholar and Poulantzas the "homo politicus," a tension characteristic of the whole opus of this author. This tension is probably one of the reasons that, in the middle of one of the most productive of scholarly carriers, he took his own life.

One virtue of how Poulantzas approaches the problem of the class structure of contemporary capitalism is that he keeps the categories of "proletariat" and "New Class" analytically distinct. According to his critics, however, Poulantzas places too much emphasis on the distinction between "productive vs. unproductive labor" and "mental vs. manual work." Indeed, in a rather orthodox manner, he states, "[I]f every agent belonging to the working class is a wage earner, this does not necessarily mean that every wage earner belongs to the working class. The working class is not defined by a simple and intrinsic negative criterion, its exclusion from the relations of ownership, but by productive labor" (Poulantzas 1975, 210). And, by "productive labor" Poulantzas means the production of "use-values that increase material wealth" (216). It is clear that Poulantzas wants to keep the workforce employed in the sphere of circulation, supervisory, and administrative positions, and the state sector, out of his concept of the working class.

He wants his conception of the working class to capture the workplace experience of what is colloquially known as a worker: the shipwright with hammer in hand, the spinner standing beside the loom, the assembly-line worker fixing a screw into a hole precisely fifteen times per minute until the bell rings once an hour and gives him or her a five-minute break to finish half a cigarette. He wants to exclude from his definition of the proletariat: the engineer who, compass in hand, walks twice every hour through the workshop to check if the turner did a precise enough job, and, when a piece of work comes off the operator's lathe half an inch too long, orders it be done again; the clerk who fills out and keeps up to date the file on the shipwright, spinner, turner, in the administration building of the corporation, in the police headquarters, the state unemployment office; and so on.

The question of whether the Poulantzian vision of the proletariat is identical to the one Karl Marx had before his eyes is, in our opinion, an uninteresting one. We do not feel the need to garner enough quotes from Marx's forty volumes to support or contradict

Poulantzas. To non-Marxists or post-Marxists, this war of quotes from the sacred texts, which was waged between Poulantzas and his critics after 1975, is of no value. Poulantzas garnered enough quotes to show that his is one possible reading of Marx, and his critics that his is not the only possible one. What is much more interesting is to explore why Poulantzas does what he does: what is his theoretical and political/ideological motivation, who are his opponents and what are their motivations, and, finally, what is the fruitfulness of these formulations for understanding class structure and formation in contemporary capitalism?

The most convincing and/or serious objection to the narrow definition of the proletariat is to suggest that it is a nineteenth-century one. Some argue that by the mid-, and especially by the late, twentieth century the "worker-with-hammer-in-hand" had disappeared. This was a widely held view in bourgeois sociology until the mid-1960s, and, in light of further automation, cybernation, and computerization, keeps re-emerging. This is the view of Daniel Bell and others, who think in terms of a "postindustrial society" with very short working hours, huge tertiary sectors, and the performance of many former manual tasks by robots.

From the mid-sixties, neo-Marxists also responded to the challenge of redefining the proletariat, with the "new working class" theories that sought to accommodate real or imagined changes in the economy. Authors such as André Gorz, Serge Mallet, and Alain Touraine attempted to work within the Marxian paradigm to redefine the proletariat to accommodate the more highly skilled workers, and even engineers, into the concept of a new working class. Braverman did a spectacular job of analyzing the actual work experience of the modern service sector, to show that people in all sorts of clerical jobs should be included among the working class. Crompton and Gubay went through a quite thorough "talmudic" analysis of the Marxian political economy to show that "surplus" and "profit" could be sufficiently twisted so that labor employed in the tertiary sector could be labeled "productive work" (basically by arguing that the production process includes the "realization" of surplus, as well).

Whenever critics of Marxism suggested that changes in the economy might make the old Marxian distinction between "capital" and "labor" useless, there were Marxists who could prove that the definition of these classes could be altered a bit, thereby preserving the logic of the classical Marxian analysis of class relations under capitalism. Such an expanding definition of the working class might be useful politically, since it allowed Marxist ideologues to classify themselves as the working class and to define all those whom they might need, to gain political power, as proletarian. If one continues to broaden the definition of the working class, however, one might end up with an extremely vague concept, theoretically uninformative.

If our reading of Poulantzas is correct, he is concerned with the obvious willingness of Marxian theorists to keep redefining their class categories, which theoretically deprives class theory of internal cohesion. This practice also represents an ideological threat to class theory, the possibility that class theory will be used solely as a political tool and lose its ability to elucidate the structures and functioning of society.

It seems that in addition to Poulantzas's more intellectually honest approach to studying the proletariat, his narrow definition of the working class has the virtue of not assuming changes in class structure that have not actually occurred. While it is true that the economy has changed since the nineteenth century, the orthodox theory of the proletariat has not lost sense at all. Curiously enough, it was bourgeois sociology, primarily John H. Goldthorpe's and David Lockwood's and the work they inspired, that rediscovered the working class. The so-called decomposition of labor that Ralf Dahrendorf was talking about simply had not happened. Manual workers in directly productive activities simply did not disappear. Critics of Daniel Bell point out that manual workers do not seem to be disappearing in any foreseeable future. The age of total robotization does not seem just around the corner.

Further, it seems that behind theories that suggest that the manual worker in directly productive spheres is disappearing are a great deal of ethnocentricity and middle-class bias. S. M. Miller's "new working class" concept, rather than include professionals in the working class, points out the dramatic changes in the ethnic composition of the manual labor force in the United States. More recent studies in Western Europe also show that manual workers are still around, but they are now "guest workers" from places like Turkey and the Philippines, instead of Germans, Swedes, etc. J. Collins in his work on labor market segmentation in Australia documents that manual labor occupations there become filled by immigrants. Further, if one keeps in mind that contemporary capitalist production has to be conceived on a world scale, then the proportion of the workforce employed in manual jobs in directly productive activities seems rather stable, given the shift in manufacturing production to the Third World.

We also find untenable the objection—which seems quite often the implicit reasoning behind the argument his critics put forward—that Poulantzas must be wrong since to adopt his definition of the working class makes that class a "ridiculously tiny minority of the population." This is an absurd view: one cannot keep changing the definition of the working class just to keep the majority or the overwhelming majority of the population within the working class. One must start with a reasonably objective criterion, apply it in empirical investigation, and wait and see what the results will be. We are convinced that the appeal of Wright's class analysis (Wright 1978, 86) is that, by his calculation, the working class is 41 to 54 percent of the population, whereas the Poulantzian definition would produce a working class that is only 19.7 percent of the population (56–57).

The important point that Poulantzas's critics seem to miss is that class theory should be able to provide us with an answer as to why there has been no proletarian revolution—and, more specifically, why such a revolution did not occur in the industrially most advanced countries. Therefore, those class theorists with techniques that succeed after all in "producing" a working-class majority, and can prove the veracity of the proletarianization thesis advanced in the *Communist Manifesto* (that capitalism increasingly divides society into "two opposing camps"), create as many problems for themselves as they solve. If Marx and Engels were actually correct, and after the "old petty bourgeoisie" has been destroyed, capitalism is composed by a "tiny minority" of capitalist oppressors and an "overwhelming majority" of the proletariat, why does the proletariat accept this absurd proletarianization?

Wright actually finds a nice compromise, from this point of view, between Poulantzas and his most extreme critics, through his notion of "contradictory class locations." He can locate about half the population in such "contradictory locations," where, being in between the bourgeois and the proletariat, they may ally with either. From this perspective, it is easier to explain why the proletarian majority (since just barely a majority) does not succeed in overthrowing the bourgeoisie.

The more vehement critics of Poulantzas, who operate with the notion of the proletariat as the "overwhelming" majority, have to resort to complex theoretical speculations about why class consciousness does not develop, as well as to complicated arguments about the working class's "segmentation and fragmentation" that they can very infrequently explain (see Boon 1978). One method for escaping this self-inflicted dilemma of the Marxist revolutionary theorist, which we especially distrust, is to resort to a neo-Leninist theory of trade union mentality and revolutionary class consciousness so as to blame the workers for not fulfilling their ascribed historic task.

Given a sufficiently broad definition of the proletariat, the neo-Leninist radical left can "sublimate themselves" into the position of the proletariat and blame the manual workers for a lack of revolutionary vigor. This is a left-wing version of the blame-the-victim strategy, no more distasteful than the right-wing versions of blame-the-victim "solutions." This is indeed the ideology of a "flawed universal class" of intellectuals. However, in the contemporary West, this "flawed universal class" is merely a bunch of powerless ideologues who gather around the tiny, so-called revolutionary parties and are nowhere near being able to challenge the power of the dominant capitalist class. If such a challenge is to come, then it will come in the West from another type of intellectual, with a somewhat different ideology, from another kind of New Class, one more likely to grow out of what Poulantzas called the new petty bourgeoisie.

The New Petty Bourgeoisie and Contradictory Class Locations

Poulantzas responds to the problem of the emergence of the New Class by theorizing the emergence of a "new petty bourgeoisie." With this notion, he can give a better explanation than any of his critics to the question of why a working-class revolution did not occur, and in fact why it is very unlikely that the Western world will move toward a "proletarian revolutionary transformation." Poulantzas's attempt at theorizing the emergence of a new middle-class position allows him to pose questions about its particularistic interests. This is in sharp contrast to Wright's vague and theoretically uniformed notion of a "contradictory class location" *defined only by what it is not*: neither fully capitalist nor fully proletarian. The identification of this "in between class's" particularistic interests makes possible an enquiry into the circumstances that must prevail for this class to ally with either labor or capital. It is precisely the vagueness of the concept of "contradictory class position" that makes Wright's type of analysis disappointing in the long run. This concept is not precise enough to work out possible strategies of class alliance or possible dynamics of the contemporary capitalist system.

If we work our way through Poulantzas, we can more easily see the seriousness of the warning that Gouldner gives us in the epilogue of *The Future of Intellectuals and the Rise of the New Class.* If we remain within the framework provided by Wright, then we face the possible danger that, if the "forces of labor" should work toward alternatives to Western capitalism, they would not recognize the potential dominant-class aspirations of some forces behind "the new petty bourgeoisie." It might happen again that the "lowliest class" would not come to power but that, on the contrary, as in the struggle between lords and serfs, the "in between" bourgeois class would emerge victorious. Thus Poulantzas is motivated not only by theoretical scrupulousness in insisting on a clear, coherent definition of the working class. As homo politicus, he also realizes, more than most of his comrades/opponents, that the agents who neo-Marxist theorists so generously and so hurriedly included in the definition of the working class may have significantly different interests than the proletariat. Party politics that offers a broad platform pretending to be the platform of *one* class, rather than a relatively shaky alliance of different class forces and class fractions, can have adverse political consequences. Such "elastic" politics raises the possibility that intellectuals could ride the backs of the "working class" into power, raising themselves into the position of a new dominant class.

In addition to providing the theoretical tools for a more democratic democratic-socialism, in which class alliances are not obscured by lumping all anticapitalist forces into one huge "working class," Poulantzas's notion of the "new petty bourgeoisie" helps explain why the "revolution" is not just around the corner. Poulantzas's theory accounts for why the Marxian forecast about the proletarianization of classes did not occur. The old petty bourgeoisie was destroyed but not proletarianized; it was replaced by a new petty bourgeoisie. This

New Class, very unexpectedly for Marxists, prevents the explosion of class conflict. The fact that this class is large and in between capital and labor, with its own mixed particularistic interests, allows it to serve as a mobility safeguard for some members of the working class, siphoning off tensions stemming from the structural relationship between capitalists and proletarians. Similarly, some of the new petty bourgeois activities, particularly those associated with providing welfare services, somewhat ameliorate class-generated antagonisms. This is a very important theoretical insight, one unavailable to those working with a broader definition of the working class, who limit the fruitfulness of their own formulations by forcing their political dreams upon their theoretical analyses. The Poulantzian concept of the new petty bourgeoisie is, to the best of our knowledge, the only serious attempt by modern Marxists to come to terms with this problem.

The Limits of the Poulantzian Analysis

Having acknowledged the originality and insightfulness of Poulantzas's "new petty bourgeoisie" concept (which required him to work with his extremely orthodox concept of the "proletariat"), we must argue that, in the final analysis, Poulantzas fails to achieve the theoretical aims he put before himself: ultimately his Marxist orthodoxy binds his hands and blinds his eyes. He is unable to locate, in any meaningful sense of the word, the new petty bourgeoisie; he is unable to account for its class character. Poulantzas describes the ideologies of the new petty bourgeoisie very accurately on the empirical level, but he cannot account for the "new middle class" structurally. The gravest problem he faces is explaining why this new petty bourgeoisie is a new middle class. His solutions are formalistic and misguided. He wrongly believes that the new petty bourgeoisie and old petty bourgeoisie form one class.

In addition, Poulantzas errs in locating the structural basis of the new petty bourgeoisie in the mental/manual distinction. This error prevents him from being able to clarify the relationship of the new middle class to the state and the changing nature of state intervention under late capitalism. As a result of these mistakes, Poulantzas in not able to elucidate the strategies that the "forces of labor" could adopt towards the New Class in their search for alternatives to contemporary capitalism.

Poulantzas acknowledges *"a considerable increase,* throughout monopoly capitalism and its various phases, of a number of non-productive wage earners, i.e., groups such as commercial and bank employees, office and service workers, etc, in short all those who are commonly referred to as 'white-collar' or 'tertiary sector' workers" (Poulantas 1975, 204). He then continues with, in our opinions, an untenable theoretical construction: "The particular question of these new wage earning groupings will form the chief object of the following analysis. *I shall refer to them as the new petty bourgeoisie, for what I am seeking to show here is that they belong together with the traditional petty bourgeoisie* (small scale production and ownership, independent craftsmen and traders) *to one and the same class, the petty bourgeoisie"* (204, all emphasis ours).

The first problem with Poulantzas's formulation is the insistence that "nonproductive" or "mental labor" is sufficient to construct a "New Class position." Poulantzas's justification relies on the worst possible Talmudic type of orthodox Marxism. For Poulantzas, "nonproductive labor" is a sufficient criterion on which to base a "new petty bourgeoisie," because it allows him to label it an "inbetween class." It is neither capitalist (because it does not own the means of production) nor proletariat (because it does not directly produce surplus). Thus, it must be "in between" these two. We do not argue that "nonproductive labor" (or even "manual labor") is an unimportant analytical term, only that what it refers to is insufficient as the basis of a New Class.

The notion of "productive work" does have meaning, if not to the intellectual ideologues, then at least to the workers themselves. The senior author remembers conducting interviews with peasant workers in a Hungarian village. He asked what kind of man the president of the village commune was. He will never forget the answer: "You know, he is one of those guys who never worked for an hour in his life." When asked to explain what he meant, the peasant worker responded, "All his life he was sitting behind desks, he was a clerk, a policeman, accountant in the cooperative, head of this department and that department." For the intellectual Marxist theorist, it might be difficult to see any meaning behind the notion of "productive work," but with a great deal of oversimplification there are workers who think that "paperwork" is not work, and that only those who work with their hands *work*. (That this is wrong, because mental workers, academics, writers, even managers and police, do work, and often rather hard, is of no consequence for the analysis.)

This phenomenon is well documented in sociological research. Harastzi's *A Worker in a Worker's State* presents a lot of in-depth interview evidence that workers on the shop floor make the distinction between "we," who actually work, and "they," who supervise, sit in an office, do not come to work at 6 A.M., but rather work 9 to 5, have proper lunch breaks, wear "white collars," and need not shower after work since they do not "dirty their hands." "We" work; "they" don't. Harastzi's evidence is from Eastern Europe, a technologically backward region, and one might argue that the contemporary West is quite different.

There is much research, however, that Harastzi's description fits frighteningly well the work experience of those who work for Ford, etc. This massive literature is common knowledge in industrial sociology. When the senior author started to do research work in a steel mill in the small southern industrial town Whyalla, what impressed him was how little difference there was between this steelworks and a Hungarian steel mill in Csepel that he had conducted research in. More specifically, there was little difference in technology as well as in the hour-by-hour, day-by-day, direct work experience of the steelworker. When the author was interviewing shipyard workers in Whylla he very soon noticed some of the same suspicious attitudes he had encountered when talking to workers and peasants in Hungary: in the workers' eyes, he belonged to "them," one who "never worked for an hour in his life" and who therefore would not understand what they had to say. While we object strongly to most "convergence theories," this is one issue where the similarity between East and West is striking.

Thus, while we acknowledge that the distinction between productive and nonproductive labor is a real one (it disappeared more in the heads of the ideologues than in the realities of the contemporary industrial world), it is not one sufficient to base a "new class," not even a "new middle class," on. From this point of view, Wright is on the right track. This distinction can be dealt with by a more parsimonious, toned-down terminology of "contradictory class locations." This distinction would not allow for more than a differentiation of strata within various classes. By labeling all those who do "nonproductive" labor members of the new petty bourgeoisie, Poulantzas lumps together the empirically most varied groups, from academics to salespersons to police to data entry clerks.

Poulantzas compounds this error with his absurd conclusion that the old and new petty bourgeoisie constitute *one* middle class. This is obviously nothing more than a formalistic solution; the only real similarity between those he labels the old and the new petty bourgeoisie is that they cannot be meaningfully classified into the class dichotomy generated according to the functioning of the main logic of the dominant capitalist mode of production. They are one only in the sense that they are neither capitalist nor proletarian. Poulantzas also uses a little dialectic to get out of his troubles when he writes about "class fractions" at great length; at no point in the analysis is empirical evidence presented that suggests that the old and new petty bourgeoisie are one class.

Surprisingly, Poulantzas is at his best, in discussing the new petty bourgeoisie, when he offers an empirical analysis concerning the ethos of this class, where he moves very close to Gouldner's analysis of a "culture of critical discourse." On pages 290–94 of *Classes in Contemporary Capitalism,* Poulantzas summarizes the main ideological features of the new petty bourgeoisie. This petty bourgeoisie "is anti-capitalist but leans strongly towards reformist illusions. This new petty bourgeoisie experiences its exploitation in the wage form, while the structure of the capitalist mode of production and the role of . . . ownership . . . remains to be hidden from it. . . . Its demands are basically bound up with the question of incomes, often focusing on a redistribution of income by the way of 'social justice' and an 'egalitarian taxation policy', the constantly recurring basis of petty bourgeois socialism. Although they are hostile to the 'rich,' the petty bourgeois agents are often still attached to wage differentials, while stressing the need for these to be more just and 'rational'. What we are faced with here is a permanent fear of proletarianization" (290).

Then Poulantzas argues that the new petty bourgeoisie, when confronted with the political and ideological hegemony of the dominant capitalist class, "leans strongly towards re-arranging these relations by way of 'participation' rather than undermining them. Demands are made on capital for a greater share of 'responsibility' in decision making powers and for a reclassification of their mental labour at its 'true value'" (291). From this point on, Poulantzas speaks explicitly about the "new class of intellectuals," with some of his analysis supportive of Gouldner's notion of the New Class as a "flawed universal class." Poulantzas writes:

> [R]ationalization of society . . . would enable "mental labor" to develop fully, without the shackles of the profit motive, i.e., in the form of a left-wing technocracy. . . . [T]he anti-authoritarian struggle that develops here, in the form of a revolt against the bureaucratization and fragmentation of mental labor, is far from attaining the scope and content of the anti-hierarchical struggle of the working class. The petty bourgeois are . . . strongly attached to a hierarchy. . . . Afraid of proletarianization below, attracted to the bourgeoisie above, the new petty bourgeoisie often aspires to "promotion" to a "career," to "upward social mobility" . . . by way of the "individual transfer" of the "best" and "most capable." . . . Hence the belief in the "neutrality of culture" and in the educational apparatus as a corridor of circulation by the promotion and accession of the "best" to the bourgeois state. . . . This leads to the demands for the "democratization" of the apparatuses, so that they offer "equal opportunity" to those individuals best fitted in the "renewal of elites." . . . The elitist conception of society, in the form of meritocracy, is closely linked with the petty bourgeoisie's aspirations for social justice. . . . An ideological aspect of "power fetishism" . . . concerns the attitude of the new petty bourgeois towards the political power of the state. . . . [T]his class has a strong tendency to see the state as an inherently neutral force whose role is that of arbitrating between the various social classes. The class domination that the bourgeoisie exert over it by way of the state apparatus is often experienced as a "technical" deformation of the state, which can be "re-arranged" through democratization. . . . This involves demands related to the "humanization" and "rationalization" of the "administration." . . . It is clear that these ideological aspects often take the form of demands for "socialism" by way of the "welfare state," the regulator and corrector of "social inequalities." (291–93)

We acknowledge that this is a rather selective set of quotes, and that we intentionally left out some of the references Poulantzas is making on these very pages to those ideological beliefs one would usually associate with the "traditional petty bourgeoisie" (for example, references to petty bourgeois anarchism, anti-statism and its combination with "bonapartism," etc.). We think, however, that we are justified in this selective reading. The conventional references to "petty bourgeois anarchism," etc. actually contradict Poulantzas's own argument, and only reflect his conceptual confusion. Our quotes form a more coherent, and in many ways powerful, description of the ideological profile, possible structural position, political strategy, and particularistic interests of the emerging New Class in the West. What is striking is the similarity to some of the more powerful propositions by Gouldner: the reference to meritocracy, the belief that if mental labor fully develops it can rationalize society without the shackles of the profit motive, the belief in the neutrality of culture, the aspirations to a career based on educational achievement, which in the metaphorical meaning of the word are references to the reproduction and accumulation of cultural capital.

The other important component in the Poulantzian description of the profile of the New Class is the importance of its relations to the state. This manifests itself through the commitment to the principle of social justice and egalitarian income policies, the belief in the state as a neutral force, the attempt to use the state as an arbiter between social classes, to put themselves (New Class actors) above particular classes by the "power fetishism" of the state (a phrase that is almost a direct reference to the aspirations of the New Class to become the "flawed universal class"), and finally demands for socialism via the welfare state.

On this point, Poulantzas is more insightful than Gouldner. Gouldner is misleading himself that the New Class's possession of cultural capital accounts for its "flawed" character. This prevents Gouldner from seeing that the real claim for class power by the New Class can only come through a qualitative change in the role of the state. The New Class cannot directly challenge the power of capital (Gouldner misses this point because he views cultural capital as real and not merely metaphorical capital). The New Class, the class of what he calls Evangelistic Bureaucrats, has to use the state—in the first instance, the welfare state, and secondarily (as we suggest later in the book), the "state mode of production" in its more advanced stage—to present a convincing claim for class power! Poulantzas does not see this, but gets closer than Gouldner to discovering it, since his theory is not blocked by a wrong emphasis on a nonmetaphorical concept of cultural capital.

For Gouldner, the education of the New Class is part of its capital because it provides class members with incomes (Gouldner 1979, 23, 28). However, capital, to be used as a criterion upon which class antagonisms are based, must be understood as a social relationship that enables those who possess capital to appropriate labor from those who are deprived from capital. It cannot be understood simply as an income-earning capacity. For example, money only becomes capital when those who have money buy the means of production and the labor power of those too poor to buy means of production themselves, and are thus able to legitimately appropriate surplus labor from the wage earner. Money is not capital because it generates personal income for the capitalist, but because it allows the capitalist to dispose with surplus, to increase capital in order to reproduce, in an extended manner, capitalist relations of production.

Highly educated labor (or culture), in an economic system where private ownership is sufficient for the appropriation of surplus, is not capital. Intellectuals in a market economy have only very highly qualified labor power that is artificially scarce as a result of credentialing. In Weberian terms, they will be "positively privileged" employees on the labor market, but they will not dispose of the "surplus" labor power of others. Even if they act like "managers," appear to be employers (they hire and fire), and appear to "dispose with surplus" (they appear to make investment decisions), they do not make their own decisions. They act on behalf of the owners, with the power delegated to them as competent managers. They are not exercising their own class power.

What bears stressing is that a top manager of a large corporation is a member of the dominant class to the extent that he or she can be understood as a capitalist—that is, as an owner of capital—and not to the extent to which he or she has "cultural capital" that entitles him or her to high income. But to define a dominant class, one must analyze the nature and logic of the power exercised by agents of that class; the personal income of the agent is secondary and, in the final analysis, basically irrelevant.

The key question is what does the manager do, not how much does the manager make (see Connell 1970, 50). To what extent does the manager exercise capitalist power and obey the logic of private capital accumulation, or to what extent can the manager have an alternative logic that would overrule the "iron law" of "economic efficiency," which is expressed in terms of long-term profit maximization? Even if Berle and Means are correct (and we do not believe they are), managers may be members of the dominant class because they control or de facto own the major means of production, but they are not members of a new dominant class, merely a functional equivalent of the old dominant class of capitalists. To the extent that the manager is an expert/professional, metaphorically an owner of "cultural capital" (perhaps embodied in a Masters of Business Administration from Harvard University), he or she cannot be regarded as a member of a "New Class," since under no circumstances can he or she challenge the power of the moneyed bourgeoisie as expressed through the logic of private capital accumulation. After all, our capitalist manager was trained to accumulate capital in the most efficient way. What Gouldner calls his or her cultural capital does not contradict the interest of private capital; to the contrary, it serves the interest of private capital. The expert-professional manager was hired to do the job because the owners, who probably inherited their wealth, are just not good enough, not well trained enough, or not clever enough, or do not care enough, to do the job themselves. But, just as the executioner who knows a great deal about hanging would not in any way challenge the power/authority of the sentencing judge simply by making sure that the convicted person dies quickly, the manager does not threaten the power of the private capitalist by making sure that the shareholders receive in the long run the highest possible dividend.

The "expert-professional industrial manager" is the most difficult example for demonstrating that professionalized intellectuals do not constitute a New Class. Quite clearly the manager of the large private corporation—precisely because he or she has a great deal of control over large organizations—is the closest among intellectuals to be identified as belonging to a new dominant class." It is far more challenging to make the case for an academic, a teacher, a painter, or a novelist. The managers (and, more clearly, the academics, teachers, painters, novelists) do not constitute a class on the basis of their metaphorical ownership of "cultural capital."

Poulantzas comes close to discovering that the formation of the New Class has to be linked to the changing nature of the state in late capitalist formations, but he cannot reach this conclusion because his conceptualization is blocked by insisting that the new petty bourgeoisie and the old petty bourgeoisie form one class. This misconception pushes him into confusion, since it is precisely in their relation to the state that these two "petty bourgeoisies" have diametrically opposed interests. It is curious that Poulantzas does not seem to realize this, although it must be clear, if one understands what the traditional petty bourgeoisie was or is, that it is exactly on the opposite side of the barricades from the "new petty bourgeoisie" in relation to the welfare state and state intervention. The "old petty bourgeoisie" is normally not reformist, is against high taxes and egalitarian income policies, does not support income differentials based on educational achievement or social promotion systems based on cultural capital, or "socialism" via the welfare state. It is not an ally of the "new petty bourgeoisie"; it opposes this bourgeoisie, the Evangelistic Bureaucrats, more than it does any other class. The old and the new petty bourgeoisie are not only not one class, but they are at least as mutually antagonistic as are the basic classes of the capitalist mode of production, capitalists and the working class. It is much more likely that the "new petty bourgeoisie" will ally with the "forces of labor" or with "capital" than with the "old petty bourgeoisie."

Nine

The Limits of the New Class Project in the West

The waves of New Class theorizing in the West, while influenced by events in the socialist world, have corresponded to real class projects that paralleled real changes in the structure of the economy and the political systems of advanced capitalist economies. New Class theorists, however, have tended to overemphasize the importance of these changes and to see them as the cause of the rise of a new dominant class capable of bringing revolutionary changes to the functioning of the capitalist economy.

The first wave of New Class theorizing in the West was responding to the rise of the dominant property form in modern American capitalism: the modern corporation owned by numerous stockholders. We agree with Maurice Zeitlin (1974) that these theorists both overestimated the extent and misunderstood the effect of the rise of share ownership and the corporate structure. Zeitlin argues that most firms are still controlled by a network of individuals representing major capitalist families. More relevant, perhaps, is that as long as the firm as a budgetary unit is market dependent for its survival, managers, engineers, and other potential New Class agents (regardless of their "autonomy" from actual owners) cannot collectively exercise rationality in any way that impinges on profits.

Managers must behave so as to maximize the price:cost ratio of the firm. If they don't, they usually go out of business or lose market share. In Polanyian terms, capital and labor are still primarily allocated through the market; America was, and is still, a market-integrated society. In Weberian terms, managers exercise instrumental rationality, not substantive rationality. The individually rational activity of units of capital are still not necessarily rational when they are aggregated. Taylor, Veblen, and Berle and Means were incorrect when they argued that scientists, engineers, or managers would occupy new structural positions in corporations such that they could exert collective rationality over the economy.

Not only was there an inadequate structural base for New Class formation in the West; there was also a failure of consciousness. The managerialists, or technocratic theorists have failed, as Gouldner would do later, to appreciate the importance of professionalization as an historical alternative to New Class formation. These theorists collapse professionalization and the New Class formation into one process, but we shall argue that these are two complementary processes, even alternatives. To do so, we shall explore Magali Sarfatti Larson's idea of professionalization as a "collective mobility project."

We argue that New Class formation, the project to overcome professional segmentation of groups of the highly educated, to reach beyond their privileged stratum position and strive for ultimate collective power of all knowledge monopolists, is an alternative strategy to professionalization. In advanced capitalism, any impulse toward teleological power by any possible New Class agents has had the negative example of actually existing socialist societies to suggest that such power may involve a significant loss of intellectual and political freedom as well as a lower standard of living. Further, the ability of professionals to have a better-than-average bargaining position in the labor market, as a result of the monopolization of certification (made possible by a plural political system), means that these professionals can have higher salaries under capitalism than in a more egalitarian society.

Neo-Marxist theories of the "new working class," like the earlier wave of New Class theories, are also responding to real changes in the structure of the economy and the workforce. Like the bourgeois New Class theorists they respond to, they misinterpret these changes. Braverman's 1974 analysis on the de-skilling of white-collar mental work emphasizes—with different political implications than has

Mallet's theory—the increasing homogenization of all wage laborers around a proletarian position. Zeitlin (1989) demonstrates that much of the "service sector" employment is composed of merely disguised manual working-class occupations. These occupations are an effect of, for one thing, the entrance of women into the workforce. Thus Braverman's and Zeitlin's analyses imply that the "new working class" is not so different from the old working class, but basically occupies the same structural position as before. Finally, just as the theory of the new working class emerges, the decomposition of the working class also seems to emerge. This decomposition, reflected in many indicators but most significantly in declining levels of union participation in most of the West, has made any upsurge in class formation that much more unlikely.

Professionalization as an Alternative to Class Formation

Gouldner's analysis of the New Class based on cultural capital, with an ideology of professionalism, is highly misleading. A manager of a capitalist corporation is an expert/professional (to the extent he or she knows a lot about macro- and micro-economic modeling, accounting, industrial relations, etc.), not a member of a class. On the contrary, to the extent that the manager is only an expert/professional, the manager relinquishes his or her claim for any kind of New Class power that could challenge the power of the capitalist class. This claim is diametrically opposed to Gouldner's: professionalism is not only not the ideology of the New Class; it is the ideology of the intellectual stratum that guarantees that this stratum does not represent any meaningful, significant challenge to the dominant capitalist class.

As we argued in chapter 4 of this book, however, the expert/professional in a socialist redistributive economy can be much more meaningfully conceived as the carrier of a new type of class power than can his or her Western counterpart. The "scientific planner" of state socialism is radically different from the (non-owner) manager of the capitalist enterprise. With the abolition of the institution of private ownership and the introduction of central planning, the scientific planner occupies a qualitatively new position.

The planner, unlike the manager in a market capitalist system, does not assume that every dollar/rouble invested will maximize the financial return in the short, medium, or long run. In the centrally planned state socialist economy, the "scientific planner" not only will dispose with "surplus" by making investment decisions, but will decide on the direction of the extended reproduction of the system. That is, the scientific planner not only allocates the social surplus, but also decides what is the rational way to use that surplus (e.g., the decision to maximize the military sector at the expense of the consumer goods sector). While, under market capitalism, the expert/ professional manager knows how to sail when the wind blows, under state socialism, at least in principle, it is the scientific planner who blows the sail! This type of decision over the use of social surplus, in Weberian terms a substantively rational decision, is never made by the manager in a market capitalist economy.

In the empirical sense, the distinction will not be that clear-cut. The daily routine work of a factory manager in the U.S.S.R. might have been frighteningly similar to the daily routine of a factory manager in Detroit (what they would do being shaped to a significant extent by factors unrelated to national political/economic social systems, such as technology, market conditions, etc.). What they would be supposed to do, however, would still be qualitatively different from, and in fact diametrically opposed to, their Western counterparts. In the long run, the manager in a capitalist market economy will lose his or her job if the shareholders receive less than the average rate of return obtained in similar businesses run by other managers. The capitalist manager has no alternative; he or she must aim to maximize profits. The manager may try to convince the shareholders for a while to be tolerant, to work with a long-term strategy, but that strategy must bear fruit sooner or later.

The scientific planner in a centrally planned economy is not supposed to maximize profits; rather, his or her job is to decide precisely where and how much loss should be allowed in the total economy. The books still have to be balanced, but this under no circumstances assumes that, in investing your next rouble as a scientific planner, you will be guided by the principle of maximum return. On the contrary: if you would do that, you would make yourself and the very system of centralized planning superfluous. After all, the system of central planning was invented to overcome the anarchy of the market, to abolish the system in which production is oriented towards exchange value rather than use value. The logic of replacing the many owners of property in a capitalist market economy with one owner (the state) in a centrally planned economy was to overcome the domination of techné over telos and create a society in which rationally selected goals would guide the economy.

It is the domination of techne over telos in market capitalist societies that provides the basis for the legitimacy of professionals. Under state socialism, intellectuals belong to the speech community identified by Gouldner as the "culture of critical discourse"—the only ultimate authority to judge the validity of a statement will be reason, making the culture of intellectuals secular and nontraditional. Obviously, when one knows that, under some actually existing socialist regimes, at various times intellectuals could be shot for writing about the "Asiatic mode of production," and a respectable way to conclude a debate in more civilized times was to have sufficient quotations from the sacred texts of Marx and Lenin, one might wonder how "critical" and "rational" such a discourse could be. It is still true, however, that the hegemonic worldview under state socialism was "scientific socialism," with a supposedly scientific ideology that would recognize no authority other than reason.

True, this reason is different from the bourgeois liberal one, which expresses a positivistic worldview. The hegemonic worldview of scientific socialism is holistic, a kind of cosmology. This cosmology claims to be secular, however, and is in fact the first secular holistic cosmology. This secular holistic cosmology (historical/dialectical/materialist/scientific socialism), which claims to be anti-positivist, was taught from kindergarten all the way up to the Ph.D. level in all possible subjects and disciplines. In principle, it gives a priority to the political-ideological component of knowledge in defining what will be accepted as intellectual knowledge. To put this in Parsonian terminology, "value-orientation" is emphasized, in contrast to professionalism where "instrumental-orientation" is emphasized. It is not sufficient to have knowhow to qualify as a "socialist intellectual." You cannot be only an expert; you must be a little bit of a red, too.

In great contrast to state socialist society is market capitalism, where the central ideology of the intellectual stratum is professionalism that even epistemologically questions the possibility of such a holistic cosmology. Professionalism emphasizes knowhow, is based on "formal rationality," and expresses the spirit of legal/rational authority and rules that regulate market economies.

Probably the most efficient way to grasp the sociological significance of professionalism is to approach it historically and to try to understand the kind of change that occurs in the relation between the consumer/client and the person who delivers the goods or services, with the emergence of "professions." When we call someone a professional rather than an amateur, we mean that this person makes a living out of his or her (professional) activity, a meaning that implies a businesslike relationship between the representative of the profession and the consumer. The consumer knows what he or she wants, but needs a professional to produce that good or service at an acceptable standard. To obtain this good or service, the consumer/client will pay a negotiated, market-regulated price/fee. It is assumed in this context that the consumer decides about the *what,* but leaves the question of *how* to the professional.

Let us not forget that the emergence of the classical "professions" in the eighteenth and nineteenth centuries is a rather small-scale operation and one oriented toward a consumer demand, which is not a mass demand but very much the demand of an emerging bourgeoisie. The professional who is emerging in this context is somebody like the architect, solicitor, etc. who will dispense the "culture of critical discourse," making the architect distinct from the bricklayer, the solicitor distinct from the petty clerk. This professional will be similar to other small businesspersons in the sense that he will be likely to work for himself without employing many persons, and will maintain a rather close but businesslike relationship with consumers. The closeness of this relationship will mean that, for example, the architect will not work for an anonymous market but with known customers who will be able to explain quite precisely what they want for their money, but then leave it to the architect to carry out the task.

This businesslike relationship is much different from the patronage relationship between the architect and the feudal lord. The aristocrat rich and powerful enough to bring architects to his or her service was likely to intervene all the time into the activity of the architect (or the biographer, composer, etc). That aristocrat usually had enough self-confidence to know not only what he or she wanted but how it ought to be produced as well. Count Eszterházy, for example, in whose court Haydn lived, was a noted composer himself. Similarly, according to gossip, when Frederick the Great hired Voltaire to write his biography, he inspected Voltaire's work almost daily, and Voltaire, who is said to have been rather fond of chocolate, received his daily chocolate portion only when the King was pleased with his work. The difference between the "architect" and the "bricklayer" was not all that clear.

An architect becomes a professional when sufficient capitalist market demand develops for architects. If this occurs, then consumers will change quite frequently and will cease to be an aristocrat/patron figure and become a bourgeois/client figure.

In this respect, professionalization means an increasing autonomy of the person who delivers the goods or services from the consumer. It is the consequence of professionalization that the consumer appears to be the client of the professional. This bourgeois/client, especially around the time when the first "professions" can be detected historically, is likely to be a nouveau-riche able to tell the professional quite specifically what is needed, but lacking the self-confidence of the aristocratic patron, and will leave the actual execution to the hired expert.

Under market capitalism, the culture of critical discourse will have to take a knowledge form, where the emphasis is placed on instrument-orientation, knowhow, or the technical component of knowledge. The dominant worldview of the professionalized possessors of the culture of critical discourse is positivistic, operating with the assumption that values or the purposes of activity are beyond reason, belonging to the domain of irrational choice. The selection of ends is a product of will. What ought to be left to rationality is to find the most efficient way to reach these irrational, willfully chosen ends. As Weber formulated so clearly in "Objectivity in Social Sciences," genuine rational knowledge cannot be value oriented: it is not the social scientists' task to tell people what they ought to do, only what they can do.

This professionalized expression of the culture of critical discourse is therefore the historical product of the development of the capitalist market economy. It reinforces its logic by complementing legal/rational authority and capitalist class domination. It is important to see that people wanting to be accepted as intellectuals will, under these circumstances, be required to look like "professionals." If not, their knowledge will not be taken seriously. It will not satisfy the criteria of the "culture of critical discourse" and be accepted as "cultural capital" unless it is dominated by the "knowhow" component. You had better learn a bit of SPSS if you want to be accepted as a proper sociologist; you'd better have many footnotes and attach long bibliographies if you want your argument to be taken seriously. It is the great joke of epistemology that you can challenge the underlying positivistic worldview and professionalism, but you have to do it in a very professional way: you have to prove with a lot of footnotes and a lot of facts that there are no facts.

Such a professionalization presumes the relative separation of a political sphere, the existence of a relatively autonomous political state from civil society. Ends are not the business of professionals. Ends are set in the sphere of politics, and the professionalized intellectuals are experts/executors hired to carry out tasks set for them. Intellectuals are only a relatively autonomous stratum in a capitalist market economy. The conflicts and diversities of ends and values find their roots in class differentiation within civil society, which find expression through the class struggles that take place at the level of the political state. When intellectuals work toward differing ends that are the product of class struggles, they express different class interests, and in this sense they will be "in between" classes. Therefore, while professionalism locks intellectuals within the logic of the capitalist system by forcing them to accept an order where telos is subordinated to technē, an order in which exchange value overrules the consideration of use value, professionalism offers them a relative autonomy from basic class determination.

Intellectuals are sometimes reluctant to be so narrowly defined as professionals, and somehow have daydreams about a more noble messianic role. In *Intellectuals on the Road to Class Power,* Konrád and Szelényi argue that the birth of the Marxist revolutionary movement at least in some respects can be explained as a revolt against such a definition of "intellectuals." In advanced market capitalist societies, however, intellectuals are compensated for their willingness to relinquish their claim to their own class power. We suggest that what Gouldner identifies as "cultural capital" is precisely this compensatory mechanism. Intellectuals who are willing to behave like professionals will be allowed to form a relatively autonomous stratum with particularistic stratum interests. This is achieved through creating "professional associations," in charge of "licensing," that create monopolies for their services within otherwise price-regulating markets.

To the extent that intellectuals behave like proper professionals, they are allowed to be involved in the kind of activity that appears to be cultural capital accumulation. Intellectuals under market capitalism are likely to develop a high level of "stratum consciousness" to defend rather petty privileges such as academic freedom; the exclusive right of academics to appoint one another; the right of medical, dental, and legal practitioners to license one another; etc. The relative autonomy of the intellectual stratum of professionalized intellectuals under market capitalism therefore has two meanings. First, they can express different, conflicting interests with reference to civil society by being "organic intellectuals" of one class or the other; second, they can pursue rather efficiently their own particularistic stratum interest in maximizing their income, prestige, and power.

There is empirical evidence that, the more evangelical or messianic intellectuals are, the less willing to accept their professionalized roles, the less likely they are to be awarded the privileges that accompany their relative autonomy. To put it rather provocatively: the more an intellectual is prepared to fit into the hegemonic worldview of the capitalist society, the more he or she will be accepted as properly professional, and, thereby, able to make himself or herself a "scarce" commodity by creating a monopolistic situation. The more disobedient intellectuals—those who for one reason or another are more interested in working out a counterhegemony by accepting the role of "organic intellectuals of the underdog"—will be less likely to share the benefits of the relative autonomy of the professionalized intellectual stratum. Accountants, lawyers, and doctors will be far more successful in forming their "professional associations" to license fellow professionals than will critical philosophers, historians, or novelists. The ability to form such associations as medical associations and dental boards shows a very high statistical correlation with average yearly income and position on the occupational prestige scales.

Social critics such as novelists and social historians, however, must compete on the price-regulating market. They cannot make themselves artificially scarce, but have to sell books in tens of thousands of copies a year to make a modest living. A few will succeed in this endeavor, but many will not. This creates an interesting paradox: while professionalism fits well into the hegemonic worldview of market capitalism and expresses the spirit of an economic system oriented toward private capital accumulation and profit maximization, intellectuals who become professionals are rewarded by being allowed to create monopolies for their services, and those intellectuals who resist professionalization and its ethic are forced to compete for their livelihood on the unregulated market. The more one likes the market and preaches its virtues, the more freedom one has from it. The more one hates the market and attempts to undermine it, the more one is subjected to the market in one's personal existence.

The Increasing Role of the State in Capitalist Economies

All theorists of the New Class in the West have failed because they were unable to specify the structural base necessary for class formation. We hold that these theories do reflect real changes in Western society, just not the ones identified by the theories themselves. The increasing role of the state in the economy does provide a structural basis for a New Class. This New Class, however, cannot be a new *dominant* class so long as the West remains capitalist. Rather it is a new middle class, based on an emergent *state mode of production*, that will stay a middle class so long as Western economies are primarily market integrated.

Gouldner's notion that intellectuals constitute a "flawed universal class" in the West as well as in the East fails scrutiny only to the extent that the West remains a market-capitalist system. However, to the extent that Western societies move away from market capitalism, to the extent that the "professionalism" of intellectuals declines, and to the extent that the relative autonomy of the political state from civil society disappears, the emergence of a New Class of intellectuals in the West becomes possible. And there are indeed trends in contemporary Western capitalisms that point beyond the "capitalist mode of production." Whether or not these changes will mean that intellectuals make a bid for class power depends on the pattern of class alliances that will emerge over time.

The Marxist theory of class that defines classes based on the ownership or lack of ownership of capital assumes the relative separation of the political state from civil society, the sphere of private economy where particularistic class relations are formed. As we saw in chapter 1, Marx (and the Marxists who followed him) insisted that, in the last instance, the state would only reflect and express class relations that are formed at the level of civil society. This Marxian view makes a lot of sense when analyzing the capitalist mode of production, an economic system that operates without much interference from the political state. The analysis begins to run into problems, however, as the political state increasingly interferes in the economy.

The orthodox Marxist theory assumed that the "revolutionary

transformation" of capitalist society, the only possible way to curb the power of the capitalist class, would necessitate the abolishment of the institution of private property via the nationalization of the means of production. Private ownership of the means of production would be replaced with collective ownership, which in practice would usually mean state ownership. In Marxist terms, this assumes a complete intrusion on "civil society" by the "political state." The old state, once the instrument of the capitalist class, would be "smashed" and rendered useless. In its place, a new state apparatus would be created to abolish the "private economy," in any meaningful sense of the phrase. Anarchic private ownership would be replaced by centralized state ownership, and production oriented toward profit making would give way to production following rationally set political considerations in which the political and the economic spheres are merged. According to this logic, without a private economy, no class antagonisms can arise within civil society. There is no real civil society as such under socialist societies; the whole society is politicized. This orthodox position also assumes that capitalism keeps reproducing itself, even if it might take new forms, so long as the "bourgeois state" is not smashed, the private economy is not replaced by state ownership, and the state does not politicize all of society and subordinate the economic system to the primacy of political considerations.

This orthodox position creates a dichotomous typology of modern societies that is extremely simpleminded. The capitalist mode of production, with a separation of the political state and civil society in which classes are formed in civil society, contrasts with socialist societies (sometimes called socialist modes of production with state ownership), with centrally planned economies in which political considerations take priority over economic decisions.

The empirical contradictions of state socialism gave way to political disillusionment with both "nationalization" and "actually existing" socialism. Attempts were made to conceive of an alternative socialist model, which stressed that nationalization did not necessarily imply socialization. Rather, a "self-managing" socialism that was not bureaucratically planned was desired. Under this system, the means of production would not be state owned but, rather, owned and controlled more directly by the "direct producers." Elements of this model of socialism were experimented with in Yugoslavia, and in China after the fall of the "Gang of Four." Empirically, however, we do not know any economic system that is genuinely self-managing, as all actually existing socialisms are, in the last analysis, state socialist.

New Class theorists of socialist societies pointed out that, while old class relations where abolished, new class relations developed. If the theorists who suggest that a New Class emerges under socialism are right, then it is precisely the state's intrusion on the economy that serves as a force to generate class antagonisms. For example, Konrád and Szelényi, in *Intellectuals on the Road to Class Power,* argue that under state socialism the basic class dichotomy is generated by the system of "rational redistribution" and the intrusion of the institution of state planning in the only relatively autonomous economy.

The theoretical payoff to this line of thought is devastating to the orthodox Marxist theory of the state: the political state does not have only to reflect class relations formed within civil society; to the contrary, the state can function as a force that generates class antagonisms. Hegel was right—the state can have genuine autonomy. Marx was also correct; however, the "genuine autonomy" of the state does not imply a universalism expressed by the state versus the particularism expressed by civil society. What we "sublimate" from Marxism and what we have learned from the historical experience of state socialism is that the universalism of the state is only appearance: it is only the universalistic expression of some other particularism.

With this hard-learned lesson in mind, we can now turn our attention to the changes that have been occurring in Western democratic societies for the last forty to fifty years. We argue that the state has gained sufficient autonomy to justify discussion of a "state mode of production"—without, however, arguing that private ownership has "dispersed" or that the capitalist mode of production has been transcended. Rather, we argue that the regulatory function of the state in modern capitalist societies may be such that a subordinate state mode of production that coexists with a dominant capitalist mode of production could conceivably generate new class relations. Figure 2 is cut horizontally into two parts. Above the line, the state is relatively autonomous from the economy/civil society. Below the line, the state should be understood as dominant and the economy/civil society as only relatively autonomous. Above the line are systems that can be conceptualized as modes of production; below the line are systems that are "embedded," meaning that the political sphere/state and the economy/civil society are not sufficiently separated to justify

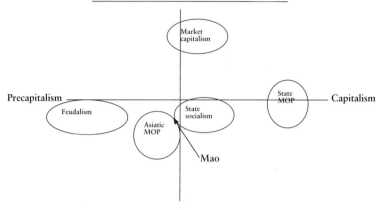

Figure 2. Typology of modern social formations, described by their underlying modes of production/models of economic integration. (MOP = mode of production.)

the "modes of production" label. The empirical realities of societies in the bottom half of Figure 2 cannot be described in any meaningful way with the Marxian "base-superstructure" dichotomy, and therefore they should *not* be called modes of production.

At the very bottom of Figure 2 is the classical "Asiatic form"— or, to use Karl Polányi's slightly modified terminology, the traditional "redistributive economic system"—where the political state is actually indistinguishable from the economy, and therefore its empirical reality cannot be described in terms of an economic base vs. a political, ideological, or cultural superstructure. State socialism is not called a mode of production, either, since it is embedded enough for the base-superstructure model not to be very helpful. Rather, state socialism is a type of "economic integration" that we call the socialist redistributive economy. We assume that the traditional Asiatic form and the state socialist systems intersect, for example in Mao's China of the late 1950s to the late 1970s, in which the relatively self-sustaining and fairly traditional commune system coexisted with a centrally planned and managed modern state redistributive system. What we call state socialism is located closer to the dividing line, since it is assumed that some of these systems, such as those in East Europe, do have some sort of embryonic civil society. The symbol that represents precapitalist modes of production intersects with state socialism as well. Communist-era Poland with its large private agricultural sector is located in this intersection, which is placed below the horizontal dividing line to emphasize the relative underdevelopment of its civil society.

At the top of Figure 2, we have put "Separation of Politics and Economics." Under the capitalist mode of production, the separation of the political state and civil society is historically the most complete of any known system, and all basic class relations are formed within civil society. Therefore, the political, ideological, or cultural sphere can be conceptualized as genuinely separate. Under these circumstances, the hypothesis that these "superstructural" spheres are the expression, "at least in the last instance," of class interests and struggles as formed within civil society, or in the economic base, is a meaningful one. We assume, however, that those empirically existing societies conventionally called capitalist cannot be described in all features as capitalist.

Historically, there will likely be mixtures of capitalist modes of production coexisting with the remains of declining precapitalist modes of production and/or systems of integration, such as Western feudalism. Since the separation of the political state and civil society is the product of a long historical process, the capitalist mode of production gradually produces the separation of the political state from civil society, with the emergence of absolutism, followed by the establishment of constitutional monarchies. Most Western societies, especially up to the 1930s, were located at the intersection of the precapitalist modes of production and the capitalist modes of production. Most Western societies up to the Great Depression still contained a precapitalist environment within themselves, which declined as it was destroyed by the expansion of the capitalist mode of production.

This relationship of capitalism to its precapitalist environment was discussed first by Rosa Luxemburg, in *The Accumulation of Capital*, where she argued that capitalist society must have a precapitalist environment to absorb excess surplus value. This line of argument, however, was most powerfully formulated in Joseph Schumpeter's *Capitalism, Socialism, and Democracy*. First published in 1943, Schumpeter's work is a diagnosis of modern capitalism based on the Great Depression, the Nazi genocide, and no experience of what the welfare state could do in late capitalist formations. Schumpeter concluded, "Can capitalism survive? No. I do not think it can. . . . The thesis I shall endeavor to establish is that the actual and prospective performance of the capitalist system is such as to negate the idea of its breaking down under the weight of economic failure, but that its very success undermines the social institutions which protect it, and 'invariably' creates conditions in which it will not be able to live" (Schumpeter 1976, 61). Later, he elaborates: "the essential point to grasp is that in dealing with capitalism we are dealing with an evolutionary process. Capitalism, then, is by nature a form or method of economic change and not only never is, but never can be, stationary" (82). The "process of Creative Destruction is the essential fact about capitalism. It is what capitalism consists of and what every capitalist concern has got to live in" (83).

However, this "progress entails . . . destruction of capital values in the strata with which the new commodity or method of production competes" (96). Further, "Private management . . . cannot be interested in maintaining the values. . . . All that private management tries to do is maximize the present net value" (97). From all this it follows that "[T]he proposition that a perfectly competitive system is optimal . . . cannot now be held with the old confidence. . . . [T]raditional theory is correct in holding that . . . profits above what is necessary [are] inimical to the growth of total output. Perfect competition would . . . eliminate such surplus profits" (105). "Neither Marshall nor Wicksell . . . saw that perfect competition is the exception" (78). In fact, in an analysis that agrees with Karl Polányi's as advanced in *The Great Transformation*, Schumpeter shows that, historically, free competition almost never existed, but was rather an abstraction that, even during the period of classical capitalism, only existed in the minds of economists. In its classical period, capitalism expanded dramatically not because competition was perfect, but rather because there was a noncapitalist environment that could not compete at all, providing the "surplus profit," supposedly inimical to growth, that is the very essence of capitalism.

Having established that capitalism needs surplus profits to survive, Schumpeter continues his analysis. "Capitalist evolution first of all destroyed . . . the feudal world . . . the world of the artisans . . . the world of the lord and the peasant" (136). For Schumpeter, however, this "victory" for capitalism was fatal: "In breaking down the pre-capitalist framework of society, capitalism thus broke not only the barriers that impeded its progress but also flying buttresses that prevented its collapse" (139). Schumpeter, unlike Luxemburg, does not limit his analysis of the effect of the disappearance of a noncapitalist environment to the economic reproduction of the system, but emphasizes the political and class implications as well.

Schumpeter does not make the errors Marx rightly accused Hegel of making; he does not think that the feudal estates who run the state are a "universal class" above capitalism. Schumpeter is well aware that "the king, the court, the army, the church, and the bureaucracy lived to an increasing extent on revenues created by the capitalist process. . . . As far as that goes, the feudal elements in the structure of the so-called absolute monarchy . . . come in only under the heading of atavism" (136). Schumpeter also establishes that "the French or German experiences with the bourgeois attempts at ruling" proved failures. "[E]conomic leadership . . . does not readily expand . . . into the leadership of nations" (137). Unlike Hegel, Schumpeter is well aware that it is not some universalism of the aristocracy that made them "good rulers." The problem with the success of capitalism is that it is likely to destroy, with the noncapitalist economic environment, all those strata that prevented the polarization of capitalist society along class antagonisms. The aristocracy that exercised political rule for the bourgeois is just an example. Other "protective strata" or "in between classes" would also disappear.

We argue that the increasing intervention of the state into the economy following the Great Depression served the same functions that the precapitalist environment provided for capitalist society in earlier periods. Why characterize this change as the emergence of a "state mode of production" as opposed to making the orthodox Marxist point that the bourgeois state intervenes in the economy in the interest of capitalist reproduction? Further, if indeed there is a state mode of production, in what ways is it different from "state socialism"? Why create a new concept when an old one might do? Is the state mode of production just a step toward state socialism, or can it lead to a society that is neither capitalist nor state socialist? And, most important for this book, how would the emergence of the state mode of production affect class relations in a new socioeconomic formation that would be the coexistence of a capitalist mode of production with a state mode of production? If a new state mode of production eventually emerges, and if it gives rise to a New Class, will this be an intellectual class? If so, how will it relate to the bourgeoisie and the working class? Can it be prevented from becoming a "flawed universal class" that implements a Soviet-style state socialism, and at the same time be prevented from only administering the state in the interest of the bourgeoisie?

We argue that state intervention in the West after World War II reached a qualitatively new stage, one that might justify the use of the term "state mode of production." This new mode of production cannot be meaningfully analyzed in terms of a capitalism-socialism contrast, because it is neither capitalist nor socialist. It can coexist with the capitalist mode of production without challenging private ownership, but in crucial respects it can overrule the logic of capitalist reproduction. Under this new mode of production, intellectuals will attempt to qualitatively increase their power by making a bid for class power, but, as long as the state mode of production coexists with a dominant capitalist mode of production, they cannot become a new dominant class. The question of to what future the new state mode of production will lead contemporary capitalism is an open one: the answer will be given by class struggle.

First, in what ways has state intervention changed sufficiently to warrant the concept "state mode of production" as opposed to simply "economic intervention by the bourgeois state"? State intervention into the economy is no novelty; the state has always intervened. Since the Great Depression, however, the state no longer only exercises legislative/regulatory intervention but budgetary intervention as well. The state disposes of approximately one-third of gross national product (GNP) in the United States and is now responsible for the employment of a large percentage of the labor force, compared to only 5 percent of the GNP and a tiny portion of the labor force before the Depression era. We learn from the Marxist structuralists, however, that increased welfare expenditure, unemployment benefits, public housing, publicly financed urban renewal, or even "nationalizing" otherwise unprofitable but still economically vital enterprises still leaves the state a bourgeois character as long as it follows the logic of capitalist reproduction.

Perhaps this reasoning sufficiently rebutted the need for a post-Marxian conceptualization of the state until the early or mid-1970s. But in the 1970s we were faced with a new situation in the stagflationary crisis, which we see as a fiscal and legitimation crisis of the state. The literature that tries to understand the meaning of this crisis seems to go, or at least lead the way, beyond the conventional Marxian theory of the state. Here, the most important works are Habermas's *Legitimation Crisis* and James O'Connor's *The Fiscal Crisis of the State*. The issues they raise, and the need for a new post-Marxian theory of the state, are far from purely academic. During the 1970s, not only was there a fiscal and legitimation crisis of the state, but a "political crisis of the theory of the state" as well (see Boris Frankel's 1978 monograph *Marxian Theories of the State: A Critique of Orthodoxy*).

In the post-Leninist epoch neo-Marxism cleansed itself from the Leninist obscurantism about the desirability of "smashing the old state apparatuses," and with Eurocommunism the obviousness of the "hundred percent more democratic nature" of the dictatorship of the proletariat a la Stalin, Mao, or even Ulbricht or Kádár lost its appeal to the Western left, even that portion of the left organized in communist parties. This allowed the left, neo-Marxist and other left-wing ideologues, to adopt a post-Leninist and comfortably anti-statist attitude. The dominant Marxist structuralism of the early 1970s was anti-statist. Many open-minded theorists of the left adopted the anti-statist attitudes of the aging Engels. They could show that the state was doing the wrong thing everywhere, subsequently disliked the traditional bourgeois state, disliked state socialism, and at the same time could even "unmask" the social democratic states by showing that, whatever they might do, in the last instance they served the interest of capital.

Knocking the state became a favorite pastime of all social analysts of the left. With great imagination, they showed that increased public housing expenditures were only indirect subsidies to capital, that free education only creates a cheaper labor force for private enterprise, and that even socialized medicine is only a method to keep labor power healthy and exploitable. Those with some experience with Eastern Europe were even inclined to "personify" the state. Konrád's *The Long Walk of Liberty* is a beautiful literary expression of this. The state, irrespective of whether it is "Mr. State" or "Comrade State," became Satan. Capitalist or socialist, left-wing or right-wing, welfare or warfare, it was the "thing" we had to gain our autonomy and freedom from.

With the upsurge of right-wing anti-statism this style of theorizing began losing its credibility, and started to create a lot of political
as well as ideological/theoretical confusion. Beginning with Malcom
Fraser of Australia, Margaret Thatcher in the United Kingdom, and
Ronald Reagan in the United States, and accelerating with U.S. Sena-
tor Newt Gingrich and the violently anti-statist militia movement,
the modest achievements of social democratic reform governments,
and of reform governments in the welfare states, were significantly
rolled back. The anti-state, antibureaucratic rhetoric of the right (for
whose members, the state appears to be the Great Satan, who over-
taxes us, who is inefficient, who wastes our money, who curbs our
freedom, etc.), *clearly necessitates a new theory of the state.*

In principle, it is possible that the Friedmans/Hayaks/Gingrichs
and other anti-statists are correct and even Keynes was wrong. In
that case, what went wrong after the Great Depression was the expansion of state budgets, the creation of welfare states, and the increase
in employment by the state. Perhaps what is needed is to dismantle
the state and go back to the 1920s. But can this be done? Can we
in the United States reduce the share of the state budget from a third
of the GNP back to 5 percent, and lay off the third of the labor force
directly or indirectly employed by the state apparatus?

Were Keynes, Schumpeter, Polányi, and the rest all fools? Was
the experiment with the "welfare state" after the Second World War,
which occurred simultaneously with the longest boom and most
prosperous period in Western capitalism, all a mistake? Alternatively,
perhaps the contemporary ideologues and politicians of the New
Right are cheats, promising goodies they will not, because they cannot, deliver. Capitalism cannot survive properly in its pure form; it
needed the welfare state, after the Great Depression, to take over the
role previously filled by the precapitalist environment. This welfare
state ran into the fiscal crisis of the state, and the stagflationary crisis,
not because there was too much state intervention by the late 1960s/
early 1970s, but because the state still retained its purely bourgeois
character and as such could not in the long run provide a sufficiently
noncapitalist environment for the capitalist mode of production. The
government right to intervene in income distribution, or in the distribution of consumer goods, is not a new mode of production because
it only affects the sphere of distribution, not that of production.

Paradoxically, one possible conclusion is that the solution to the fiscal crisis of the state might not be smaller state budgets and less state intervention but, to the contrary, tighter government control of, and intervention into, the private economy. There is some empirical indication that this might not be as paradoxical as it sounds. After all, the record of the "anti-statist" conservative parties once they get into power is not particularly successful. These conservative politicians have been spectacularly unsuccessful in cutting state budgets. When they cut taxes, they increase indirect taxes; when they fire teachers, they hire police; when they cut expenditures on public health and education, they increase defense spending. They seem to be more successful in redistributing some income from the poor to the rich, from the wage earners to the owners of capital, and from welfare to warfare, but they are less successful in decreasing the percentage of GNP that flows through the government budgets. The state all over the West by the 1990s, after years of neoconservatism, seemed to be more warlike, but not any smaller, than in 1975. There is no indication that George W. Bush's administration is any different, combining the old Reagan formula of tax giveaways and expansion of the military. Is it possible that there is, then, no way back to the 1920s?

But if this time machine of laissez-faire capitalism does not work, we might have to move towards the future instead. If so, we must attempt to understand the role of the state in late capitalist society.

Two of the most insightful thinkers dealing with this topic are Clause Offe and Jürgen Habermas. For Offe, one of the central concepts necessary to grasp the essence of capitalism is "commodification." This concept distinguishes Offe's understanding of capitalism from structuralist Marxist understandings. The major weakness in the Althusserian Marxist-structuralist conception of capitalism is that it tries to understand the essence of capitalism as a set of structural relations. This in the last analysis locks structuralists into a nondynamic view, the well-known and widely criticized circular argument. Whatever happens in capitalism will only reproduce it, making forces pointing beyond capitalism difficult or impossible to identify; it is necessary to break up the whole structure before one can create a new structure; without the "big Bang," nothing will really change.

By focusing on the concept of commodification, Offe focuses on a process, rather than on fairly static structural relationships that just keep reproducing themselves. If the essence of capitalism is actually the process of commodification, then one can argue that capitalism will work efficiently as long as this "commodification" process can expand. This is another way to suggest that capitalism's healthy survival depends on a noncapitalist environment that is not thoroughly commodified, where, through "Creative Destruction" (to use Schumpeter's terminology), noncommodity relations can be destroyed and turned into commodities. With the notion of commodification and de- and re-commodification, Offe can describe in a quite imaginative way the activities of the state in state-regulated capitalism. Using his logic, one can suggest that in a fluctuating manner the state will de-commodify, and at later stages re-commodify, things according to the needs of private capital accumulation.

Moreover, Offe can now consider whether "permanent," or "irreversible," de-commodification can be conceived. If it can be conceived through certain kinds of state activities, then we might meaningfully suggest that the state indeed could move beyond what normally can be expected from the bourgeois state, and gradually build up an irreversibly de-commodified sector of the economy. In this sector, production and/or investment activities are not guided by "exchange value" anymore, but rather the purpose of the activity is to maximize use value.

It is important to realize that such a role for the state is far from identical with state ownership. The state as an owner can behave like a capitalist and own sectors of the economy where the purpose is profitability or exchange value. The state follows this logic when it keeps an industry nationalized as long as it is not profitable, and, when it turns profitable again, reprivatizes it. This would be a classical cycle of de- and recommodification, and a maneuver in the capitalist business cycle. The state might, on the other hand, make commitments to provide certain use values under all circumstances. In a way, these processes point to the possibility of a "state mode of production," by implying state economic activity that is beyond the logic of private capital accumulation and is not guided in the long run by the iron law of capitalist production (according to which, the purpose of production has to be exchange value rather than use value). Socialized health care, a free education system, provision of electricity, water, telecommunication services, etc. are examples.

Habermas, in *Legitimation Crisis*, adopts similar reasoning. He notes that, although earlier state involvement in the economy could have been adequately described as generating or complementing the market, by the 1970s the state seems to be involved in market-replacing activities in advanced capitalist countries. Under classical capitalism, the purpose of involvement in the economy was to create favorable conditions for the creation of capitalist markets. A good example is the British Crown's sending convicts to Australia to help develop a labor market. Once sufficient domestic capital was accumulated, Australian pastoralists could afford market prices for labor power, and convict labor was replaced with a labor market. On other occasions, the state complements markets, and intervenes in the economy, where private capital cannot provide goods and services necessary for the maintenance of capital reproduction and/or private capital accumulation. Examples would be retraining schemes financed by the government, or the creation of public housing projects when capital is more likely to be involved in investment activities where the return to capital is safer and faster.

At some stage, however, the state can conceivably move into replacing market functions, permanently and irreversibly. It can also be conceived—and this makes Offe's and Habermas's type of analysis even more attractive—that market replacement, or irreversible decommodification, might occur not simply out of economic necessity but as the product of class struggle. At least in this sense, it can be conceived as genuinely postcapitalist, as the consequence of a long-term and strategic, rather than merely tactical, victory by the forces of labor. In light of the possible consequences of the Offe-Habermas analysis, Boris Frankel insightfully notes, we have the kernel of a new theory of the state in which we can look at the state as a possible instrument of progressive change without implying that the "smashing of the bourgeois state" and massive nationalizations are absolutely necessary. We can now assume, at least theoretically, that private ownership might survive the establishment of such a reformist state apparatus that might be under the political hegemony of the forces of labor.

The Offe-Habermas reasoning remains, on the other hand, theoretically ambiguous, for from their position one cannot clearly establish to what extent and for how long such a permanent decommodification, or market replacement, is possible by the state without massive state ownership. Is decommodified production or market replacement only conceivable in the state-owned sectors? Theoretically this is vitally important, since without clarifying this issue very clearly one could not decide to what extent a "state mode of production" is simply a Trojan horse that is gradually smuggling into modern capitalism state socialism (possibly with a slightly more human face than the Soviet version, but still with massive state ownership that might well lead to the penetration of civil society by the political state).

Lefebvre's conceptualization of the "state mode of production" (1978) is helpful with these problems. Lefebvre's claim concerning the emergence of a new mode of production, which is not the "capitalist mode of production" and must be called a state mode of production, focuses the analysis precisely on the relation between civil society and the political state. He is very much in harmony with our analysis, which defines as the most crucial characteristic of the "capitalist mode of production" the radical separation of the political state from civil society. Lefebvre also acknowledges that, under such a capitalist mode of production, it is civil society where classes are formed, and the political state that will be the arena of the struggle between these classes.

We have good reason to believe that, as long as the capitalist mode of production is dominant, in the last instance the political state will express the interests of the dominant class. But, with late capitalism, the state gradually gains increasing autonomy from the dominant class, and begins to exercise a new function and re-intrude in a qualitatively new manner in civil society. In Lefebvre's analysis, which is more political-science oriented and rather less informed by political-economy concerns, this state autonomy is more a question of class relations than of ownership. What follows from Lefebvre's analysis is that the new state mode of production emerges not by spreading state ownership, but by changing the nature of political hegemony expressed in the state. In this light, one could conceive a state mode of production that does not assume state ownership and does allow a significant independence of civil society and the existence of a private economy. It is a state mode of production because it does not express an intervention by a state dominated by capitalists, but by a state that genuinely has become autonomous from the dominant capitalist class and does not express the hegemony of the class that is dominant in the private economy. The state now may express the political hegemony of the class that is *dominated* in the private economy.

Iván Szelényi's paper "The relative autonomy of the state or state mode of production" is in many respects an attempt to achieve a synthesis of the analyses of Offe/Habermas and Lefebvre. The crucial common element in these two works is the assumption that capitalism, with the emergence of new types of state intervention in the economy, will probably move into a new socioeconomic formation. This new formation can be most accurately described by the coexistence of a capitalist mode and a state mode of production. The key questions addressed in Szelényi's paper are: public control of what? decommodification of what? replacement of market logic, in what respect? And what is the meaning of such market replacement without state ownership? Precisely where does the political state intrude in the economic sphere?

To sum up Szelényi's argument in one paragraph, a state mode of production is a meaningful concept if the state, in its economic intervention, puts forth an alternative to capitalist logic while regulating expanded reproduction. It will cease to be a capitalist mode of production if the state can gain rights to plan investment decisions without being concerned with maximizing profits. Put another way, the state mode of production will emerge when governments gain the power to control private investment decisions by overruling private corporations' profit-maximizing decisions, in the name of public interest. These actions might include forcing capital investment in areas to create jobs, maintaining employment and income levels, utilizing existing infrastructure, taking into account environmental considerations, etc. In Offe-Habermas terminology, the state mode of production means the replacement of market logic, the decommodification of the investment of private capital (but possibly without the changes in legal ownership of these goods). In Lefebvre terminology, this means the intrusion of political/social considerations into investment decisions. In political terms, this assumes the granting of these investment rights to governments, and possibly trade unions, rights that would be exercised by technocratic central planning agencies perhaps similar to income tax bureaucracies. It is clear that such a state mode of production (private ownership combined with government planning and control of investment decisions) does not exist empirically, at least not yet. But in theory it may be possible.

Having established the possible meaning of a "state mode of production," and why such a mode is neither capitalist (since investments are government planned and not regulated by the profit motive) nor state socialist (since the means of production are privately owned and the state does not rule civil society), we can come back to the central theme of this book: how would the emergence of the state mode of production affect class relations? This question is not as fanciful as it may sound, for the New Class in the West is in a state of development; it is the structural basis underlying much of the theorizing discussed in the previous two chapters. As Gouldner proposed, "there is no reason to suppose that the New Class . . . in the 'West' will 'overthrow' capital. . . . [This class] will [require] hundreds of years of development" (Gouldner 1979, 31).

While a state mode of production does not exist yet, it is in the process of formation. Kernels of such a new state mode of production can be found within the womb of the welfare state apparatus, where a "new middle class" is actually in formation. It is possible to empirically grasp this class's real existence in government welfare or planning bureaucracies. The army of social workers, multiple types of state planners, "evangelistic bureaucrats," academics-as-advisers (to government bureaucracies, trade unions, and political parties) are the agents that may develop into this New Class if political conditions become more propitious. These agents, members of classes and "strata," are not passive products of the development of a "thing" that is the state mode of production, but are social-historical forces. In their struggles for their own interests, in alliance with others with complementary interests, they not only reflect how the new mode of production develops, but play an active role in creating the mode of production in which they genuinely have a New Class position.

In late capitalist formations, intellectuals are more and more split into two types of contradictory class locations or strata. One is the conventional "professionalized intellectual" class that fits so nicely into the logic of Western capitalism; these intellectuals are usually self-employed or function as experts/executives. The other intellectual stratum is most characteristically composed of people working for government policymaking bodies or planning agencies, or as academic advisors to government institutions. This stratum of "bureaucratized intellectuals" may also be understood as the very top of the "new middle class." These intellectuals, as they move closer to class power, will resemble professionalized intellectuals less and less; they will trade some of their cultural capital for political power. As the state mode of production emerges, there will be increasing state and bureaucratic mediation between intellectuals and their "clients." The intellectuals will lose some of the "relative autonomy" and the

clients will lose the consumer power that characterized the old relationship between professionalized intellectuals and bourgeois clients
(see Johnson 1972; Davies 1972).

With the increasing consolidation of the new state mode of production, this upper stratum of the new middle class will gain more
self-confidence and may begin to claim power on its own, and at one
stage may even attempt to enter real bargaining with the dominant
capitalist class, even challenge the power monopoly of the capitalist
class. As (some) intellectuals move toward class power, they become
increasingly different from professionalized intellectuals. Evangelical
bureaucrats are the purest expression of this. They are evangelical
in the same sense as evangelists: they begin exercising "substantive"
or "teleological" rationality, claiming to know not only *how* things
ought to be done, but *what* ought to be done.

This movement from technological to teleological knowledge
can be illustrated with a discussion of the changing position of the
architect/planner. We have already discussed how the architect became a planner with the emergence of market capitalism. With the
emergence of market demand for the architect's services, the architect
was confronted with his or her client: the bourgeois consumer. As the
state mode of production begins to emerge, the architect is asked to
provide services for state housing projects, large-scale urban redevelop-
ment schemes, and so on. The close relationship between the consumer
and the architect begins to disappear; the architect has to design for
an anonymous consumer, and less and less guidance is given to the
architect about what ought to be produced. Now the architect's responsibilities include deciding what the consumer's needs are, and
indeed what needs are legitimate.

As this process unfolds, the architect is gradually changing into a
planner. With the development of planning, of government-regulated
social, spatial, and economic systems, we enter into an increasingly
paradoxical situation. Is there such a thing as a planning profession,
or is this actually a contradiction in terms? Is planning really possible under market capitalism? Jon Gower Davies makes a number
of insightful comments on these issues, although he does not seem
aware of the class implications and theoretical consequences of this
paradoxical development of modern capitalism. Davies notes that, as
long as planners regard themselves as members of a profession, rather
than as evangelistic bureaucrats, they see themselves as not supposed

to make decisions (Davies 1972, 89, 230). Davies also observes, however, that as long as planners do not make decisions, but merely follow the dictates of the market, they are not doing much planning (228). To the extent that planners exercise real planning by overruling the anarchy of the market and the irrational back-and-forth shifting of elected political leadership, they cannot be "professionals" but are agents of an emerging class of intellectuals.

To return to Figure 2, it seems that, above the horizontal dividing line, those societies located in the intersections of modes of production, such as nineteenth-century Britain and contemporary Sweden, are the most stable. Western societies faced their most serious challenges around the 1930s, when they were probably closer to a completely pure capitalist mode of production than before or since. The noncommodified sectors of the economy, such as self-employment in agriculture and in artisan industries, were already largely destroyed, but there was no autonomous state to complement the functioning of the capitalist economy. In this pure capitalist system, classes formed in the private economy stood in plain opposition to each other. The old precapitalist ruling class lost most of its power by the 1930s, but a new evangelistic state bureaucracy still had not developed. Suddenly the bourgeoisie had to exercise political power directly. During this epoch, modern capitalism came the closest in its history to breaking down.

Conclusion

The "Third Way" as the
Fourth Wave of New Class Projects?

In this book we have offered a review and critique of the history of New Class theories. We have sought to sustain two major arguments concerning this body of ideas. First, we have argued that these theories serve as the ideological accompaniment to failed "collective mobility projects" in which various types of intellectuals have sought to advance their own interests by claiming to represent the interests of others. This accounts for the constant rebirth of these theories over the past 150 years or so. Second, we maintain that each of these class projects has failed because it was incomplete in some way. We advanced a theory of successful class formation in the first chapter, which postulated a tripartite requisite: for a New Class to come into being, there must exist a suitable group of people; these people must have the proper consciousness; and, simultaneously, they must have a proper structural position from which to transform society. All New Class projects have failed along one or more of these dimensions.

Our hypothesis in this conclusion is that, with the fall of the Cold War, new versions of New Class projects were born. These projects belong to two types; the first we call "neo-socialist real utopia," and the second we call "Third Way" or "actually existing social democracy." In analyzing these New Class projects, we will offer our own advice, tongue in cheek, to would-be New Class actors about the conditions under which a New Class movement could develop.

Neo-Socialist Real Utopias

We begin our analysis by discussing the thought experiments associated with the neo-socialist real utopia projects. These are not interesting as social movements. None of the real utopias we describe below causes any sleepless nights for the "old dominant class" (or for that matter for anybody—readers of some of these utopias are likely to fall asleep rather than become agitated). But these neo-socialist real utopias are nevertheless of theoretical interest, at least for the tradition from which this book also receives intellectual inspiration. Their very existence demonstrates that the end of the Soviet Union does not imply the end of the socialist idea. After an initial shock, socialist intellectuals began to develop new concepts for the socialist project, this time casting them as "utopian." Wright explains that "real utopias" are "utopian ideals that are grounded in the real potential of humanity, utopian destinations that have accessible way stations, utopian designs of institutions that can inform our practical tasks of muddling through in a world of imperfect conditions for social change" (Wright 1999, 1. Wright's examples include van Parijs 1992; Cohen and Rogers 1995; Roemer 1994; Bowles and Gintis 1999).

These utopias often accept features of modern capitalist society that previous socialists generally claimed would be transcended by socialism. Most important, some of these utopias not only accept markets as the proper economic integrative mechanism, but also in some ways suggest that "free markets" are only possible under socialism, when property monopolies are eliminated. For the purpose of this chapter, the main question we have to ask is whether these utopias are new versions of New Class theory or not? And if so, why do they cut so little ice? Will they ever cut any ice? And finally: they are utopian all right, but in what sense of the term are they real?

Real Utopias

What is the alternative to capitalism, now that state ownership and central planning no longer seem viable? One group of utopian authors makes the key concession to the critics of "old-style" socialism that markets are inherently more efficient at providing information than planning, and therefore must be harnessed to achieve socialist ideals. These are the market socialists. We find some of these authors to be the farthest, among the neo-socialists, from a realistic proposal that could potentially serve a successful New Class movement. Again, while no such actual movement exists beyond the professors contributing to this academic debate, these particular academicians present ideas that are particularly utopian.[1]

The paradigmatic example of this tendency toward the utopian is John Roemer's influential theory of market socialism, as most recently expressed in *A Future for Socialism* (1994). Roemer's utopia involves two structural changes in the economy. The heart of his proposal would be to redistribute wealth and allow markets to create the most efficient outcome. Roemer calls this "coupon socialism" because he advocates that the ownership of corporations would be split up and distributed so that all persons would have equal shares of the economy. People could trade shares in one company for shares in another, but could not sell shares for money or commodities. Roemer would also reorganize corporations into Japanese- or German-style conglomerates headed by large banks with ownership and creditor relationships with a number of companies. The banks would monitor managers to ensure profit maximization.

Roemer claims that, because of the first change, society would be far more equal. Because of the second change, investment funds would be allocated according to profitability criteria, ensuring that they result in the most efficient allocation of resources possible. Thus, resources would be both equally distributed and efficiently employed. The New Class nature of this argument is extremely obvious—capitalists would be literally stripped of all of their wealth (or of all above their equal share—that is, above the level of abstract capital that makes them capitalists), and the control of that property would be vested literally with company managers. Roemer acknowledges this by also referring to his ownership scheme as "managerial market socialism." This has more than faint echoes of Veblen's soviets of engineers or Taylor's scientifically trained managers.

Hypothetically, even if there were the political force to make Roemer's vision a reality, to have this utopia as the goal of the transformation seems a disastrous use of time and energy. It would do nothing to reduce the destructive externalities that are the inevitable side effect of market competition by profit-maximizing agents. The problem identified by Hegel, Saint-Simon, and Marx, and by all

subsequent New Class theorists, the unrestrained competition of actors in civil society, is not addressed by Roemer's utopia. Roemer's
plan also seems to concede too much to procapitalist forces, not even
attempting to soften the alienation inherent in the capitalist productive process. Finally, it is almost certain that even the equality gained
by the wealth redistribution called forth by this utopia would not be
enduring. Eventually, if there actually was trading in these coupon
shares, this would create inequalities even if the shares could not be
sold. People with luck, skill at trading, or insider connections would
wind up with better stocks, which would create a group owning high-
dividend-bearing stocks and a group owning low-dividend-producing
stocks.

Roemer's utopian coupon socialism, while hopelessly fanciful in
Western capitalism, bears a remarkable similarity to "voucher capitalism" as practiced in some postcommunist societies, most notably
the Czech Republic and Russia. In the Czech Republic, citizens were
indeed given the right to buy shares of the nation's productive wealth
for a nominal fee (about one month's wages). While they were allowed
to sell their shares (contra Roemer's plan), most did not, choosing to
invest their shares in investment companies. As a result, the second
part of Roemer's utopia was also created. Large government-owned
banks owned investment companies that in turn had ownership in
many industrial companies. Thus, the economy was divided up into
conglomerates consisting of large state-owned banks with ownership
and creditor relations with many firms. Despite the distribution of
corporate ownership to citizens, the differential endowment of individuals with human capital as well as network connections (social
capital) quickly created a concentrated ownership structure typical
of capitalist economies (see King 2001a, 2001b for illustrations of
this process). And despite the bank-conglomerate form of ownership,
monitoring of managers was notoriously weak and firm performance
was quite unimpressive.

In addition, Roemer's model, as well as other models of market
socialism that envision completely abrogating capitalist ownership,
seems hopelessly utopian to us. Thus, while the theories are certainly
New Class in spirit, they are removed from political and economic
reality. Thus they fail by Wright's own criterion for real utopias:
that they "inform our practical tasks" of transforming the economy
under inhospitable conditions. In contrast, some other new market-

socialist visions are premised only on the redistribution of *some* assets, a program that seems far more likely to have some modicum of success than abrogating all capitalist ownership. Prominent among these advocates, Sam Bowles and Herb Gintis (1999) argue that market integration itself is not a problem for the economy; rather, it is the unequal distribution of assets that makes markets irrational and destructive. They maintain that inequality produces inefficiency because it creates disjunctures among incentive structures. For example, they claim, employee ownership creates more efficient firms because monitoring costs are reduced and incentives to work hard are increased. Other examples of asset redistribution that they advocate include housing vouchers and even school vouchers to increase school responsiveness to parents' needs. What this program boils down to in practice would be some redistribution of assets, and supporting current trends toward employee ownership and charter-style school reform.

The New Class character of this theory is less pronounced than is that of Roemer's version of market socialism. The Bowles-Gintis scheme relies on the state to redistribute some assets, but in ways that benefit all wage earners. However, it is not hard to imagine school vouchers disproportionately benefiting those with more human capital and institutional connections—such as are possessed by professional intellectuals and managerial personnel.

Still, our hypothetical New Class movement might more profitably orient around such an idea, as many people support some redistribution along these lines. Therefore, an incremental increase in economic decisions devolved from both the state and private corporations to citizens could be strived for. However, we feel that a potential New Class movement that relied exclusively on this structure for class formation would probably fall short of reaching its goals. Economic decisions that affect everyone would still be made by individuals maximizing personal interests, making many dynamic externalities—like overcompetition resulting in slow growth—just as likely as under traditional capitalist relations.

This critique of market socialism informs another variant of neo-socialist real utopia: that envisioned by the associationists. These scholars do not seek to redistribute assets as a substitute for having socialist planning mechanisms. Rather, they seek to build alternatives to market integration and private ownership by a revival of the classic Durkheimian position on the desirability of "voluntary associations" as regulators of political and economic processes. Influential examples of this approach can be found in Joshua Cohen's and Joel Rogers' *Associations and Democracy* (1995) as well as in Paul Hirst's *Associative Democracy* (1994). Both advocate devolving as many decisions as possible to the local level, where voluntary but publicly funded organizations would provide "governance." These organizations would overcome the problems of private competition without creating the even greater harm of a repressive bureaucratic state. A real existing example of such associational behavior can be found in organizations that constitute the consumers rights movement (such as Consumer's Union). These organizations serve the interests of New Class actors as well as of other salaried employees, at the expense of the interests of corporations. For instance, university professors and truck drivers have identical class interests as consumers vis-à-vis obtaining information about corporate products that the corporations do not provide. Having associations like Consumer's Union even provides a structure from which intellectuals can exercise some teleological power. The associationists want to increase the size, number, and resources of these institutions by publicly funding them.

The associationist position, like the redistributive position of Bowles and Gintis discussed above, also seeks to build on employee ownership. "The spread of cooperative and mutual ownership would tend to reduce the current gap between the wage worker, who sees the firm as a mere means to earn a living, and the manager, who acts as a steward of external providers of capital. . . . Such forms of ownership would also help facilitate the rational collaboration of firms and public-private partnerships" (Hirst 1994, 121). This worker ownership would, therefore, also give rise to nonprofit financial cooperative endeavors, based on workers' savings, that would facilitate regional economic performance (121). In terms of the sustainability of such a structure, for the transformation sought by our theoretical New Class project, the associationists would seem to have a clear advantage over the market socialists: the associations explicitly seek to overcome externalities caused by market competition.

Still, as we argue in regard to the market socialists, we doubt that the associationist ideal is an adequate basis for the success of a hypothetical New Class movement. We believe that this "real utopia" is unrealistic about the cooperation such a scheme would elicit from corporations. Indeed, the capitalist is quite capable of dominating voluntary associations. Most important, as critics can argue, these associations would only go part of the way in neutralizing capitalists' trump card, the structural dependence of the state on capitalist accumulation. The publicly funded associations would be equally dependent on the investment decisions of corporations for their funding.

The Third Way, or Actually Existing Social Democrats

The irony of history is that, soon after the fall of the Berlin War II, the neoliberal political forces began to lose political ground. While George Bush the First claimed credit for victory in the Third World War, he lost the election to the New Democrat Bill Clinton. Thatcherism suffered a humiliating defeat from the New Labor Tony Blair, and the German reunifier Helmut Kohl was unseated by the New Social Democrat Gerhard Schroeder. Ten years after the end of the Cold War, thirteen out of the fifteen governments of the European Union were led by social democratic or socialist parties. In fact, it is the neoliberal center right that is in a deep crisis in many advanced countries of the West. This is arguably the single most important political development for decades. The loss of a sense of mission by the center right gives rise to the far right from Austria to Germany, from Italy to France.[2]

What is the reason for the crisis of the right and the rise of New Social Democracy? And what is New Social Democracy, neoliberalism in sheep's clothing or the most recent wave of a New Class project? Our next task here is to try to answer this question.

First, what is the reason for the crisis of neoliberalism? "The economy, stupid," as then-President Clinton might have put it. By the early 1990s, it appeared that the neoliberal economic policies were not working, and the electorate began to punish the neoliberals by backing the politicians that the reformed Democratic, Labor, or Social Democratic parties began to offer.

A quick look at the economic record under the neoliberals, led by Reagan and Thatcher, demonstrates the limits of this program. The neoliberal economic policy objectives were to limit credit and government borrowing in order to eliminate inefficient firms slowing down the economy. They would also eliminate "supply-side" obstacles to growth, such as strong unions, high wages, heavy taxes, and "too much" government regulation.

They did indeed eliminate some supply-side constraints, most spectacularly on the labor front and in the realm of taxation. However, monetary restriction seemed to weed out good firms as well as bad, and by the summer of 1982 there was the deepest recession since the 1930s. Real interest rates were at record highs and profitability plummeted, especially in the manufacturing sector, where profitability was 50 percent less than in 1978. Most important politically, unemployment skyrocketed to 11 percent.

Reagan's success, the so-called Reagan boom, ironically succeeded when he abandoned the monetarist experiment and primed the economy with a massive arms buildup and tax cuts. This fiscal expansion was matched on the monetary front as Paul Volker expanded credit.[3] However, the neoliberal emphasis on decreasing taxation rates and labor costs was not abandoned. In essence, Reagan led an antiworker, pro-military, pro-corporate-rich, Keynesian explosion. Overall taxation as a percentage of GDP (gross domestic product) decreased 5.3 percent from 1980 to 1992, and total wages and salaries as a percentage of total expenditures fell by 9 percent. The U.S. economy recovered from the recession, but the recovery was not particularly impressive. The United States grew at an average rate of only 1.33 percent from 1981 to 1992, as measured in growth of GNP per capita. This was significantly less than the Japanese growth of 3.33 percent and about equal to the French rate of 1.42 percent. Unemployment in the United States averaged 7.33 percent, up from the 6.5 percent of the Carter years and the 5.8 percent of the Nixon-Ford era.

This growth was the result of the most massive Keynesian expansion in the nation's history. Naturally, as a result of these tax breaks and military spending, there was a massive increase in the weight of the state in the economy. The federal government deficit as a proportion of GDP averaged 4 percent in the 1980s (more than 5 percent in 1982–87), compared to 2.3 percent for the 1970s and 1.1 percent for the 1960s. In 1995 dollars, total government spending increased a massive 27.3 percent. This was paid for with debt, primarily, and the central government debt as a percentage of all debt ballooned from 27 percent in 1981 to 50 percent in 1992. There was generally a massive increase of borrowing of all types. From 1982 to 1990, total borrowing (public and private) was 22.1 percent, compared to 17.4 percent for 1973–90 and 11.8 percent for 1960–73 and 8.5 percent for 1952–60. While moderate growth levels were being achieved through massive transfers from the government to the private sector, investment growth managed to fall. The average annual growth of net capital stock in the private business economy fell to 2.9 percent, from 3.4 percent in 1973–79 and 4.3 percent in 1965–73. Overall, the economy seemed in major decline. The overall competitiveness of the U.S. economy deteriorated, and, as a result, the trade deficit skyrocketed; it went from a positive $5 billion in 1981 to a staggering negative $168 billion in 1986 before declining back to a negative $52 billion in 1992 (in 1999 US$). Further, neoliberal financial deregulation also seemed to lead to financial instability, as financial crises started occurring with disturbing frequency (crises occurred in Argentina in 1980–82, Chile 1981–83, Uruguay 1981–84, and Israel 1980–83). If anything, it seemed that resources "trickled up," as the U.S. government would step in to guarantee the losses of major financials.

As we mentioned, even though the economic growth seemed weak and premised on debt, Reagan and Bush did deliver in terms of wages and taxes. The rate of taxes on nonfinancial corporations fell massively. This tax averaged 40 percent between 1967 and 1980. Between 1980 and 1990, it fell to 26 percent.[4] The story is similarly clear on the labor front. The pivotal event was the destruction of the air traffic controllers union (PATCO). After this defeat, the retreat of labor was underway. The absolute numbers of unionized workers fell an average of 817 thousand per year between 1979 and 1983, 361 thousand per year between 1983 and 1987 (Brenner 1998, 191). During this same period, there was a massive increase in unfair labor practice claims, even as workers had seemingly lost their capacity to fight back. From 1982 to 1990, the average number of strikes with more than one thousand workers fell to about 60, compared to 142 from 1979 to 1983, 280 for 1973 to 1979, and 325 for 1950 to 1973 (191).

Not surprisingly, with organized labor in retreat, wages fell dramatically. Hourly real wages and salaries (excluding benefits) fell at an average annual rate of 1 percent (Brenner 1998, 192). Compared to rates during the Carter administration, average wages for nonsupervisory workers actually decreased by 5.1 percent (from $13.51 to $12.82, in 1998 dollars). Indeed, these wages were down 2.6 percent over the Nixon-Ford years. The average wage for the bottom percentile of wage earners decreased a full 10.1 percent compared to the Carter years ($6.32 to $5.68, in 1998 dollars) (Pollen 2000, table 5). Considering that the consumer price index increased 53.33 percent during this period, the real wages of these workers declined dramatically. While wages fell, inequality skyrocketed. The ratio of the ninetieth percent to the tenth percentile in wages increased 13.9 percent from the level of the Carter administration. Predictably, the individual poverty rate increased a massive 17.6 percent after the Carter years (from 11.9 percent to 14 percent) (Pollen 2000, table 5). It generally became clear that very little ever trickled down.

It is quite possible that the inability of the neoliberal movement to deliver what was promised led to a severe voter backlash. After more than a decade of electoral success, the neoliberal movement started to run into problems. In the heart of the neoliberal world, the United States and England, new versions of the Democratic and Labor parties, explicitly advocating a "Third Way," came to power. In a loose sense, this political program has appealed to the New Class and is analyzable as a New Class movement. New Democrats have had solid support among intellectuals and the technocratic intelligentsia, and at times genuine New Class actors, such as Robert Reich and Laura Tyson in the United States and Anthony Giddens in Britain, have served as the advisors/ideologues of these movements. The New Labor and New Democrats created a broad class alliance including labor, minorities, women, and, in the United States, Reagan Democrats.

Before considering the rhetoric of the politicians who led this movement, we should review the most prominent theorist of the Third Way, Anthony Giddens. His "third way programme" can be analyzed as a neosocialist real utopia. Giddens, like Roemer and other market socialists, seeks to increase the realm of "choice" and reliance on the market for meeting the traditional goals of the left—in this case, the goal of social democracy. While the market socialists sought to redistribute resources to make markets function better, Giddens saw a need to substitute market solutions for traditional welfare programs. According to Giddens: "A high rate of business formation and dissolution is characteristic of a dynamic economy. This flux is not compatible with a society where taken-for-granted habits dominate, including those generated by welfare systems. Social democrats have to shift the relationship between *risk* and *security* involved in the welfare state, to develop a society of 'responsible risk takers' in the spheres of government, business enterprise and labour markets" (Giddens 1998, 100; emphasis in original). This position moves extremely close to the culture-of-poverty position long espoused by conservatives, stating, "Leaving people mired in benefits tends to exclude them from larger society" (110). Redistribution should instead take the form of investing in human capital, to "as far as possible replace 'after the event' redistribution" (101). Along with this reform of traditional welfare redistribution, new social democrats should focus on local, or community-based, approaches (110).

Is Gidden's theory a New Class theory? In a weak sense, it is. What better way to advance the interests of intellectuals than by generally increasing government expenditure on education—which will provide new jobs for intellectuals while creating more intellectuals as well. However, again, we believe that any such New Class movement based on education reform to provide the structure to transform the current system of corporate capitalism would be doomed to failure. Indeed, this would be just more of the same—and it would not increase the "teleological power" of intellectuals, but rather just create more professionals. This would arguably be beneficial to those members of the working class and excluded minorities who might become professionals under such an expanded system, and may even be beneficial for the economy at large by encouraging business formation in high-tech or high-value-added sectors. Still, no New Class formation would follow from such a vision of Gidden's "investor state."

What of the actual agents leading this hypothetical New Class movement? What political program was advocated by Bill Clinton, Tony Blair, and Gerhard Schroeder? There must have been something distinctive about their appeal that distinguished them from the traditional left. Critics might charge that their appeal lay in highlighting (and co-opting from the right) certain conservative themes that had long resonated in Western, particularly Anglo-American, political culture—the very same themes that promote the ethic of individualism that has long buttressed capitalist legitimacy. Most prominently, Clinton and Blair gave up defending the traditional welfare state. Indeed, like the neosocialists discussed above, the New Democrats made drastic revisions of left-wing or democratic visions of what the state could accomplish.

One thing is clear, this New Social Democracy or new Third Way is very compatible with corporate capitalism. For example, Schroeder and Blair coauthored a paper on the future of social democracy that bluntly states, "We have to create conditions under which existing corporations can prosper and new businesses can form and grow." Further, "the weaknesses of markets have been overestimated, the strengths underestimated," and what is really needed is the "entrepreneurial spirit." If that isn't clear enough, the two leaders state that "Modern Social Democrats must be the advocates of the bourgeoisie" (Schroeder and Blair 1999).[5] The classic liberal emphasis on choice and individual responsibility at the expense of collective responsibility for structural problems was explicitly embraced from the very beginning: "Modern Social Democrats want to transform the safety net of claims into a launching pad for individual responsibility."[6]

And yet, at least originally, the position was not identical to the right-wing position. For example, Clinton's "Putting People First" campaign manifesto stressed public investment and an active partnership between government and the private sector. Clinton had stated, in response to arguments that he should just cut the deficit, "All spending is not the same. There is plainly a difference between spending money and investing it. We have got to change the character of federal spending"—toward investment.[7] Clinton was advocating a kind of "investor state" in which, unlike the ideal of Monetarists and Keynesians, the state should intervene in specific ways to overcome specific problems in the economy.

Does not the record reveal that the Third Way was the right way, all along? Did not the New Democrats not only win political power, but deliver the economic goods? Was Fukuyama ironically trumpeting the wrong "end of history" just as the real "end of history" emerged? In support of this position, one could argue that the United States during the last half of the 1990s experienced the longest economic boom in history, with inflation almost nonexistent, economic growth dynamic, and unemployment at a thirty-year low (averaging 5.8 percent between 1993 and 1998, down from the 7.1 percent of the Reagan-Bush eras [1981–92]). Even the picture for those at the bottom perhaps improved, overall. The poverty rate shrank to 13.8 percent from 14 percent (through 1989), which remained significantly greater than the rate during the Carter years of 11.9 percent. Real wages increased for the first time in two decades. The percentage of the population on welfare was declining (it had fallen by one-half since 1994), as was teenage pregnancy, the crime rate, and drug use). For the first time in decades, the nation had a balanced budget, and for the first time in its history it would start reducing the national debt. Even productivity growth was restored in the two years 1998 and 1999, averaging 2.9 percent. However, overall the average productivity growth of 1993 to 1999 was 1.81 percent, which was actually lower than the 1.86 percent average from 1981 to 1992 (Bureau of Labor Statistics, data extract, 5 May 2000).

This success was achieved by an increase in inequality, as the growth did not reach down to the very bottom. The most that can be said in defense of the Third Way is that the *rate of increase in inequality slowed* compared to the neoliberal years. This was not a record to be proud of, especially given the "longest economic boom ever." The average wage for nonsupervisory workers actually fell a bit in constant dollars, the average wage of the tenth percentile was also down from the Reagan-Bush era. The ratio of the ninetieth to the tenth percentile in wages actually increased by 7 percent. And this was only wages, and excluded gains in wealth through the stock market. Thus, absolute levels of inequality in the United States actually increased under Clinton in comparison to the Reagan and Bush era. In the tenth percentile of income earners, there was no gain from 1996 to 1998. In the fifth percentile, the average income, including the value of food stamps and housing subsidies, fell to $6,400 in 1997 and 1998, down from $6,900 in 1995 and 1996 (all figures in 1997 dollars). Indeed, after nearly eight years of Clinton's new Third Way, *the real median net worth of families fell significantly* from 1989 to 1998 (by 9 percent for families headed by persons under thirty-five— a fall from $9,900 to $9,000). By the end of Clinton's "boom," the minimum wage did not bring a full-time worker with one child even above the poverty line. There were 11 million more people without health insurance than at the beginning of the boom. There were more people living in extreme poverty (defined as less than half the poverty level) than at the beginning of the boom. The portion of the homeless consisting of families with children had increased from 27 percent to 37 percent in five years. Meanwhile, in 1999, Wall Street bonuses were up by a record 18 percent.

Of course, supporters of the Third Way could argue that the problems of the Clinton administration were not the New Democrats' fault, but rather the inevitable price of the inability to push the full Third Way program through a hostile Congress. Thus, the positive accomplishments were claimed to be the result of Clinton's policies, and the negative achievements the fault of the Republicans.

Should Clinton have been blamed for the increase in the number of Americans without health insurance, or should the Republicans who blocked his reform?

In response, critics of Clinton could counter that Clinton and the Third Way supporters actively took steps that hurt the poor—most importantly through "welfare reform." This issue was not forced only by the Republicans, who probably never believed they would get their way on it. The reform (really, abolition) was perfectly congruent with the metatheoretical position that embraces "choice" and "responsibility" over old-style welfare provisions.

In this light, the lower welfare rates were not such an unambiguous success. In the United States, "welfare reform" serves to shift the poor from "welfare" to "work." Thus it explicitly seeks to increase the "commodification" of labor, in Offe's sense. The empirical results from Clinton's reform have so far confirmed this analysis. Welfare-to-work programs succeeded in moving many recipients into work (though not as many as it might seem, since many former welfare recipients were working but not reporting income). However, even in the most favorable situation possible (in Wisconsin, a state with robust economic growth and a tight labor market), the program moved the poor into jobs at the cost of making the life of the average poor person more difficult and making the fate of the worst-off poor people even more worst-off. For example, demand at soup kitchens doubled.

Evidence from a broader-based random sample throughout the country of all single mothers, not just those on welfare, gave similar findings. Christopher Jencks and Joseph Swingle argue that, although the number of welfare recipients has fallen since 1994, almost one-half of single mothers would have left the rolls anyway because their children got older, they found jobs, or they got married. But they are no longer replaced, because states have made it much more difficult to get on the rolls.[8] Further, while most who leave welfare find jobs, a large minority do not (Jencks and Swingle 2000, 38). It is therefore no surprise that the poorest had less money. The fifth percentile of income averaged $6,400 in 1997 and 1998, down from $6,900 in 1995 and 1996 (these figures, all in 1997 dollars, include value of food stamps and housing subsidies). Kathryn Edin and Laura Lein, in *Making Ends Meet*, have shown that individuals earning in the fifth percentile typically work off the books or receive gifts from family. Once they have been kicked off welfare and must declare their actual earnings, they have significantly less total money. Also, once they work, they have to pay for transportation to work, childcare, and office clothes (Edin and Lein 1997, 38). They also have declining access to healthcare. A single mother on welfare would automatically qualify for Medicaid; once she is kicked off welfare, this is no longer the case. Finally, there is a major problem in providing childcare for these women's children; thus, "welfare reform" could end up hurting children even if it did help parents.

What Did the "Third Way" Do?

When Clinton came into office in 1993, the recession of 1991–92 was over. The recession helped Clinton get elected, but he also inherited the debt that resulted from the Keynesian explosion of the Reagan and Bush years. Net government debt as a percent of GDP went from 21.8 percent in 1980 to 46.4 percent by 1993. Clinton, as noted above, initially advocated state investment in the economy. To this end, he proposed a modest $16 billion stimulus package, which could not pass Congress. After this, he made balancing the budget the central goal of his administration. He signed legislation in the summer of 1993 that Congress could not increase expenditure anywhere without cutting an equivalent amount elsewhere. From 1992 to 1996, the federal budget as a percent of GDP fell, from 4.7 percent for 1992–93 to 1.4 percent in 1996 and to 0 percent in 1997, and generated a surplus thereafter. Clinton's fiscal responsibility was matched by a restrictive monetary policy. The Federal Reserve Board raised interest rates, between February 1994 and 1995 alone, by 3 percent.

The argument that the New Democrats were merely neoliberals in sheep's clothing goes beyond arguing that they were more successful budget-balancers than were Republicans. The pressure on organized labor continued, and union density and strike activity continued to fall. Of course, defenders of Clinton could argue that labor declined not because of the New Democrats but because of the globalization of the economy.

Can we conclude that the New Social Democrats are the agents of change and the Third Way the revolutionary consciousness the neo-socialists have been seeking? Clearly, the answer is no. The electoral victory of the New Social Democrats during the 1990s signals the potential for such a movement; it is not the movement itself. The new Social Democrat and New Labor parties of Blair, Clinton, Schroeder,

Jospin, and others are no more the agents of this new movement than the Communist Party was the agent of real socialism. Just as most of the Western left insisted that the socialism of the Soviet Union was so far in practice from socialist ideals that it was not "real socialism" but only "actually existing socialism," we insist that the New Social Democrats should be considered "actually existing new social democrats." In spite of their rhetoric of the Third Way, it is far from clear that they represent a revitalization of social democratic forces. Critics could find ample evidence that the New Democratic and New Labor parties have accommodated the same interests as have the neoliberals and conservatives: the dominant corporations and financial institutions and the people who own them. Further, while the Third Way advocates claim to maintain their allegiance to the values of the left, they have made the crucial metatheoretical concession to the right in unconditionally espousing voluntary action and choice in explaining social outcomes.

These critics would point out that, in terms of who the agents are in the new governments, there seems no substantial change away from filling these spots with people from the highest echelons of the corporate and financial elite. This is probably more the case in the United States, less the case in Germany. However, even in the latter case, officials in the government who can be seen as defenders of old-style social democratic programs, or newer anticapitalist ideologies based in ecology, have been purged, as demonstrated by the replacement of the German Finance Minister Oscar Lafontaine with the super-rich entrepreneur Hans Eichel, who proceeded to reduce social spending and moved to introduce more corporate-friendly taxation laws estimated to provide an $8–15 billion tax break for large corporations.[9]

Thus, how do we evaluate the economic performance of the New Democrats? Does their countries' good economic performance have anything to do with a new social democracy? It is hard to find evidence for this position—quite the contrary. Paradoxically, it is more plausible that Clinton and Blair demonstrated the correctness of the neoliberal formula, since it was they, ironically, who actually implemented the conservative program, because the neoliberals were too busy being military Keynesians and giving away vast sums of money in tax breaks to the rich. The main argument against this position is that the economic success of the Clinton administration had nothing to do with anything that Clinton did so much as with structural change in the economy induced by new information technology. However, Clinton defenders could argue this point: the Clinton 1992 program addressed the central issues of the new economy, from the internet to publicly funded research, and public funding of research increased substantially during the Clinton administration. However, others claim that the "new economy" was very long in the making, going back to public funding of research and education since World War II, and protectionist measures in decades past (like the anti-dumping measures taken against the Japanese in semi-conducters in the 1980s) (Bluestone 2000; Chomsky 2000). Further, according to Bluestone, there is a relatively long period of learning during which a new technology will not be fully utilized; thus, the benefits of the "new economy" are unlikely to have been caused by the Third Wayers (Al Gore did not invent the internet—but he is right that the government did).

Reform of the Pension System

The issue of pension reform has been squarely thrust on the national agendas of much of the advanced capitalist world, and it holds particular interest for us because it gets to the heart of controversies about how the economy should be organized. Neoliberals are leading a new charge to privatize the social security system. George W. Bush made creating private pension funds out of some portion of Social Security a major platform for the 2000 presidential elections (although the stock market crash has effectively killed this idea). However, this position has been put forward in the advanced capitalist countries more generally. For example, in 1994 the World Bank released an influential report, *Averting the Old Age Crisis*. Like Bush, the World Bank argued that the increase in the average age of the population will eventually mean too many people collecting pensions on the contributions of too few earners. This will require a greatly increased rate of payment to fund then-current recipients, eventually becoming unsustainable and bankrupting the system.

The World Bank advocated transforming pay-as-you-go systems into individually funded pensions invested within the private sector. This would decrease the amount that individual workers would have to pay because investments in equity markets historically yield much higher returns than the placement of surplus funds in low-yield public bonds (which in essence subsidize current expenditures). In addition, such pensions would provide additional resources for investments, thereby spurring increases in labor productivity and thus economic growth. These benefits, such advocates maintain, would outweigh any disadvantage stemming from higher administrative charges in the private sector, as well as the resources that would have to be spent on nonlabor productivity to enhance competition, an expenditure that would not be present with a state-owned scheme.

The Third Wayers also break with the traditional Democratic or labor position, which supports publicly funded provisions. Defenders of the current system[10] hold that the demographically induced crisis of the Social Security system is a myth. For example, Rasell and Faux (1999) argue that the projections of disaster do not add up. According to the 1999 Social Security Trust Fund, which every year is mandated to project the fund's finances for seventy-five years, there will be no problem making payments until 2034, after which the fund will still have enough money to pay 73 percent of benefits in 2035 and 67 percent of benefits in 2075.[11]

Thus, some additional funds will be necessary. How much will this cost? It is estimated that the increased cost of Social Security will equal 2.5 percent of GDP over the next seventy years. This hardly seems earth-shattering. Education as a percent of GDP increased almost 3 percent from 1946 to 1966. Social Security expenses increased by a similar percentage between 1960 and 1995, without destroying the economy. The fund will have to redeem $2.8 trillion of the Treasury Bonds that make up its surplus. But the economy is projected to grow from $8 trillion in 1997 to $24 trillion in 2020 and $38 trillion in 2030. There is no reason that the United States cannot absorb this expenditure. Moreover, this shortfall could easily be paid for by progressive taxation that would hardly be excessive and seems easily justifiable on the grounds that people are living longer and thus their contributions to Social Security taxes should be greater. Critics could also argue that there is ample room for cutting defense expenditures—and now that the United States spends more than the thirteen next largest militaries combined, the "peace dividend" could be used to pay for Social Security shortfalls.

According to Faux, the president of the Economic Policy Institute (a left-Keynesian think tank), a full 89 percent of this shortfall could be raised by "raising the 'cap' on taxable wages back to the level it was in the early 1980s, $97,000 in 1998 dollars." A modest payroll tax, indexed to increases in longevity, could also help pay for the increase: to pay for the rest of the shortfall, this tax would only have to be 0.02 percent for both employer and employee contributions (Faux 1998).

What are the assumptions of the estimated shortfall predicted by the Social Security Trust Fund? First, it reports that two-thirds of this deficit will be caused by the projected increase in life expectancy. Only one-third is attributed to the assumption of a slowdown in the rate of growth as a result of population growth, and a lowering of productivity growth to a rate lower than that of the past seventy-five years. While the first assumption, on longevity increase, seems undeniably sound, the latter assumption seems overly pessimistic. Even accepting this gloomy scenario, it does not seem that the shortfalls would be such a burden on the economy. The Fund's own pessimistic projection of GDP growth is that GDP will increase from $8.4 trillion in 1998 to only $14.2 billion by 2035. In addition, real wages are projected to rise 17 percent. Thus, even in a very pessimistic scenario for growth, the country would be much richer, and should be able to pay for the shortfall without great difficulty.

What is the position of the "actually existing social democrats" on how to deal with this system? Clinton, while still the leader of the most powerful new democratic party in the world, would not argue for increasing taxes by even the relatively modest amounts that the above analysis indicates would be necessary to fund the gap. This is understandable, since Clinton/Gore and indeed all New Social Democrats made balancing the budget and fiscal austerity the cornerstone of their economic policy—and the chief way they wished to distinguish themselves from the Republicans. In essence, they have sought to be more "conservative" than the conservative party itself.

Clinton's proposal was that $2.7 trillion be transferred to the Fund over fifteen years out of projected budget surpluses. This would extend the Fund's solvency to 2049. Clinton also suggested that 20 percent of the $2.7 trillion be invested in the stock market. These investments would be limited to 14.6 percent of all Trust Fund assets, and would average 3.4 percent of the capital on the stock market over the next fifty years. The Clinton administration estimated that the stock market would average 6.75 percent yield as opposed to 2.8 percent from the bonds, bringing an additional six years of Social Security funding. Gore espoused a similar program.

The Republicans countered with their own proposal, which centered on the privatization of Social Security. An example is the Feldstein-Samwick plan, which seeks to establish individual accounts funded by federal surpluses. Upon a person's retirement, the individual fund would be turned into an annuity. Bush has announced a commitment to some version of a private plan.

The proposals have different advantages and disadvantages, and their relative desirability depends to a significant extent on assumptions about economic growth and the returns on equity investments. For the purposes of this chapter, we need not actually take a position on the inevitability of the Social Security crisis. However, we argue that any hypothetical New Class movement might well consider using Social Security investments in the stock market as a structural platform for a movement. Indeed, just as many advocates of Social Security privatization desire the massive opportunities for profits for the financial service providers that would handle these individual accounts, these same advocates seem horrified by the potential for a non–individually based investment of retirement funds into the equities market. Milton Friedman declared in the *Wall Street Journal,* "I have often speculated that an ingenious way for a socialist to achieve his objective would be to persuade Congress, in the name of fiscal responsibility, to (1) fully fund obligations under Social Security, and (2) invest the accumulated reserves in the capital market by purchasing equity interests in domestic corporations" (26 January 1999). Perhaps this is not simply the usual hyperbolic rhetoric of archconservatives and libertarians, but the recognition of an unforeseen development in the ownership patterns of contemporary capitalism that could provide an additional structural base for a New Class movement, a development that seems as if it must be seized if any New Class movement could ever hope to be successful. It could be the structural base that the reviewed neosocialists theories lack.

Using pension funds to collectively purchase equities could provide the structural basis that a hypothetical New Class movement could use to maintain class formation. Pension ownership could be limited by law to remain in national bounds or be used to stave off financial speculation. For example, in Chile these funds were at first required to invest exclusively within Chile, although this limitation was, as of 1998, relaxed to allow a limit of 10 percent of assets to be held abroad (Blackburn 1999, 44). Thus, the New Class would have a weapon against capital flight and capital strike, and an instrument that could be used to restructure the economy.

Unlike the schemes of various market socialists, this transformation of the economy along the lines of a potential New Class movement is already well under way. Contemporary capitalism has witnessed the international mega-mergers of firms that were formerly national oligopolies. Thus, the economy is more and more "planned" within huge hierarchies by New Class actors such as technical and managerial workers. These giant hierarchies are now owned mostly by institutional owners, the biggest portion of which is held by labor and especially other noncapitalist classes (such as the new middle class) in the form of pension funds. Institutional ownership in the United States, for example, exploded from about 12.6 percent of all stock ownership in 1960 to 47 percent in 1996, with pension funds accounting for 26 percent of this ownership (Ambachtsheer and Ezra 1998, 224–25).

This development of employee pension ownership occurred over the last two decades, as the long-term economic downturn in profitability rates around the world since 1973 induced employers to find ways to limit the growth of wages. One such method was to encourage employees to take shares in firms in lieu of wages (Minns 1996). By 1994, total world assets in pension funds totaled $10,000 billion (in U.S. dollars). This is equal to the value of all companies listed on the world's three largest stock markets. Already in 1976, pension funds owned 25 percent of the equity capital of U.S. businesses (Drucker 1976, 1). By 1994, U.S. pension fund assets were worth more than $600 billion, more than 60 percent of the nation's GDP and more than one-third of the stock market; in Australia, state-run pension funds in 1995 were equal to 45 percent of the GDP; in Singapore, they were worth 75 percent of the GDP (Minns 1996, 50). In the United Kingdom, pension funds owned 27.8 percent of all shares, insurance companies another 21.9 percent in 1994, up from 6.4 percent and 10 percent, respectively, in 1963.[12]

This unprecedented evolution of ownership creates a *potential* structural basis for New Class power (or, more precisely, "employee" power—a combination of "working class" and "New Class" actors' collective ownership of the means of production). This basis is only potential, because currently employee ownership does not bring with it any control rights. Rather, in the United States, the United Kingdom, and Switzerland, the rise of institutional ownership actually increases the power of the traditional financial institutions that advise and administer these funds. Indeed, in 1996, Morgan Guarantee, Bankers Trust, Citibank, Mellon Bank, and Harris Trust and Savings Bank held 80 percent of these assets in the United States and the United Kingdom (Minns 1996, 47). Dialectically, perhaps, the rise of employee ownership increases the wealth, power, and control of those finance capitalists who are at the very heart of the capitalist class (Zeitlin 1974; Scott 1997). These financial institutions are interested only in managing their investments to maximize short-term profitability.

We should therefore distinguish between "actually existing wage-earner ownership" and a future political strategy of giving real substance to such ownership rights in a way that can correct for the problems of capitalist ownership. While the control of these ownership rights are effectively captured by the super-rich that control the biggest financials that serve as the asset managers of pensions, control could be democratized without actually taking away any legal ownership rights, just by altering the way ownership rights are managed. Thus, there is a perfectly legal and democratic way for this ownership to be transformed.

The collective ownership of assets allows for the exercise of teleological power by intellectuals. For example, the obvious New Class actors composed of teachers and college professors, as represented by TIAA-CREF, are collectively among the largest owners in the world. The Teachers' Insurance and Annuity Association and the College Retirement Equities Fund held over $140 billion worth of assets in 1996. The California Public Employees Retirement System is worth more than $100 billion. Thus, teachers collectively are a huge owner of capital. If these existing ownership rights were brought under the real control of their legal owners, capitalist ownership of the means of production would be at least partially limited. To run with this fantasy: there is nothing that could legally stop all college professors with their pensions in TIAA-CREF from changing TIAA-CREF policy to refuse to invest in companies that significantly damage the environment or violate fair labor practices. This would be an enormous incentive for corporations to conform to these standards. This would therefore be a democratizing force over the economy—only not through the outright nationalization that the old socialist pattern envisioned and new versions of market socialism advocate.

The most ambitious experiment in this regard was that, never fully adopted, of wage-earner funds, as proposed by Swedish Social Democrats in the 1970s. The first concrete proposal to create these funds was a report submitted to the LO (Landsorganisationen) Congress in 1975. This report was seen as a move to bring capital under democratic control. The idea was to use a payroll tax or a tax on profits to invest in companies by buying shares of enterprises to be run collectively by employee funds. Thus, ownership would be slowly transferred to democratic collective control.

From the beginning, business groups, like the Federation of Swedish Industries, spent a huge sum to defeat the legislation. Business spent as much on the campaign against the wage-earner funds in 1982 as the five parliamentary parties combined spent in the parliamentary election (Pontusson 1992, 228). Eventually, in 1983, a very watered-down version of the plan was adopted. Five regional funds were established through a 0.2 payroll tax or a 20 percent tax on profit, the purpose of which was to purchase existing shares of enterprises. Each fund had a nine-member board appointed by the state, with five seats on each given to labor representatives. However these boards were passive, and only allowed to own 8 percent of any given firm. By the end of 1990, they only had 3.5 percent of the shares on the Stockholm exchange (Minns 1996, 45). By 1998, the funds had been closed, their assets serving as endowments for social research, a testament to the New Class inspiration of the funds.

Using pension funds to alter the behavior of private corporations is one strategy of a potential New Class movement. A complementary strategy would be to embrace the notion of an "investor state" as originally advocated by Clinton. Some did not appreciate the radical nature of this policy. It would be an extension of traditional social democratic policy to the extent that the state gains the right to intervene directly in production to spur economic growth. This type of intervention most sharply contrasts with traditional Keynesian intervention to pump up aggregate demand. Many argue that Keynesian policy no longer is effective in reversing slow growth and high unemployment (Brenner 1998; Hirst 1994). A state with the capacity to directly intervene in production is the type of investor state that a New Class movement could advocate. Gidden's notion of an investment state that invests in the human capital of the population before people enter the labor market is fine but does not go nearly far enough. Of course spending on education is a good thing, and even a conservative like George W. Bush increased spending on the U.S. Department of Education, but a more radical investor state would be able to directly intervene into production as a response to economic downturns or other market externality.[13]

Can a New Class Movement Come to Power?

We are perfectly aware that, despite a revival of theoretical interest in new ideas about socialism, and despite the electoral success of various new social democratic parties, there is no social movement on the horizon. It is not that intellectuals on the left have simply run out of ideas. The ideas are there, but at present there is no political force that could make these ideas a reality. Still, since we have spent a few hundred pages discussing several waves of New Class theory, we will summarize the advice, to a hypothetical New Class movement, that has emerged from our review of the Third Wayers and the neosocialist "real utopians."

For one thing, such a New Class movement would have no reason to completely expropriate the capitalist class: there are many capitalists who are not part of the hegemonic segment, and these could possibly serve as New Class allies from within the bourgeoisie. Such a movement could advocate some type of mixed system combining private ownership with different forms of noncapitalist ways of organizing economic activity. This is good, because we are doomed to a mixed economy whether this is advocated by anyone or not. The devil is in the details, of course; exactly what type of mix should a New Class strive for to be successful in formation? There would remain a large role for capitalist private property; still, the economy could be significantly democratized through a variety of possible mechanisms that would probably include direct state ownership and intervention, social ownership through wage-earner funds, and associational forms (e.g., voluntary institutions). And, of course, income and assets could be partly redistributed and traditional social democratic welfare state practices could be expanded. Capital's ability to mold the shape of capital accumulation could be significantly curtailed without massive nationalization and centralized planning.

In the long run, there seems little doubt that the structural conditions of advanced capitalism allow for the possibility of the formation of a New Class. Most importantly, the economic processes of advanced capitalism systematically generate potential New Class actors. The potential agents are still around in record numbers, given the technological evolution of corporate capitalism and the fact that the state will remain crucial to the functioning of advanced capitalism. Neoliberals like Gingrich failed to significantly shrink the state; massive corporations are still dependent on the state in fundamental ways. In the advanced capitalist countries, an average of 45.1 percent of the GDP flowed through the state in 1996, 36.7 percent in the United States and 42.3 percent in the United Kingdom.

Just as important, all the major new technological advances that have led to the most dynamic center of capital accumulation have originated within the state or through state-funded research. Examples include the development of key technologies such as the internet, computers, information processing, lasers, and satellites. Almost the entire basis of the "new economy" has been designed, developed, and funded by the public sector (such as the Pentagon and the National Science Foundation) (Chomsky 1999). Publicly funded science and highly skilled technical labor continue to drive this development—precisely the economic processes that create large groups of professionals in private and public institutions as well as the critical intellectuals who inevitably find a home in the universities that train these professionals. Thus there will be the same raw material of New Class actors around for the rest of capitalism. Indeed, the clear developmental tendency within capitalism is to increase the absolute numbers of these actors as capital accumulation proceeds. At the same time, the ownership of property through pension funds will continue to gain dominance. Capitalism can be said to produce not only its own *potential* gravediggers but their tools as well.

Notes

Introduction

1. See Kuron and Modzelewski, *Il Marxismo Polacco all'Opposizione* (Roma, 1968), quoted in Carlo 1974.

2. For a critique of this view, see Zeitlin 1974, 1073–1119.

3. See in particular H. Marcuse, "Some implications of modern technology," and F. Pollock, "State capitalism: Its possibilities and limitations" in Arato, ed., 1978.

4. The term "adversary culture" was initially a concept of L. Trilling (1965).

5. Bell is certainly less critical and more sympathetic to the emergent New Class thesis than are the theorists of the New Right.

6. Veblen had similar ideas about the future role of engineers, and Galbraith, following Veblen, developed a parallel analysis about technostructure. See T. Veblen, *Engineers and the Price System,* and J. K. Galbraith, *The New Industrial State.*

7. See G. Konrád and I. Szelényi, *The Intellectuals on the Road to Class Power,* and N. Berdayev, *The Origins of Russian Communism.*

8. We call these agents "archaic" to emphasize that they are unable to achieve a rational form of social domination. They rule in traditional ways; they can more accurately be called an estate or an order than a class.

2. The Vanguard Project

1. Kolakowski has a point (see Kolakowski 1981, 248): Bakunin, unlike Marx, "had not the gifts of a theoretician, or a founder of systems." Bakunin is quite sloppy and unsystematic, but we still appreciate his sparkling originality.

2. From Bakunin, *Statism and Anarchism,* 289.

3. In Bakunin, "Marx, the Bismarck of Socialism," 87.

4. In his *Federalism, Socialism, and Anti-Theologism*. Reprinted in *The Political Philosophy of Bakunin*, 189.

5. As far as we know, the only text in English by Machajski (excerpted from his book *The Intellectual Worker*, originally written around 1905) is in V. F. Calverton, ed., *The Making of Society* (1937). Max Nomad wrote on Machajski's work in some of his books; see for instance his *Rebels and Renegades* (1932) and *Apostles of Revolution* [1933] (1961). Machajski received better treatment in France, where, during the 1970s, a significant portion of his work was translated and published.

6. See Nomad, *Rebels and Renegades*, 208.

7. According to Nomad, the similarities between Machajski's and Trotsky's analyses are far from accidental. Nomad seems to know that they spent some time together in Siberian exile and that Trotsky may have been influenced by Machajski in formulating both his theory of permanent revolution and his much later-elaborated theory of a "deformed workers' state."

8. This concept is borrowed by Trotsky from Marx's *The Critique of the Gotha Program*.

9. Nomad, *Apostles of Revolution*, 319

10. We find this quite an astonishing accomplishment. Machajski sets the agenda here for most of the coming state capitalism theorizing, from Tony Cliff to Charles Bettelheim.

11. From Machajski, *The Intellectual Worker*, 427.

12. Ibid., 435.

13. Prior to the late fall of 1918, Lukács's critical analysis is directed against modernity. As he turns into a Marxist, the problem of "second nature," formulated during his pre-Marxist period, is redefined as the problem of "bourgeois reified consciousness"—redefined, that is, in reflection of the world governed by the logic of commodity production, and thus of capitalism.

14. We are grateful to David Bathrick, who brought this to our attention.

3. A Bureaucratic Class in Soviet-Type Society

1. Trotsky therefore called upon the Soviet working class to organize itself, overthrow the Stalinist bureaucracy, and regain political power. The social revolution, for Trotsky, had been completed with the transformation of relations of production and the class structure.

2. Decades later, Miklos Haraszti, in his brilliant *Workers in a Worker's State*, demonstrated empirically that socialist workers on the shop floor see bureaucrats as "them" and develop an oppositional identity as "us" (Miklos Haraszti 1977; Michael Burawoy 1985, 156–208).

3. The Trotskyist argument that the U.S.S.R. had successfully completed its social revolution meant that in the last instance the U.S.S.R. must be considered more progressive than the best of the capitalist countries. The Hitler-Stalin pact made this position untenable.

4. The sentence does not make much sense. We assume that this must be a typo or a translation error. We suppose that Djilas wanted to say: "the new class was *not* born in the revolutionary struggle. . . ."

5. Castoriadis preferred to call the U.S.S.R. "total bureaucratic capitalism" rather than "bureaucratic collectivist," a pedantic but not substantive difference (Castoriadis 1978–79, 46).

6. The book belongs to the "bureaucratic collectivism" school, although Heller,

Feher, and Markus in this brilliant essay used the somewhat awkward term "dictatorship over needs" as the synonym of "bureaucratic collectivism."

4. Beyond Bureaucratic Power

1. Bahro did not recommend a violent revolution, but his "alternative" was fundamentally different from "actually existing socialism"; it was such socialism's revolutionary alternative in *this* sense.

2. The anarchists saw the new order as a "despotism of scientists," a phrase Konrád and Szelényi would feel uncomfortable with, though in essence it is not that far from their position.

3. This is analogous to Julien Benda's view of what intellectuals should do, although Benda believed that intellectuals betrayed their historic mission by accepting a professional role in bourgeois society (see his *La trahison des clercs*). Benda was very influential in Eastern Europe during the interwar years. László Németh, probably the most polished Hungarian populist theorist, also took the position that socialism can only be conceived as a society of intellectuals. It is ironic that this type of analysis would return to Eastern Europe during the late 1980s and 1990s, this time not as a theory of socialism, but as a reformulated theory of "civil society." As the idea of civil society as a critique of socialism lost power with the transition to postcommunism, the idea of civil society has become recast in positive terms. During state socialist times, it was a critique of socialism; now it is seen as the "society of intellectuals." For a criticism of the theory of civil society along these lines, see Bill Lomax, "The Strange Death of 'Civil Society' in Postcommunist Hungary" (unpublished manuscript, 1995).

4. One puzzling phenomenon of the 1960s was the convergence of critical intellectual thinking in the West and East. While Western critics of capitalism and Eastern critics of state socialism should have been on a collision course, in certain respects they were not. In some sense there was an East-West 1960s phenomenon. The Western New Left and the East European reform movement of the 1960s differed in fundamental ways (commitment to Marxism, attitudes toward the Soviet Union and the United States, and, in particular, the assessment of the role of markets), but they shared strong antibureaucratic and anti-authoritarian values; therefore they were rather close to each other in the search for alternative lifestyles.

5. Radovan Selucky makes a distinction between market reform and technocratic reform, along similar lines; see Selucky 1972, 43–55.

6. Sutela 1984.

7. Kornai for instance started his career as a journalist for the central party newspaper. When he became disenchanted with Communist policies, as early as 1953, he began to learn economics, especially its mathematical aspects. Some of his early publications belong to this mold. See, for instance, Kornai, *Economics of Planning* 1965, 5 (3):3–18.

8. Liberman [1962] 1972, 309–18.

9. Lange 1936, 53–71; Lange 1937, 123–42.

10. Von Mises [1920] 1935, 87–130.

11. Liska [1964] 1988.

12. János Kornai 1992.

13. There was quite a concern about consumerism during the 1960s in Eastern Europe. While it may not have been as central a concern for East European reformers as it was to the New Left in the West, the 1960s was still the decade of the "limits to

growth," and the ideas of the Club of Rome found their way into East European intellectual thinking, too. In particular, the East European revisionist neo-Marxists—for instance, the theorists of the so-called Budapest School (Ágnes Heller, Mihály Vajda, György Markus, János Kis, and György Bence)—responded to the idea of the market's capacity to generate "false needs" and excessive consumption, thus distorting "human essence."

14. Feher, Heller, and Markus come close to this position in their *Dictatorship over Needs*. They regard East European socialism as illegitimate, though they consider the Soviet Union a legitimate system of authority, a system of traditional domination. Quite independently from Feher, Heller, and Markus, Ken Jowitt also called the Soviet social order "neotraditional," coining the term about the same time that *Dictatorship over Needs* was written. Jowitt's "neotraditionalism" was adapted by Andrew Walder for the study of Maoist China.

15. There were forces in the Soviet Union pointing in the direction of the emergence of traditional authority. Especially in the Soviet Union, but to some extent even in Eastern Europe, clientelism grew with the consolidation of communist power, in part building on the habits formed already in precommunist societies. Thus it is fair to suggest that Stalinism was a mixture of charismatic and traditional authority, although we believe that the more explicit claim by the rulers for legitimacy was based on charisma.

16. To put it with Weber: goal-rational authority is *Zielrationalitat* (rationality of goals, or aims), rather than *Zweckrationalitat* (the exploration of goals in light of the availability of means by which they can be attained—so that in the last instance the rationality of goals is subordinated to the rationality of the means).

17. Although many more were Marxist-Leninist than now recall. With the fall of communism, people are busily repressing their past ideas, creating a new historical identity for themselves.

18. Al Szymanski, one of the last true believers in the Soviet dictatorship of the proletariat, in his *The Red Flag Is Still Flying* explains this by the generosity of the proletariat. The working class is so generous that it pays those who serve them better than it pays themselves. Fair enough, except that salary levels were set not by the proletariat, but by bureaucrats.

19. Eventually it was published (in 1984) as *Urban Inequalities under State Socialism*, by Oxford University Press.

20. See Feher, Heller, and Markus 1984; Castoriadis 1977–78; Carlo 1974.

21. Karl Polányi, "The Economy as Instituted Process," in *Trade and Market in Early Empires* (1957).

22. For a recent restatement of this theme, see Andrew Walder, *American Journal of Sociology* (January 1996).

23. János Kornai's *Economics of Shortage* (1980) pursues the same type of analysis, but it offers the institutional specificities at the micro-economic level with the theory of hard and soft budget constraints. Kornai's analysis culminates in a fascinating social psychology of state socialism. He calls it a paternalist system, with a great deal of insight.

24. In the Hungarian original, the Weberian term "uralkodó rend" ("ruling estate") was used, which was translated as "elite" into English, making the analysis more accessible to Anglo-Saxon readers but making it less theoretically accurate.

25. We use the term "political capital" as a special form of "social capital." Social capital refers broadly to assets accumulated in interpersonal networks, which often are rather informal. Social capital can be institutionalized in different ways. One such

way is to use political institutions, in communist societies primarily membership in the communist party, to "store" social capital. When this happens, we speak of political capital.

26. We call these procedures "ritualistically agreed upon" since the application of procedures—e.g., how an academic argument is reasoned out, how therapy is conducted—is usually defended against ongoing critical scrutiny. An "appropriate" procedure is decided by convention, and those who would try some radically different procedure are likely to be rejected as charlatans or nonprofessionals; they even could be found unethical. With the term "ritual," we would like to indicate that a deeper, ethical meaning is involved when one calls a procedure appropriate.

27. Weber's distinction between "commercial" and "social" classes tries to deal with this problem. His "commercial" classes are identified by market position, while his "social" classes are defined by typical patterns of social mobility, lifestyles, and the like. Undoubtedly, for Weber, "social classes" stood halfway, in terms of their "classness," between pure, or "commercial," classes and "stand" (rank or status) groups.

28. This is a major theme in late-nineteenth-century and early-twentieth-century left social thought, and it shapes in consequential ways the thinking of the Frankfurt School theorists, mainly under the impact of Georg Lukács.

29. Weber's distinction between "formal" and "substantive rationality" in *Economy and Society* is greatly influenced by the idea of socialism and also by what he saw as the emergent socialist reality in Soviet Russia. As, in Soviet Russia, planning began to replace markets, Weber saw this as the violation of the rules of "formal rationality," and, while he did not reject (as irrational or even nonrational) the "substantive rationality" pursued by planners, he did believe that, in some respect, substantive reality had, in comparison with formal rationality, irrational elements—even though he emphasized that formal rationality also can be seen as irrational, if analyzed from the perspective of substantive rationality.

5. The Fall of the Class Project of the Socialist Reform Intelligentsia

1. Interestingly, bourgeois liberalism—the project not to move Hungary back where it had been but to push it ahead in the direction of Western Europe or North America—which was the major ideological force in 1989 and after, was almost absent in 1956.

2. The theory of civil society generated a great deal of interest in the Western left, which surely did not have any reason to hide pro-capitalist views. The Western left imported the new, East European version of the theory of civil society because it enabled the left to distance itself from the paternalistic and oppressive features of the Soviet system without accepting bourgeois or capitalist society as an ideal.

6. Intellectuals under Postcommunism

1. But Slovakia, among the Central European countries, seems to have much more of this phenomenon (see Miklos 1995).

2. Windolf 1996.

7. Bourgeois and Post-Marxist Theories of the New Class in the West

1. The Pullman Upheaval in 1894, the Homestead Strike in 1892, and the Haymarket Riot in 1886 represented the crest of this wave.

2. Veblen was greatly influenced by the writings of Taylor's two most prominent disciples, Henry L. Gantt and Morris L. Cook.

3. Gouldner 1979, 7.

4. Trilling 1965; Podhoretz 1979, 31. Trilling also influenced Bell; see Trilling's *The Cultural Contradictions of Capitalism.*

5. Bell 1973, 20.

6. Konrád and Szelényi 1979, 24–35.

7. See his trilogy, *The Dark Side of the Dialectic.* The three volumes are *The Dialectic of Ideology and Technology, The Future of Intellectuals and the Rise of the New Class, The Two Marxisms.*

8. Mallet 1963; Parkin 1967; Mann 1973.

9. Schelsky 1974.

10. Mannheim [1936] 1972, 137–46.

11. Habermas, *Knowledge and Human Interest* 1971, 43–63, 301–17.

12. See Gouldner 1979, 9.

13. Neo-Marxism is a bit of a strawman here; other approaches with less economic determinism would analogously treat knowledge as basically "epiphenomenal." However, the other approaches' "existential base" would be more flexible, more broadly defined as status, or position in social structure, or by other structural characteristics.

14. The conceptually clearest statements are in essays published in Foucault, *Power/Knowledge* 1980, in particular chapters 5, 6, and 7.

15. Poster 1984, 151.

16. Horkheimer and Adorno [1947] 1982.

17. Habermas 1981, 2:171–293, 548–93.

18. Habermas 1984, no. 33:79. See also Habermas 1985, 279–312.

19. Poster 1984, 130.

20. See Ágnes Heller's Habermas critique in her "Habermas and Marxism," in *Habermas—Critical Debates* (MIT Press, 1982), 24.

21. This account relies on Robert Brenner's massive 1998 compilation of data in *International Economic Turbulence.*

Conclusion

1. If the academics who engage in this debate constitute a "movement," then the activities of this movement consist primarily in agitation during guest lectures and free dinners.

2. Of course, the election of George W. Bush over the New Democrat Al Gore might potentially temper this claim. However, it seems that Gore lost the election more than Bush won the election. Decisive in this election was the contingent factor of Clinton's scandal-plagued administration. Moreover, Bush claimed to be a new kind of conservative, of the "compassionate" variety. This can be seen as a concession of defeat for the old ideological formula, an acknowledgment that traditional neoliberalism has serious problems. Bush's policies, far more reminiscent of his father's and especially of the Reagan administration's, should eliminate "compassionate conservatism" as a viable new ideology. Still, with Silvio Berlusconi's election there may prove a trend towards traditional parties.

3. Friedman 1988,148–49, 173.

4. Mishal et al. 1997, 121–24.

5. "Der Weg vorne fuer Europa's Sozialdemkraten—Ein Vorshlag von Gerhard

Schroeder und Tony Blair" ("The way forward for Europe's Social Democrats—a proposition by Gerhard Schroeder and Tony Blair").

6. Gundsatzprogramm der Sozialdemokratischen Partei Duetschlands. Beschlossen vomProgramm-Parteitag der Sozialdemokratischen Partei Deutschlands am 20. December 1989 in Berlin, geaendert auf dem Partaig in Leipzig am 17.04 (1989), 45.

7. Quoted in Bluestone 1998, 18.

8. Jencks and Swingle 2000, 37–41.

9. *Speigel Online,* 5 June 1999, "Staatsfinanzen—'Das müßt ihr schlucken'" (23/1999); *Speigel Online,* 27 October 1999, "Unternehemesteuerreform—Eichel präsentiert Entwurf im Januar" (43/1999).

10. From the initial legislation in 1935 until 1982, recipients were funded by taxes from current workers. Each cohort would thus pay for the retirement of the cohort that proceeded it. In 1982, Congress raised social security taxes and delayed the age of retirement, which created a surplus that would go to pay for the cost of retirements in the future. With this surplus, the Social Security Trust Fund purchases U.S. Treasury bonds that can later be used to pay benefits.

11. Social Security and Medicare Boards of Trustees, "A Message to the Public" (1999), http://www.ssa.gov.OACT/TRSUM/trsummary.html.

12. *Promoting Prosperity: A Business Agenda for Britain,* Report of the Commission on Public Policy and British Business (London 1997), 97.

13. Such a policy need not look only to Sweden for such a proposal, as exactly this policy had been advocated by the Democrats during the Great Depression and gained widespread bipartisan support in the U.S. Senate. The Employment Act of 1946, when passed by the Senate by a vote of 71 to 10 on 28 September 1945, contained the following amendment: "(4) to the extent that continuing full employment cannot otherwise be attained, [the Federal Government shall,] consistent with the needs and obligations of the Federal Government and other essential considerations of national policy, provide such volume of Federal investment and expenditures as may be needed, in addition to the investment and expenditure by private enterprises, consumer and State and local governments, to achieve the objective of continuing full employment" (quoted in Domhoff 1990, 198). Business networks like the National Association of Manufacturers, local and state Chambers of Commerce, and the conservative coalition in the House mobilized to weaken this legislation.

Works Cited

Abercrombie, Nicholas, and John Urry. 1983. *Capital, Labor, and the Middle Classes*. London: Allen and Unwin.

Ambachtsheer, Keith, and D. Don Ezra. 1998. *Pension Fund Excellence: Creating Value for Stakeholders*. New York and Chichester: Wiley.

Ansart, Pierre. 1970. *Sociologie de Saint-Simon*. Paris: Presses Universitaires de France.

Arato, Andrew, and Paul Breines. 1979. *The Young Lukács and the Origins of Western Marxism*. New York: Seabury Press.

Bahro, Rudolf. 1978. *The Alternative in Eastern Europe*. London: NLB.

Bailes, Kendall E. 1978. *Technology and Society under Lenin and Stalin: Origins of the Soviet Technical Intelligentsia, 1917–1941*. Princeton: Princeton University Press.

Bakunin, Mikhail A. 1953. *The Political Philosophy of Bakunin: Scientific Anarchism*. New York: Free Press.

———. 1966. "Marx, the Bismarck of Socialism." In *Patterns of Anarchy*, ed. L. Krimmerman and L. Perry, 882–93. New York: Anchor.

———. [1871] 1972. "The KnotoGermanic Empire and the Social Revolution." Selections published in *Bakunin on Anarchy*, ed. Sam Dolgoff. New York: Alfred Knopf.

Bauman , Zygmunt. 1974. "Officialdom and Class: Bases of Inequality in Socialist Society." In *The Analysis of Class Structure*, ed. Frank Parkin, 129–48. London: Tavistock.

Bazelon, David T. 1967. *Power in America: The Politics of the New Class*. New York: New American Library.

Bell, Daniel. 1976. *The Coming of Postindustrial Society*. New York: Harper and Row.

Benda, Julien. 1969. *The Treason of the Intellectuals (La Trahison des clercs)*. Original in French, Paris: B. Grasset, 1927. New York: Norton.

Berdayev, N. 1972. *The Origins of Russian Communism*. Ann Arbor: University of Michigan Press.

Berend, T. Ivan. 1985. *The Hungarian Economy in the Twentieth Century*. London: Croom.

Berle, Adolf A. 1959. *Power without Property: A New Development in American Political Economy*. New York: Harcourt, Brace.

Berle, Adolf A., and Gardiner C. Means. 1932. *The Modern Corporation and Private Property*. New York: MacMillan.

Bettelheim, Charles. 1976. *Economic Calculations and Forms of Property*. Original in French, Paris: F. Maspero, 1970. London: Routledge and Kegan Paul.

Bian, Yanjie, and John Logan. 1996. "Market Transition and the Persistence of Power: The Changing Stratification System in China." *American Sociological Review* 61: 739–58.

Blackburn, Robin. 1999. "The New Collectivism: Pension Reform, Gray Capitalism, and Complex Socialism," *New Left Review*, no. 233: 3–66.

Bluestone, Barry. 2002. "Clinton's Bequest Reconsidered." *American Prospect* 11 (4): 18–21.

Bourdieu, Pierre, and J. C. Passeron. 1977. *Reproduction in Education, Society, and Culture*. Beverly Hills, Calif.: Sage.

Bowles, Sam, and Herb Gintis. 1999. *Recasting Egalitarianism*. New York: Verso.

Braverman, Harry. 1974. *Labor and Monopoly Capital*. New York: Monthly Review Press.

Brenner, Robert. 1976. "Agrarian Class Structure and Economic Development in Pre-industrial England." *Past and Present* 70: 30–75.

———. 1998. "The Economics of Global Turbulence." *New Left Review*, no. 229 (special issue).

Bruce-Briggs, B., ed. 1979. *The New Class?* New York: McGraw Hill.

Bruzst, Laszlo, and David Stark. 1991. "Remaking the Political Field in Hungary." *Journal of International Affairs* 45 (1): 201–46.

———. 1998. *Postsocialist Pathways: Transforming Politics and Property in East Central Europe*. Cambridge: Cambridge University Press.

Buci-Glucksmann, Christine. 1980. *Gramsci and the State*. London: Lawrence and Wishart.

Burawoy, Michael. 1985. *The Politics of Production: Factory Regimes under Capitalism and Socialism*. London: Verso.

Burch, Philip. 1972. *Managerial Revolution Reassessed*. Lexington, Mass.: Lexington Books.

Burnham, James. 1962. *The Managerial Revolution*. Bloomington: Indiana University Press.

Calverton, V. F., ed. 1937. *The Making of Society*.

Campeanu, Pavel [Casals]. 1980. *The Syncretic Society*. White Plains, N.Y.: M. E. Sharpe.

Carlo, Antonio. 1974. "The Socioeconomic Nature of the U.S.S.R." *Telos* 21: 2–86.

Carter, Bob. 1985. *Capitalism, Class Conflict, and the New Middle Class*. London: Routledge and Kegan Paul.

Castoriadis, Cornelius. 1978. "The Social Regime in Russia." *Telos* 38: 212–48.

Central Committee of the Communist Party of China. 1967. *How the Soviet Revisionists Carry Out All-Around Restoration of Capitalism in the U.S.S.R.* Peking: Foreign Language Publishing.

Chandler, Alfred D., Jr. 1962. *Strategy and Structure: Chapters in the History of the American Industrial Enterprise*. Cambridge, Mass.: MIT Press.

Chomsky, Noam. 1999. *Profit over People.* New York: Seven Stories Press.

Cliff, Tony. 1974. *State Capitalism in Russia.* London: Pluto Press.

Cohen, Joshua, and Joel Rogers. 1995. *Associations and Democracy.* New York: Verso.

Commission on Public Policy and British Business. 1997. *Promoting Prosperity: A Business Agenda for Britain.* Report.

Cousin, Mark, and Althar Hussain. 1984. *Michel Foucault.* New York: St. Martin's Press.

Dahrendorf, Ralf. [1957] 1976. *Class and Class Conflict in Industrial Society.* London: Routledge and Kegan Paul.

Davies, Jon Gover. 1972. *The Evangelistic Bureaucrat.* London: Tavistock Publications.

Djilas, Milovan. 1966. *The New Class: An Analysis of the Communist System.* London: Unwin Books.

Domhoff, G. William. 1990. *The Power Elite and the State : How Policy Is Made in America.* New York: A. de Gruyter.

Dreyfus, Hubert L., and Paul Rabinow. 1983. *Michel Foucault: Beyond Structuralism and Hermeneutics.* Chicago: University of Chicago Press.

Drucker, Peter. 1976. *The Unseen Revolution. How Pension Fund Socialism (or Society?) Came to America.* Oxford: Oxford University Press.

Durkheim, Emile. 1957. *Professional Ethics and Civic Morals.* London: Routledge and Kegan Paul.

Edgell, Stephen. 1975. "Thorstein Veblen's Theory of Evolutionary Change." *American Journal of Economics and Sociology* 34 (July 1975): 267–80.

Edin, Kathryn, and Laura Lein. 1997. *Making Ends Meet: How Single Mothers Survive Welfare and Low-Wage Work.* New York: Russell Sage Foundation.

Ehrenreich, Barbara, and John Ehrenreich. 1979. "The Professional Managerial Class." In *Between Labor and Capital,* ed. Pat Walker, 5–47. Boston: South End Press.

Eyal, Gil, and Eleanor Townsley. 1995. "The Social Composition of the Communist Nomenklatura: A Comparison of Russia, Poland, and Hungary." *Theory and Society* 24: 723–50.

Eyal, Gil, Ivan Szelényi, and Eleanor Townsley. 1998. *Making Capitalism without Capitalists: Class Formation and Elite Struggles in Post-Communist Central Europe.* London: Verso.

Faux, Jeff. 1998. "Making Social Security Work." Statement to the National Conference on Social Security. http://www.epinet.org/statement.html.

Fehér, Ference, Agnes Heller, and George Márkus. 1983. *Dictatorship over Needs.* Oxford: Blackwell.

Foucault, Michel. 1972. *Archaeology of Knowledge.* New York: Pantheon Books.

———. 1979. *Discipline and Punish.* New York: Vintage Books.

———. 1980. *Power/Knowledge.* New York: Pantheon Books.

Frankel, Boris. 1978. *Marxian Theories of the State: A Critique of Orthodoxy.* Melbourne: Arena Publications.

Friedman, Benjamin M. 1988. *Day of Reckoning: The Consequences of American Economic Policy under Reagan and After.* New York: Random House.

Fukuyama, Francis. 1989. "The End of History?" *The National Interest,* summer, 3–18.

Galbraith, John Kenneth. 1973. "Introductory Note" to *The Theory of the Leisure Class,* by Thorstein Veblen. Boston: Houghton and Mifflin.

———. 1985. *The New Industrial State.* 4th ed. Boston: Houghton Mifflin.

Giddens, Anthony. 1998. *The Third Way.* Oxford: Polity Press.

Goldthorpe, John H., et al. 1964. *The Affluent Worker in the Class Structure.* Cambridge: Cambridge University Press.

Gorz, André. 1967. *Strategy for Labor.* Boston: Beacon Press.

Gouldner, Alvin. 1962. "Anti-Minotaur: The Myth of a Value Free Sociology." *Social Problems* 9 (3): 199–212.

———. 1968. "The Sociologist as Partisan: Sociology and the Welfare State." *American Sociologist* 3 (2) (May): 103–16.

———. 1974. "The Metaphoricality of Marxism and the Context-Free Grammar of Socialism." *Theory and Society,* no. 4: 387–414.

———. 1975–76. "Prologue to a Theory of Revolutionary Intellectuals." *Telos* (winter 1975–76): 3–36.

———. 1976. "The Dark Side of the Dialectic: Toward a New Objectivity." *Sociological Inquiry,* no. 1: 3–16.

———. 1976. *The Dialectic of Ideology and Technology.* New York: Seabury Press.

———. 1979. *The Coming Crisis of Western Sociology.* New York: Basic Books.

———. 1979. *The Future of Intellectuals and the Rise of the New Class.* New York: Seabury Press.

———. 1980. *The Two Marxisms.* New York: Seabury Press.

Gramsci, Antonio. 1971. *Selections from the Prison Notebooks.* Ed. Quintin Hoare and Geoffrey Nowell Smith. New York: International Publishers.

Habermas, Jürgen. 1970. *Toward a Rational Society.* Boston: Beacon Press.

———. 1971. *Knowledge and Human Interest.* Boston: Beacon Press.

———. 1974. *Theory and Practice.* London: Heinemann.

———. 1975. *Legitimation Crisis.* Boston: Beacon Press.

———. 1979. *Communication and Evolution of Society.* Boston: Beacon Press.

———. 1981. *Theorie des Kommunikativen Handelns.* Frankfurt: Suhrkamp.

———. 1984. "The French Path to Postmodernity: Bataille between Eroticism and General Economics." *New German Critique,* no. 33: 79.

———. 1984. *The Theory of Communicative Action.* Boston: Beacon Press.

———. 1985. "Vernunftkritische Entlarvung der Humanwissenschaften: Foucault." In *Der Philosophische Diskurs der Moderne.* Suhrkamp Verlag: 279–312.

Halmos, Paul, ed. 1973. *Professionalization and Social Change. Sociological Review* Monograph no. 20.

Hankiss, Elemér. 1990. *East European Alternatives.* New York: Oxford University Press.

Hanley, Eric. 2000. "Cadre Capitalism in Hungary and Poland: Property Accumulation among Communist-Era Elites." *East European Politics and Society* 14 (1): 143–78.

Hanley, Eric, Lawrence P. King, and Janos István Tóth. 2002. "The State, International Agencies, and Property Transformation in Postcommunist Hungary." *American Journal of Sociology* 108: 1 (July): 129–67.

Haraszti, Mikos. 1977. *Workers in a Worker's State: Piece-Rates in Hungary.* New York: Penguin.

Haug, M. R. 1973. "De-professionalization." In *Professionalization and Social Change, Sociological Review* Monograph no. 20, ed. Paul Halmos.

Hayek, F. A. 1960. "The Intellectuals and Socialism." In *The Intellectuals,* ed. G. B. de Huszar. Glencoe, Ill.: Free Press.

Hegel, G. W. F. 1942. *Hegel's Philosophy of Right.* Oxford: Clarendon Press.

Heller, Agnes. 1982. "Habermas and Marxism." In *Habermas—Critical Debates.* Cambridge, Mass: MIT Press.

Hirst, Paul Q. 1994. *Associative Democracy: New Forms of Economic and Social Governance*. Cambridge: Polity Press.

Hohendahl, Peter. 1985. "The Dialectic of Enlightenment Revisited: Habermas' Critique of the Frankfurt School [and Foucault]." *New German Critique*, no. 35: 3–26.

Horkheimer, Max, and Theodor W. Adorno. [1947] 1982. *Dialectic of Enlightenment*. New York: Continuum.

Jay, Martin. 1973. *The Dialectical Imagination*. Little, Brown and Co.

———. 1984. *Marxism and Habermas: The Adventures of a Concept from Lukács to Habermas*. Berkeley and Los Angeles: University of California Press.

Jencks, Christopher, and Joseph Swingle. 2000. "Without a Net: Whom the New Welfare Law Helps and Hurts." *The American Prospect*, January 3, 37–41.

Jerome, W., and A. Buick. 1967. "Soviet State Capitalism? The History of an Idea." *Survey* 1: 58–71.

Johnson, Terrence. 1972. *Professions and Power*. London: Macmillan.

———. 1977. "Professions and Class Structure." In *Industrial Society: Class, Cleavage, and Control*, ed. R. Scase. London: Allen and Unwin.

Jowitt, Kenneth. 1983. "Soviet Neotraditionalism: The Corruption of a Leninist Regime." *Soviet Studies* 30 (3): 275–97.

Kautsky, Karl. 1920. *Terrorism and Communism: A Contribution to the Natural History of Revolution*. London: G. Allen and Unwin.

Kellner, Douglas. 1977. *Karl Korsch: Revolutionary Theory*. Austin: University of Texas Press.

King, Lawrence P. 2001a. "Making Markets: A Comparative Study of Postcommunist Managerial Strategies in Central Europe." *Theory and Society* 30 (4) (August): 494–538.

———. 2001b. *The Basic Features of Post-Communist Capitalism: Firms in Hungary, the Czech Republic, and Slovakia*. Westport, Conn.: Praeger.

Kocka, Jürgen. 1993. *Bourgeois Society in Nineteenth-Century Europe*. Providence: Berg.

Kolakowski, Leszek. 1981. *Main Currents of Marxism: Its Origins, Growth, and Dissolution*. New York: Oxford University Press.

Konrád, George. 1978. *The Long Walk of Liberty*.

Konrád, George, and Ivan Szelényi. 1979. *The Intellectuals on the Road to Class Power*. New York: Harcourt Brace Jovanovich.

Kornai, János. 1965. "Mathematical Programming as a Tool in Drawing up the Five-Year Economic Plan." *Economics of Planning* 5 (3): 3–18.

———. 1980. *Economics of Shortage*. New York: North Holland Publishing Co.

———. 1992. *The Socialist System*. Princeton, N.J.: Princeton University Press.

Korsch, Karl. 1971. *Marxism and Philosophy*. New York: Modern Reader.

Kristol, Irving. 1978. *Two Cheers for Capitalism*. New York.

Kuron, Jacek, and Karol Modzelewski. 1968. *Il Marxismo Polacco all'Opposizione*. Roma.

Lange, Oskar. 1936. "On the Economic Theory of Socialism." Part 1. *Review of Economic Studies* 4 (1): 53–71.

———. 1937. "On the Economic Theory of Socialism." Part 2. *Review of Economic Studies* 4 (2): 123–42.

Layton, Edwin T. 1971. *The Revolt of Engineers*. Cleveland, Ohio: The Press of Case Western University.

Lefebvre, Henri. 1977. *De l'Etat*. Paris: Inedit.

Lenin, Vladimir I. 1960. *Collected Works.* Moscow: Foreign Language Publishing House.
————. [1917] 1970. "Left-Wing Childishness and the Petty Bourgeois Mentality." in *Selected Works* [by V. I. Lenin], 682–705. Vol. 2. Moscow: Progress Publishers.
Liberman, Evsey G. [1962] 1972. "The Plan, Profit, and Bonuses." In *Socialist Economics,* ed. Alec Nove and Domenico M. Nutti, 309–18. Middlesex: Penguin Books.
Liska, Tibor. [1964] 1988. *Okonosztat.* Budapest: Kéözgazdasági és Jogi Kiadó.
Lomax, Bill. 1995. "The Strange Death of Civil Society in Postcommunist Hungary." Unpublished manuscript.
Lukács, Georg. 1971. *History and Class Consciousness: Studies in Marxist Dialectics.* Cambridge, Mass.: MIT Press.
Luxemburg, Rosa. 1951. *Accumulation of Capital.* New Haven, Conn.: Yale University Press.
Machajski, Jan W. [1905] 1937. "The Intellectual Worker." In *The Making of Society: An Outline of Sociology,* ed. V. F. Calverton. New York: The Modern Library.
Mallet, Serge. 1963. *La Nouvelle classe ouvrière.* Paris: Edition Seuil.
————. 1975. *Essays in the New Working Class.* St. Louis: Telos Press.
————. 1975. *The New Working Class.* Nottingham: Bertrand Russell Peace Foundation, for Spokesman Books.
Mandel, Ernest. 1974. "Ten Theses." *Critique* 3: 5–22.
Mann, Michael. 1973. *Consciousness and Action among the Western Working Class.* London: Macmillan.
Mannheim, Karl. 1940. *Man and Society in the Age of Reconstruction: Studies in Modern Social Structure.* New York: Harcourt, Brace, and World.
————. 1968. *Ideology and Utopia: An Introduction to the Sociology of Knowledge.* New York: Harcourt, Brace, and World.
————. [1925] 1971. "The Problem of a Sociology of Knowledge." In *From Karl Manheim,* ed. Kurt H. Wolff, 59–115. New York: Oxford University Press.
————. 1972. *Essays on the Sociology of Knowledge.* London: Routledge and Kegan Paul.
————. [1936] 1972. *Ideology and Utopia.* London: Routledge and Kegan Paul.
Mao-Zedong. 1957. *On the Correct Handling of Contradictions among the People.* Peking: Foreign Languages Press.
Marcuse, Herbert. 1964. *One Dimensional Man.* Boston: Beacon Press.
————. 1968. "Aggressiveness in Advanced Industrial Society." In *Negations: Essays in Critical Theory,* by Herbert Marcuse. Boston: Beacon Press.
————. 1978. "Some Implications of Modern Technology." In *The Essential Frankfurt School Reader,* ed. Andrew Arato, 138–62. Cambridge, Mass.: Blackwell.
Marx, Karl, and Frederick Engels. [1845–46] 1972. "The German Ideology." In *On Historical Materialism,* by Karl Marx, F. Engels, and V. Lenin, 14–76. Moscow: Progress Publishers.
————. 1975. *Collected Works.* New York: International Publishers.
————. 1978. *The Marx-Engels Reader.* 2d ed. Ed. Robert C. Tucker. New York: Norton.
McCarthy, Thomas. 1981. *The Critical Theory of Jürgen Habermas.* Cambridge, Mass.: MIT Press.
Mészáros, István. 1971. *Aspects of History and Class Consciousness.* London: Routledge and Paul.

Miklos, Ivan. 1996. "Corruption Risks in the Privatization Process." Bratislava: Klub Windsor.

Minns, Richard. 1996. "The Social Ownership of Capital." *New Left Review*, no. 219 (September-October): 42–61.

Mishal, Lawrence., et al. 1997. *The State of Working America, 1969–1997*. Armonk, N.Y.: Economic Policy Institute.

Moynihan, D[aniel] P. 1982. "Equalizing Education: In Whose Benefit?" *The Public Interest*, fall 1982.

Nee, Victor. 1989. "A Theory of Market Transition: From Redistribution to Markets in State Socialism." *American Sociological Review* 54 (5): 663–81.

Nicolaus, M. 1975. *The Restoration of Capitalism in the U.S.S.R.* Chicago: Liberator Press.

Nomad, Max. 1932. *Rebels and Renegades*. New York: MacMillan.

———. 1939. *Apostles of Revolution*. Boston: Little, Brown and Co.

Nove, Alec. 1979. "Market Socialism and Its Critics." In *The Political Economy of Soviet Socialism*, ed. Alec Nove, 112–32. London: Allen and Unwin.

O'Connor, James. 1973. *The Fiscal Crisis of the State*. New York: St. Martin's Press.

Oppenheimer, M. 1973. "The Proletarianization of the Professional." In *Professionalization and Social Change*. *Sociological Review* Monograph no. 20, ed. Paul Halmos.

Orwell, George. 1968. "James Burnham and the Managerial Revolution." In *Collected Essays, Journalism, and Letters* [of George Orwell]. Vol. 4. London: Harmondsworth.

Parkin, Frank. 1967. *Middle Class Radicalism*. New York: Praeger.

Phillips, Kevin P. 1975. *Mediacracy: American Parties and Politics in the Communication Age*. Garden City, N.Y.: Doubleday.

———.1982. *Postconservative America: People, Politics, and Ideology in a Time of Crisis*. New York: Random House.

Podhoretz, Norman. 1972. "Laureate of the New Class." *Commentary* 54, no. 6 (December): 4–7.

———. 1979. "The Adversary Culture and the New Class." In *The New Class?* ed. B. Bruce-Briggs, 19–33. New York: McGraw Hill.

Polányi, Karl. 1957. "Economy as Instituted Process." In *Trade and Market in the Early Empires*, ed. Karl Polányi, Conrad M. Arensberg, and Harry W. Pearson, 243–70. Glencoe, Ill: Free Press.

Pollin, Robert. 2000. "Globalization, Inequality, and Financial Instability: Confronting Marx, Keynes, and Polányi: Problems in the Advanced Capitalist Economies." Paper presented at conference on Globalization and Ethics, Yale University, Department of Political Science, New Haven, Conn.

Pollock, Friederich. 1978. "State Capitalism: Its Possibilities and Limitations." In *The Essential Frankfurt School Reader,* ed. Andrew Arato, 71–94. Cambridge, Mass.: Blackwell.

Pontusson, Jonas. 1992. *The Limits of Social Democracy: Investment Politics in Sweden*. Ithaca, N.Y.: Cornell University Press.

Poster, Mark. 1984. *Foucault, Marxism, and History*. Cambridge: Polity Press.

Potoéka, Jan. 1976. "Wars of the Twentieth Century and the Twentieth Century as War." *Telos* 30: 116–26.

Poulantzas, Nicos. 1975. *Classes in Contemporary Capitalism*. London: New Left Books.

Rassel, Edith, and Jeff Faux. 1999. "Fixing Social Security." Economic Policy Institute Briefing Paper. http://www.epinet.org/breifingpapers/fixsocsec.html.

Richta, Radovan. 1969. *Civilization at the Crossroads: Social and Human Implications of the Scientific and Technological Revolution.* White Plains, N.Y.: International Arts and Sciences Press.

Rizzi, Bruno. 1985. *The Bureaucratization of the World.* London: Tavistock.

Roemer, John. 1994. *A Future for Socialism.* Cambridge, Mass.: Harvard University Press.

Róna-Tas, Ákos. 1994. "The First Shall Be the Last? Entrepreneurship and Communist Cadres in the Transition from Socialism." *American Journal of Sociology* 100 (1): 40–69.

———. 1998. "Path Dependence and Capital Theory: Sociology of the Postcommunist Economic Transformation." *East European Politics and Societies* 12 (1): 107–31.

Rorty, Richard. 1980. *Philosophy and the Mirror of Nature.* Princeton, N.J.: Princeton University Press.

Saint-Simon, [Claude] Henri. [1813–25] 1952. *Selected Writings.* Oxford: Blackwell.

Sarfatti-Larson, Magali. 1977. *The Rise of Professionalism: A Sociological Analysis.* Berkeley and Los Angeles: University of California Press.

Schelsky, Helmut. 1974. *Die Arbeit tun die Anderen: Klassenkampf und Priesterherrschaft der Intellektuellen.* Koln: Oppladen.

Schumpeter, Joseph. 1942. *Capitalism, Socialism, and Democracy.* New York: Harper and Row.

Scott, John. 1997. *Corporate Business and Capitalist Classes.* Oxford and New York: Oxford University Press.

Selucky, Radovan. 1972. *Economic Reforms in Eastern Europe: Political Background and Economic Significance.* New York: Praeger.

Shachtman, Max. 1962. *The Bureaucratic Revolution: The Rise of the Stalinist State.* New York: Donald Press.

Stabile, Donald. 1984. *Prophets of Order: The Rise of the New Class, Technocracy, and Socialism in America.* Boston: South End Press.

Staniszkis, Jadwiga. 1991a. "Political Capitalism in Poland." *East European Politics and Societies* 5 (1): 127–41.

———. 1991b. *The Dynamics of Breakthrough.* Berkeley and Los Angeles: University of California Press.

Stark, David. 1996. "Recombinant Property in East European Capitalism." *American Journal of Sociology* 101 (4): 993–1027.

Sutela, Pekka. 1984. *Socialism, Planning, and Optimality: A Study in Soviet Economic Thought.* Helsinki: The Finnish Society of Sciences and Letters.

Szalai, Erzsébet. 1989a. *Gazdasági mechanizmus, reformtökvések, s nagyvallalati érdekek.* (Economic Mechanisms, Reform Scenarios, and Interests of Large Firms). Budapest: Kéözgazdasági és Jogi Kiadó.

———. 1989b. "The New Elite." *Across Frontiers* 5: 25–31.

Szelényi, Iván. 1978. "Social Inequalities in State Socialist Redistributive Economies: Dilemma for Social Policy in Contemporary Socialist Societies of Eastern Europe." *International Journal of Comparative Sociology*, no. 1–2: 63–87.

———. 1982. "Gouldner's Theory of the Flawed Universal Class of Intellectuals." *Theory and Society* 11 (6): 779–98.

———. 1983. *Urban Inequalities under State Socialism.* New York: Oxford University Press.

———. 1988. *Socialist Entrepreneurs: Embourgeoisement in Rural Hungary.* Madison: University of Wisconsin Press.

Szymanski, Albert. 1979. *Is the Red Flag Flying? The Political Economy of the Soviet Union Today.* London: Zed Books.

Taylor, Frederick W. [1911] 1947. *The Principles of Scientific Management.* New York: Harper.

Ticktin, H. 1976. "The Class Structure of the U.S.S.R. and the Elite." *Critique* 9.

———. 1979. "The Ambiguities of Ernest Mandel." *Critique* 12: 127–37.

Treiman, Donald J., and Iván Szelényi. 1993. "Social Stratification in Eastern Europe after 1989." *Proceedings of Workshop: Transformation Processes in Eastern Europe.* The Hague: NOW-SSCW.

Trilling, Lionel. 1965. *Beyond Culture: Essays in Literature and Learning.* New York: Viking Press.

———. 1976. *The Cultural Contradictions of Capitalism.* London: Heineman.

Trotsky, Leon. [1937] 1962 . *The Revolution Betrayed: What Is the Soviet Union and Where Is It Going?* New York: Pathfinder Press.

van Parijs, Philipe. 1993. *Arguing for Basic Income.* New York: Verso.

Veblen, Thorstein. 1963. *Engineers and the Price System.* New York: Harcourt and Brace.

Von Mises, Ludwig. [1920] 1935. "Economic Calculations in the Socialist Commonwealth." In *Collectivistic Economic Planning,* ed. Friedrich A. Hayek, 87–130. London: Routledge and Kegan Paul.

Walder, Andrew. 1992. "Property Rights and Stratification in Socialist Redistributive Economies." *American Sociological Review* 57: 524–39.

———. 1996. "Market and Inequality in Transitional Economies: Toward Testable Hypotheses." *American Journal of Sociology* 101 (4): 1060–1073.

Walker, Pat, ed. 1979. *Between Labor and Capital.* Boston: South End Press.

Weber, Max. [1922] 1978. *Economy and Society.* Berkeley and Los Angeles: University of California Press.

———. 1949. "Objectivity in Social Sciences." In *Methodology of the Social Sciences.* New York: The Free Press.

Wellmer, A. 1971. *Critical Theory of Society.* New York: Herder and Herder.

Windolf, Paul. 1996. "The Transformation of the East German Economy." Manuscript.

World Bank. 1994. *Averting the Old Age Crisis.* Oxford: Oxford University Press.

Wright, Erik O[lin]. 1978. *Class, Crisis, and the State.* London: New Left Books.

———. 1999. *Real Utopian Projects: A General Overview.* Available online at http://www.ssc.wisc.edu/~wright/OVERVIEW.html.

Zagorski, Krzysztof, and Janina Frentzel-Zagorska. 1989. "East European Intellectuals on the Road to Dissent." *Politics and Society* 17: 89–113.

Zeitlin, Maurice. 1974. "Corporate Ownership and Control." *American Journal of Sociology* 79: 1073–1119.

———. 1989. *Large Corporations and Contemporary Classes.* Oxford: Polity.

Zinoviev, G. [1925] 1960. Excerpts from "Minority Report to the Fourteenth Party Congress." In *A Documentary History of Communism,* ed. R. V. Daniels, 274–77. New York: Random House.

Index

LAWRENCE PETER KING is associate professor of sociology at Yale University. A comparativist who studies the intersection of political processes, social structure, and economic institutions, he has published on economic change in postcommunist societies, including articles in the *American Journal of Sociology, European Journal of Sociology, Theory and Society,* and *Politics and Society.* He is the author of *The Basic Features of Postcommunist Capitalism.*

IVÁN SZELÉNYI is William Graham Sumner Professor of Sociology and professor of political science at Yale University. He is a fellow of the American Academy of Arts and Sciences and a member of the Hungarian Academy of Sciences. He is author or coauthor of *Intellectuals on the Road to Class Power, Urban Social Inequalities, Socialist Entrepreneurs,* and *Making Capitalism without Capitalists.*